Jar ~~~~

POLICE SERGEANT
EXAMINATION PREPARATION GUIDE

EARNING YOUR STRIPES!

Larry F. Jetmore, Ph. D.

Captain, *retired*
Hartford, CT Police Department

Looseleaf
Law Publications, Inc.

43-08 162nd Street
Flushing, NY 11358
www.LooseleafLaw.com
800-647-5547

This publication is not intended to replace nor be a substitute for any official procedural material issued by your agency of employment nor other official source. Looseleaf Law Publications, Inc., the author and any associated advisors have made all possible efforts to ensure the accuracy and thoroughness of the information provided herein but accept no liability whatsoever for injury, legal action or other adverse results following the application or adoption of the information contained in this book.

Library of Congress—Cataloging-In-Publication Data

Jetmore, Larry F.
    Police sergeant examination : preparation guide : earning your stripes! / by Larry F. Jetmore.
        pages cm
    ISBN 978-1-60885-068-6 — ISBN 978-1-60885-156-0 (mobi, epub)
    1. Police—United States—Examinations, questions, etc. I. Title.
HV8143.J479 2014
363.2076--dc23   2014040560

Cover by Tin Box Studio, Inc., Cincinnati, Ohio

Contents

About the Author

Larry F. Jetmore, Ph.D., is a twenty-one-year veteran and former captain and commander of the Hartford, Connecticut Police Department. Upon his retirement from the police department, Dr. Jetmore became a member of the full-time faculty and Director of the Criminal Justice Program at a Connecticut college. He has published six books and over a hundred and fifty articles in various magazines on a variety of topics in the field of criminal justice. He is now the Director of the Connecticut Police Testing Service, LLC and has created and administered hundreds of police examinations ranging from entry level to Chief of Police. A nationally recognized expert in police testing, Dr. Jetmore works with the Connecticut Chiefs of Police Association to create and administer entry level and lateral police tests. Dr. Jetmore has dedicated his life to the philosophy that there is no more important function in government than selecting those individuals entrusted to protect its citizens and enforcing its laws.

Other Popular Books by Larry F. Jetmore

Police Management Examinations Preparation Guide
(*Lieutenant/Captain/Assistant Chief*)

Police Officer Entrance Examination Preparation Guide (2015)

Path of the Warrior—
*An Ethical Guide to Personal & Professional Development
in the Field of Criminal Justice*

Path of the Hunter—
Entering and Excelling in the Field of Criminal Investigation

Foreword

The method by which people are selected for supervisory positions in police departments is gradually shifting from the traditional 100-question written exam and subsequent oral examination to a variety of innovative testing systems. Progressive police chiefs and personnel directors have recognized the limitations of traditional testing and are searching for ways to make the examination process more job-related and a better indicator of which candidates have the knowledge, skills, abilities, and personal traits necessary to be a successful police sergeant. Although written exams and oral boards continue to be the most frequently used tests, many cities and towns are now incorporating modified assessment center testing and situational exercises into the examination process. Such additions to the testing process often include structured essay questions or video recordings recreating an incident requiring supervisory action (such as a hostage situation), followed by candidates taking written tests or oral examinations that assess how they would handle the incident as police sergeants. Other testing processes use exercises in which candidates assume the role of police sergeants who must resolve situations through interaction with actors playing the parts of civilians or police employees. Because of these changes to testing procedures, this edition has been updated to show you how to achieve high scores, whether traditional examinations or these new types of tests are used in your city or town.

1 The Path to the Way

First Steps

Now that you fully understand how vital it is to commit yourself to achieving your goal, it's time to take some preliminary steps. First, get yourself a set of sergeant's stripes—from your department's supply clerk, the store that has your uniform account, or a military-supply outlet. While you're out shopping, also pick up the following supplies:

1. Some highlighters. Get red, yellow, and blue not little skinny ones, but the nice, big, fat ones.
2. A package of rubber bands, the thick kind.
3. Three or four large, loose-leaf notebooks, the ones that have three giant rings.
4. About 300 three-by-five, white index cards.
5. Three stuffed animals. Get large ones, preferably a lion, a tiger, and a bear.

Sound silly? It gets worse! Now take one of the sergeant's stripes and tape it on your bathroom mirror. From now until test day, it will be the first thing you see in the morning and the last thing you see at night. Take the second sergeant's stripe and carry it with you wherever you go, on or off duty. In the martial arts, we call this technique *continuous concentration*. In psychology, it's termed *visualization*. This simple process will help keep your mind focused on your goal. In today's fast-paced world, there are many people and many things that distract you—that can keep you from concentrating on your objective. You need to develop a variety of techniques to increase both your attention and your motivation so that you'll stay focused on your studies. See yourself as a sergeant; *convince* yourself that you have what it takes. Getting promoted to the rank of police sergeant is *more difficult than achieving other ranks*. There are more competitors, and you may not have had the advantage of taking previous promotional exams. By making sergeant at your first opportunity, you start building the time in grade necessary to become eligible for the lieutenant's exam.

Take a long, slow look around at who's wearing sergeant's stripes right now in your department. If they can do it, so can you. We both know that you sneaked that sergeant's stripe up on the sleeve of your uniform to see how it would look. If you're willing to pay the price by studying and perfecting your craft, the next person wearing sergeant's stripes in your department will be you!

The purpose for the other items on your shopping list will be explained later.

> *When a man is no longer anxious to do better than well, he's done for.*
>
> —ANONYMOUS

Before the Test Announcement

Many officers make the mistake of waiting for a "test announcement" to be posted before they begin to study. Achievers, on the other hand, are *always* studying for the next test, and you can't afford to wait if you want to be competitive. If your organization's rumor mill is rumbling about a sergeant's test coming up, it's probably true. In most jurisdictions, the sergeants' list (those who took the last test are put on an eligible list according to their final test scores) is kept in effect for two and sometimes even three years before expiring. Naturally, if lieutenants or above are promoted or retire, the sergeant's level will eventually have some vacancies. It's also common for departments to allow for the extension of the eligible list for one additional year, mainly because of the cost of creating and administering promotional examinations.

Check your department's seniority list to see how many officers have the necessary tenure to be eligible for sergeant (know who your competitors are) or who currently are sergeants and could retire soon. Historically, raises and other benefits specified by the labor-management contract have a bearing on when officers choose to retire, creating vacancies that may motivate your agency to administer a promotional exam.

> *Everything comes to him who hustles while he waits.*
>
> —Benjamin Franklin

What's on the Test

There are other significant things you can do before the promotional examination announcement is *officially* posted. Find out the names of the officers who took the last sergeant and lieutenant exams and who came out No. 1 and No. 2 on each list. Officers who've been promoted are eager to talk about how they "aced the test." They'll usually be willing to answer any of your questions, and there's nothing wrong with picking the brains of people who've already succeeded. Your competition will be doing the same thing. Ask these people the following questions:

1. What type of examination did you take? Was it a written test, consisting of multiple-choice questions? Did it contain any true/false or essay questions?
2. What were the major subject areas covered? Was it patrol-supervision oriented? Did it ask questions about criminal investigation, crime scenes, lost-time management, etc.?
3. What type of marking system was used to correct the written exam? Did wrong answers count against you or were only correct answers totaled? Were those who scored less than 70% allowed to take the oral examination or were they eliminated from the process?
4. How long did you have to wait to receive your score? Was it immediately corrected by computer or was there an extended wait?

5. What type of oral examination was given—one oral with three panelists or a series of different orals scheduled throughout the day or over a series of days? Was it a "technical" oral or a "traditional" oral?

6. Were assessment center situational exercises used? If so, what type of exercises? Were role-players used? Videos?

7. What books were listed on the examination reference posting? Do you still have them? If so, may I borrow them? From which books were most of the questions taken?

8. Was a physical examination part of the promotional process? What did the physical exam cover: blood pressure, eyesight, sugar test, height/weight restrictions, body fat composition?

9. Did the test cover department orders and procedures, rules and regulations, department manuals?

Because the source material that promotional examinations are derived from (books on policing, department orders, rules and regulations, procedural manuals, training bulletins, etc.) change infrequently, it's likely that the material used on the last test will also be used on yours. Promotional exams are extremely costly to create and administer, and given the reality of shrinking city budgets, it's not always cost-effective to create a new test. Undoubtedly, there will have been new court decisions and department orders or procedures since the last time the test was given; however, concepts evolve slowly in our profession. For example, topic areas, such as "span of control" or "unity of command" have changed very little over the past ten years. So it's worth the investment to obtain these materials and begin to study *before* the official examination announcement. In larger departments, you can find promotional reference material in the police academy library. In smaller organizations, check with your department's training officer to see if you can get a copy of the last test announcement. The books and materials used for that exam will be listed. You can buy or order the books at your local bookstore or online and find the other study material in department binders or manuals. The following reference sources have often been used in the past by test analysts in creating police promotional examinations and are a valuable addition to any police officer's library.

- Supervision of Police Personnel, Nathan Iannnone, Marvin Iannone, and Jeff Berstein, Pearson Publishing, 2014, ISBN# 978-0-13-29-382-3

- Effective Police Supervision, Harry More and Larry Miller, Anderson Publishing, 2011, ISBN# 978-1-4377-5586-2

- Police Administration, Gary Cordner and Kathryn Scarborough, 7th Edition, Anderson Publishing, 2010, ISBN# 978-1-4224-6324-6

- Effective Police Supervision—Moving Beyond Management, 3rd Edition, Thomas E. Baker, Looseleaf Law Publications, 2011, ISBN# 978-1-60885-020-4

A head start in the studying process will pay you large dividends on test day. It's been my experience that high promotional test scores are directly related to the amount of effort expended in preparing and studying.

Generic and Procedural Questions

Ordinarily, there are two types of test questions used in written and oral police examinations—*generic* and *procedural*. Generic questions are not specific to the duties performed by a sergeant in your department. They are broad in scope and deal with a generalization of what *all* sergeants should do in any police department. Procedural questions *are* specific to what a sergeant in *your* department would be *required* to do based on its orders, guidelines, procedures, and rules and regulations. For example, if the exam question deals with setting up a command post in an emergency situation, there are general things all first-line supervisors would do (whether in Los Angeles, Chicago, or Memphis) and specific responsibilities for sergeants in your department. The former are *generic*, and the latter *are procedural*. Consider the following test question:

> Officer Steven Jones signed out for portable radio No. 19 at 1600 hours. An inspection by Sergeant Lawson at 0020 hours revealed that portable radio No. 19 was not turned in. Officer Jones was contacted and submitted a report indicating he "lost the radio." The proper action for Sergeant Lawson to take is to
>
> (A) advise Officer Jones that his failure to properly care for department property will result in a referral for disciplinary action against him.
> (B) advise Officer Jones that he has 24 hours to locate the missing radio or he will be brought up on charges.
> (C) determine the cost of the radio and deduct the amount from the officer's salary.
> (D) immediately issue a written reprimand to Officer Jones for failure to properly care for department property.

Whether you're answering this question from a generic or procedural viewpoint, both answers (B) and (C) are incorrect. Answer (B) doesn't address the officer's failure to care for the radio and implies that, if it is located later by the officer, any negligence will be negated. Answer (C) improperly places a monetary value on officer negligence and doesn't address future behavior other than to indicate that a fine will be assessed for negligence—a procedure contrary to the principles of effective discipline.

After eliminating answers (B) and (C), you have only two remaining possibilities, either of which may be correct depending on whether you're answering the question generically or as required by your department's policies and procedures. Answer (A) is correct in all police agencies *unless* your department regulations mandate that sergeants issue discipline for lost property. If that's the case, the correct answer is (D).

It's critical to determine whether the test you'll be taking will have generic questions, procedural questions, or a combination of both. Many personnel agencies send away for "canned" promotional examinations, which are devised by companies that specialize in creating police tests. If your test wasn't created by your own city or town, the "canned" exam will have only generic questions. On the written test, it often comes down to choosing the *most* correct answer between two similar alternatives. Knowing whether your selection should be based on the requirements of your department, as opposed to a generic response, will add points to your final score.

The Test Announcement

The test announcement will be posted in a prominent place in your department. Usually, it's the union bulletin board or the roll-call room. The announcement contains a wealth of information vital to you in planning your study program. If it's not distributed, take it down and make yourself a copy. A description of each section follows, with an explanation of how you can use the information to plan your studying.

Eligibility Criteria

One of the reasons the Civil Service testing system was created was to protect police selection and promotion systems from political interference. Central personnel agencies now go to great lengths to ensure that promotional exams and the process under which they are created will withstand court review. The minimum requirements for promotion are becoming more stringent. Many departments require a combination of job position, tenure, and advanced education. Invariably, the minimum standard will include a length-of-service requirement, which varies from city to city. However, if the time in grade requirement is three years, for example, and you fall several months short, immediately begin petitioning your personnel department to be allowed to take the test using the following rationale: Your tenure may qualify you for eligibility at the time the test is actually *given*. The cut-off date for applying may be in March, for instance, but the written test won't be given until May and the oral until June. Will you have enough tenure by the time the testing process is *completed* to meet the seniority requirement? You have nothing to lose and everything to gain by asking questions or contacting your union representative. This is especially true if many other officers also fall within this category. Union officials can apply pressure to revise the length-of-service restriction because of the effect the flexibility will have on a large number of their members.

Duties and Responsibilities

This area outlines what those giving the test have determined are the duties and responsibilities of a sergeant in your department. Using one of the highlighters you bought, mark the major topic areas. You'll see general headings such as "Patrol," "Deployment of Personnel," and "Supervision of Patrol Officers." Write each of these major headings across the top of an index card. You'll have to use several to complete this process.

Example of Duties

The promotional announcement illustrates the types of duties (job tasks and functions) that sergeants perform in your department. Highlight these and write them on the index cards directly under the major topic areas that apply. In every department, there's an order or procedure outlining the duties of a sergeant. Get a copy and correlate it with this section of the job announcement.

Knowledge, Skills, and Abilities

This section is of particular significance because in many ways it tells you what's going to be on the test. For the examination to be *valid*, it must be *job-related*. Both criteria are especially important in the creation of police tests and will be explained later.

This part of the test announcement outlines the basic knowledge a sergeant should have and be able to demonstrate (skills and abilities). Many personnel analysts confuse these two terms. An *ability* is an individual trait you possess. You're either born with it or develop it as you mature. A *skill* is your ability to do something after you receive training in a specific area. The reason this distinction is so important is that many police tests evaluate officers for *skills* that wouldn't be present until they've been *trained* to be sergeants. This area on the test announcement may be quite specific, giving further clues to what the test will cover. Highlight these topics and place them on your index cards next to the appropriate *example of duties*. Your index cards now look like this:

DIRECTS

Directing

Guiding subordenates toward job task accomplishment.

MANAGES

Management
The process of directing human and equipment resources in an efficient and effective manner so that the goals and objectives of the organization can be accomplished.

Methods of Selection

This is the most important part of the announcement. It explains the type and various parts of the examination, the skill level and depth of understanding required, the relative weights of each type or part of the test, and the minimum passing score, if there is one. It also explains how the test will be graded. Methods of selecting officers for promotion vary from city to city, but here's an example of how this section might look.

Parts	Weight	Passing Score
Written Test	55%	70
Oral Test	30%	70
Time in Service	5%	—
Performance Evaluation	10%	—

In some jurisdictions, the oral examination counts for up to 50% of the final grade. Others add points for veterans' preference, education, residency, seniority, performance evaluations, and being a member of a protected class. This section informs applicants of the "suggested reference material" from which the test is constructed. Invariably, there's also a caveat that states that the examination will "not be limited to these announced sources." Listed will be books, manuals, department procedures, rules and regulations, etc. Obtain all of these materials as quickly as you can and begin studying.

Qualification processes for different phases of the examination are also explained. A minimum passing grade on the written test is often required in order to be eligible to take the oral examination. Any *physical examination* requirements or eliminators will be explained, along with the date of expiration of the promotion list.

The date and location of the first phase of the test will also be given. Usually, there's a sentence stating that further information on test specifics will be mailed to candidates.

Submitting Applications

This section explains where applications may be obtained and the deadline for their submission. *Do not* write out your application unless the directions specifically require you to do so. Type it. The application will be reviewed at many different levels and may eventually end up at your oral exam board. Be certain that *all* of the blocks are filled in completely. Make yourself a copy and, if possible, hand-deliver your application. Obtain the name of the person that you give it to and request that it be dated and time-stamped in your presence. In some departments, ties on the exam are broken by the time the application was submitted—a fact usually not mentioned on the test announcement or by the person to whom you hand your application. In other departments, job-classification seniority breaks ties. Your standing on the department's seniority list is often determined by your date of appointment and further classified by your final standing in the police academy. You can verify whether either of these methods is used to break ties on your promotional tests by reviewing your state, city, or town *personnel rules*. Familiarize yourself with the process and photocopy the relevant sections.

The following is an example of a typical test announcement:

THE CITY OF SMITH FALLS

An Equal Opportunity Employer
Announces a Promotional Opportunity for

POLICE SERGEANT
Weekly Salary Range $1200.00-$1281.00

POSITION

Supervises and directs the work of law enforcement personnel in the protection of life and property and the enforcement of criminal and traffic laws and local ordinances. Responsible for the efficient and prompt performance of the work of an assigned patrol unit; supervises and participates in the work of booking and communications operations. May also supervise and participate in the work performed by the various investigative and inspectional units in the police department. Performs other related work as required.

QUALIFICATIONS

Four years of experience as a regularly appointed police officer in the Smith Falls Police Department or four years combined experience as a regularly appointed police officer on special assignment in the Smith Falls Police Department.

EXAMINATION

The promotional procedure for police sergeant will consist of a written test and an oral examination. The written test will be given a weight of 49%. The oral examination will be given a weight of 51%. The written test will consist of questions based solely upon the Police Sergeant Reading List attached. Scores from the written test and oral examination will be combined to obtain a total score.

Candidates will be required to pass a physical examination administered by a city physician before appointment and will be required to also pass a working test period of one year. This examination is subject to all municipal, state, and federal laws, rules, and regulations. The written examination is scheduled for Saturday, October 28.

APPLICATIONS WILL BE ACCEPTED UNTIL 4:30 P.M. FRIDAY, OCTOBER 6.
Exam No. 1457   Issued 914

Applications are obtained from and submitted to
DEPARTMENT OF PERSONNEL
Municipal Building
550 Main St.

Resumes

In some departments, applicants are required to attach a resume to their applications. Submission of resumes will be covered later in this book.

> *By working faithfully eight hours a day, you may eventually get to be a boss and work twelve hours a day.*
>
> —ROBERT FROST

2 Footprints Along the Path

Written Tests

As well as the personnel rules, one or more of the following sources—which may have a different name in your area—may explain the manner in which your department tests candidates for promotion:

1. city charter
2. labor agreements
3. labor board decisions
4. court decisions

In most police organizations, there are strictly regulated procedures for administering promotional examinations, outlining the who, what, where, when, and how of testing. Obtain a copy of everything related to testing, promotions, filling vacancies, appeals, eligible lists, etc. Highlight all pertinent material and place it in your own "promotional file," along with a copy of your application. If your test score ends up tied with another officer's or if the mandated process hasn't been followed, you may need this research material if you decide to file an appeal or protest.

Appealing Written Tests

Police promotional examinations are only as good as the people who create and administer them. You have a right to question any part of the test process. Ordinarily, the city's personnel rules outline a formal procedure for protesting various parts of the examination. For example, after the written test is administered, most departments supply candidates with a tentative answer key to the test. Protests of specific questions are then submitted, which may result in the elimination of particular questions from the exam. This is usually the case when study reference material contradicts the answer key. If you're not satisfied with the test administrator's decision, you can take the matter to court, but this course is often time-consuming and costly. It may take years before your case is heard. It's important to keep carefully documented records on the entire testing process in case the test isn't administered properly.

Constructing Written Tests

One of the reasons that so many officers fail written examinations for promotion is that they study the wrong material or use the wrong study techniques. *Do not* make the mistake of studying for a promotional test the same way you studied for exams in high school or college. Those tests usually required you to recall specific facts from a relatively narrow band of subject matter. Promotional exams cover much wider topic areas, and to be successful on them, you must emphasize basic principles and concepts rather than specific facts. For instance, in studying criminal investigation, you'll eventually come to a section that lists the stages the body goes through after death. Definitions of "muscular flaccidity," "rigor mortis," and "postmortem lividity," among others, will be given along with a timetable in which these effects can be expected to occur. Memorizing these definitions will result in a correct answer on the test only if the question is phrased like this: "How soon after death is rigor mortis most likely to occur?" The question you should be asking yourself when you study is "Why?" Why is it important for a sergeant to be familiar with the various stages the body goes through after death? What supervisory and investigative concepts and principles are involved here? It's important to memorize some material, but if the fact you memorized isn't one of the questions on the test, it will be of little help to you. Gear your studying to the understanding of basic principles and concepts. Using this technique will ensure that regardless of whether the question concerns supervision, patrol techniques, administration, or principles of investigation, you'll have a better chance of choosing the correct answer.

O. W. Wilson's famous book, *Police Administration,* first published in 1963, is as valid today as it was back then. He wrote, "In promotion to sergeant, supervisory content should be stressed in written examinations. A good balance of subject matter might provide 40 percent of material on supervision, 20 percent on principles of administration, 10 percent on departmental procedures, 10 percent on criminal law and procedures, and the balance on police investigation and procedures." You'll find that the majority of test analysts creating sergeant's exams follow his advice.

Knowing "how to play the game" can make the difference between getting promoted and not getting promoted. Knowing how police tests are constructed, what process is used, and with which criteria your performance will be judged is of immense help to you. In fact, by the time you've finished this book, you'll be able to write a 100-question, multiple-choice test of your own and find that it contains most of the subject matter that will be on *your* test.

Test Validity and Reliability

There are two theories of testing essential to the creation of any exam: validity and reliability. Tests which successfully withstand the increasing civil litigation have both. A 1968 Supreme Court decision, *Griggs v. Duke Power;* mandates that promotional examinations have some relationship to success on the job and that a "test which fails a higher percentage of minority applicants is discriminatory." The Police Foundation's research indicates that "what is prohibited is the use of tests and other selection techniques which tend disproportionately to reject members of various classes heretofore discriminated against (minorities, women, etc.) and which cannot or have not been demonstrated by the employer to measure and reflect occupational requirements." In another important court decision, *Brito v. Zia,* the Tenth Circuit Court ruled that a "performance evaluation" is a "test" and must be "validated according to the Equal Opportunity Employment Act of 1972 relative to employment testing."

For a test to be *valid,* the questions must specifically relate to "job performance." In a sergeant's exam, for example, it would be improper to ask a test question involving the specific duties performed by a captain. There are several ways that those who create the written examination can be sure that the test is related to job performance and that the exam is measuring what it's supposed to measure. One method is for the tester to perform a "job task analysis"—a systematic process that defines the exact tasks and/or behaviors needed to perform a job successfully over a period of time. In conducting a job task analysis, the test analyst writes down the steps, in logical sequence, which must be taken by the person completing a job in order to perform it properly. The person creating the test must be careful to differentiate between the characteristics an individual must possess before assuming the position of sergeant and those normally obtained through experience and training after promotion. One of the problems with police testing is the tendency to promote people before determining whether they have the characteristics necessary to perform the job—one of the primary disadvantages of using seniority as a criterion for promotion. Tenure doesn't necessarily mean that an officer possesses the traits necessary to be a good supervisor.

To be valid, a test must show a distinct relationship between the process used to promote officers and job performance. What is it that sergeants do in your department and how do they do it? What steps are required? What unique characteristics are important? What job tasks do sergeants spend most of their time performing? Test developers ensure that exams are job-related through observation (actually observing people in the position performing job tasks), by completing behavior checklists, and through job surveys. In conducting a job survey, the analyst meets with individuals who hold the rank of sergeant and ask them predetermined questions in order to find out how often they perform a specific job function and what degree of importance they attach to it. Correlate a job task analysis, a sampling profile of sergeants currently performing the job assignment, and your department's orders and procedures outlining the duties and responsibilities of a sergeant, and you have a potentially valid test. All police departments include the sergeant's job description in their orders and procedures—a document that's one of the basic tools used in the creation of a sergeant's examination.

Your test will compare your performance (on a multiple-choice test, for example) with predetermined criteria as described earlier in the "Test Announcement" section. The promotional tests used most often are *criterion-type examinations*, which measure your responses on the written test against a predetermined, presumably correct standard. For example, if your department has an order concerning the use of deadly physical force, it then becomes a standard, or criterion, on which a test question and its answer selection can be based.

The second requirement is that the test be *reliable*. For an exam to be *reliable*, it must consistently and dependably measure what it's supposed to measure, producing about the same results each time the test is given. Without reliable and consistent test-measuring techniques, the exam will not be valid as a prediction instrument.

Advantages of Multiple-Choice Tests

The reason that multiple-choice tests are most often used in promotional testing is that they have the following advantages:

- These tests lend themselves to more *reliable* answers through standardized test items.
- Guessing, which may come into play with true/false questions, is reduced.

- Answers that are feasible can be added to require a discriminating choice between two close answers, only one of which is correct.
- They can be quickly administered and are easier to score and more difficult to challenge than other test instruments.
- They provide the ability to rank order officers by numerical score.
- They provide a permanent record of test performance, which is available for review.

Predicting Future Competence

Police promotional examinations are often part *achievement* and part *aptitude* test. An achievement test measures present proficiency, mastery, and understanding of general and specific knowledge. An aptitude test *predicts* the capacity for achievement and competence. All tests for promotion attempt to predict whether you have or will have the ability to be a sergeant (are you trainable?). How well the test functions depends on to what extent the test is valid and reliable. Many police officers confuse promotional examinations with intelligence tests. Your IQ has little to do with the score you ultimately receive on a promotional exam. That's not what the test is designed to measure.

Remember, your test will have questions relating to the skills you need to perform the job of a police sergeant in your department. If you determine what duties a sergeant in your department performs most often and correlate them with the duties that are most important for a sergeant to accomplish organizationally, you can make a good guess/estimate about what you should be studying. For example, don't spend a lot of time studying what a sergeant in charge of a specialized division does if the majority of sergeants in your organization are in patrol. Know the broader points of specialization, but spend most of your time studying what's most likely to be on the test.

> *There is no gathering of the rose without being pricked by the thorns.*
>
> —Pilpay

Motivation

Superior intelligence, exceptional job performance, and longevity have little to do with how well police officers perform in promotional testing. These characteristics are not what the test is designed to measure. What really matters is

1. self-motivation—how much you want it
2. perseverance—how often and how well you study
3. test-taking skills
4. reading comprehension

I'm firmly convinced that the final ranking of the top 10% of officers taking promotional examinations has more to do with individual motivation than with any other single criterion. Consider the following: If 100 officers take a written test for sergeant, the final rank ordering of at *least* the top 10% is often so closely spaced that there's no real difference in the test's predictive ability. Add the oral examination score to the written test mark, average the two, and the gaps between individuals widen considerably. Here's a sample promotion list.

PROMOTION LIST

	Name	Written Exam	Oral Exam	Final Score
1.	Richard Brown	96%	95%	95.5%
2.	Jeffrey Stone	94%	90%	92.0%
3.	Enrique Gonzalez	91%	88%	89.5%
4.	Paul Johnson	90%	88%	89.0%
5.	Pamela Stone	87%	90%	88.5%
6.	Anthony Lorenzeti	84%	80%	82.0%
7.	Phillip Jones	90%	74%	82.0%
8.	Jose Martinez	81%	76%	78.5%
9.	John Gotling	78%	76%	77.0%
10.	Judith Fleming	70%	80%	75.0%

The difference between the officer who came out No. 1 on this list (Brown, 95.5%) and the one who came out No. 5 (Stone, 88.5%) is only seven points. However, notice the widening gap as the list gets larger. The difference between No. 5 (Stone, 88.5%) and No. 10 (Fleming, 75.0%) is 13.5 points. The first four or five people on this particular promotion list are so close that any of them could have come out No. 1. The only real difference between Officer Brown and Officer Stone is that he was, perhaps, more highly motivated, had better test-taking skills, and knew how to "play the game" better on the oral examination.

No one can really motivate another person to *do* anything—motivation must come from within. In studying for the sergeant's test, you're seeking recognition, advancement, a sense of achievement, and personal growth. To succeed, you must have a specific plan and the ability to motivate yourself consistently towards a visualized goal. You're the only person who really knows what fuels your fire. Galileo put it this way: "You cannot teach a man anything; you can only help him find it within himself." Create the vision and establish a plan to achieve your goal.

We've all used self-motivational techniques since the time we were children. Some people become motivated by leafing through their high school yearbooks or reviewing newspaper clippings of their careers as police officers. Others use family, the need for recognition, or the pursuit of power. Whichever technique you use, make a contract with yourself, take a solemn oath, develop a routine, master self-discipline, buy into the vision, and establish a plan of action. These simple steps will do more to assure that you do well on your test than any other study aid.

> *Genius is 1% inspiration and 99% perspiration.*
>
> —THOMAS A. EDISON

Studying

Arranging Study Material

By this time, you'll have obtained all of the reference material listed on the promotional examination announcement. Arrange these books and materials in a logical sequence grouped by subject matter. Place all your departmental orders, procedures, training bulletins, and rules and regulations in order of descending importance by major topic area. Put this material into the three-ring notebooks you purchased. All of the job tasks associated with being a sergeant in your department should be filed together and an index placed in front of each notebook. Set these notebooks aside; we'll come back to them later. The test questions involving technical and procedural data specific to your department will come from this material.

The books listed on the promotional announcement as references contain the generic information from which your test will be constructed. First, select the book that has the most content related to the index cards you've made out based on the major topic areas of a sergeant's responsibilities, examples of duties, and required knowledge, skills, and abilities as listed in the test announcement. Read the book—but *not* as you would a novel. Read the text very slowly. Consciously make yourself pay strict attention to every word. Obviously, there are some words, terms, and phrases in these textbooks that are more important than others. If you read a textbook the same way you read the newspaper, you'll understand it in only a limited way. Make a deliberate effort to note key words and spend time reflecting on what it is that the author is trying to tell you. At the end of each paragraph, cover the text with an index card and mentally ask yourself the following questions:

- What were the most important thoughts?
- What is the author trying to tell me?
- Why is this section important and how does it relate to the other areas covered in this paragraph?
- How would a test question about this idea be phrased?

Now, restructure the main ideas of the paragraph in your own words. As you're reading, use a dictionary to look up each word that you can't define. Write the definition on a sheet of paper. You'll better understand the ideas expressed if you compare them with your real-life police experiences. This procedure is called making a "positive mental transfer" and is discussed more fully later. Using this technique will improve both your reading comprehension and your vocabulary. Use this method to read the book a second time. The next stage in this process is more analytical.

Highlighting Material

On your third run-through, use a highlighter, and go through the text page by page, sentence by sentence, marking key phrases and sections. Use the red highlighter for any information that is particular to *your* department (procedural information found in your department's manuals, bulletins, etc.). Use the yellow highlighter for books and other reference material listed on the test announcement (generic information). Use the blue highlighter for material found in any other reference source (this book, magazines, other police books, etc.). Look for important ideas and for terms that the author uses repeatedly. Note the sometimes subtle changes in word meanings when they're used in different areas of policing. If the word or key phrase has several meanings, depending on how it's used, think about how the different concepts are related to one another. For instance, you might highlight terms such as *span of control, unity of command, delegation of authority, positive discipline, negative discipline,* and *lost-time management.* Also highlight subtopics of obvious importance such as *supervisory responsibilities at a crime scene, the sergeant's role in emergency situations,* and *motivation of personnel.* When in doubt, highlight the word or phrase. After you complete this task, begin writing all of the areas that you've highlighted on separate index cards. Place a heading in bold print on the top of each index card listing these topic areas. A representative index card may look like this:

DIRECTS
Span of Control
The number of officers a sergeant can effectively supervise.
Factors Influencing
1. Sergeants experience and abilities
2. Type of tasks performed by subordinates
3. Conditions under which job tasks are performed
4. Physical resources available

The reason this procedure works is that you learn by using your five senses. The more senses you stimulate while studying, the more likely you are to retain the information. Studies indicate that we learn about 75% through the sense of sight and about 13% through the sense of hearing. We remember only about 30% of what we see and 20% of what we hear. Combining these two senses works out to a retention level of, at best, about 50%. However, by using "positive mental transfers" in your studying process, you can greatly increase your ability to retain the principles and concepts on which you will be tested. Relate new study material to a fact or experience you already know. For example, the definition of the term *inspection* used in the text you're studying is "a systematic review of department procedures,

systems, methods of operation, equipment, and human resources in order to improve efficiency, effectiveness, and productivity." Your study reference books may have entire chapters
devoted to the sergeant's role in the inspection process. To better retain the definitions and
concepts involved, relate *inspection* to something you know at the officer level.

You've undoubtedly been inspected at roll call, on the beat, in the cruiser, and on calls
for service. Your service revolver was checked; your reports were inspected; the manner in
which you handled a particular case was reviewed; and the time you took on calls for service was analyzed. So, you do know something about the inspection process that you can relate directly to the material you're studying. Create a mental picture of new study material
that connects it to something that is familiar to you.

Writing the material you've highlighted will increase your ability to learn and retain it.
Later, when you have all of your index cards compiled from the reference materials, you'll
use another process that combines seeing and hearing to boost your efficiency even further.

Repeating the Process

After you complete this procedure for the first book, repeat it for the rest of your reference
material, including all the items you put in your three-ring binders.

1. Read slowly, sentence by sentence.
2. Read for meaning.
3. Highlight key material.
4. Copy the material onto your index cards.

While you're reading, don't allow your mind to wander. It's useless to move on to another
topic before you thoroughly understand the one you've just read. Slower comprehension
often happens with technical material, such as budgets or managing by objective. Pay attention to charts and graphs; they further explain the text. Take the time to study them, and
you'll find that your understanding improves.

There's a big difference between being able to repeat a definition and understanding what
it means. Always state the concept in your own words. If you can't, you don't know what it
means. Learning definitions by memory will help you only if that particular term is on the
test, but understanding meanings will enable you to answer questions no matter how they're
worded. By the end of this procedure, you will have assembled an impressive stack of index
cards divided into major topic areas and subdivided by specific classification. Time-consuming? Yes. Boring, difficult, hard work? Yes. **But it works!**

Now, after assembling all your index cards, put one of the rubber bands you purchased
around each stack, dividing them by topic area. You'll carry them with you from now until
test day. *Every single free minute (in the car, while walking around, at lunch, etc.) read the
cards until you know the material cold.* Do this pick-up studying in addition to your planned
sessions. You must master the subject matter to the extent that you can read the top of the
card (Span of Control, for example) and without looking, repeat what you had previously
written. Continue doing this day in and day out, hour after hour. Return to your reference
material often and reread constantly. Repetition improves memory. Understand key principles, know the theory behind topic areas, and study consistently. This is what it takes to be

No. 1. You get only one chance on a promotional test. After all, if it were easy, you wouldn't need superior motivation in order to succeed.

> *One today is worth two tomorrows.*
> —Benjamin Franklin

Other Important Tips

1. Teach. It's long been an axiom that the best way to learn a subject is to teach it. As a patrol officer, you may not be able to teach supervisory concepts, but you can still teach subjects, such as criminal investigation or patrol techniques at a variety of places. Approach your police academy commander and offer to teach at the academy. Also, many departments have "citizen academies," and if your department does, teaching at one of these is a good way to gain experience. Additionally, if you have a college degree, call local colleges that have criminal justice programs. Over the years, I've found that preparing lesson plans and tests is a great way to augment studying for promotional exams. At the very least, teaching will significantly improve your oral examination score.

2. Police promotional tests are extremely competitive. Often, only tenths of a point separate the candidates and make the difference between promotion and failure. So don't study with others; they are your competition! Although there are advantages to group study, such as feedback, any leverage you gain is offset by your helping people who'll be competing directly against you on test day. Study alone in a quiet setting for a minimum of two hours every day. It's very difficult to study at home—too many interruptions and the constant temptation to take breaks. Two hours of study at a library, park, or other quiet place is often better than four hours of study at home. Remember, these two hours are *in addition* to your index card work. Remember also to consistently write out your material while you're studying.

3. Don't waste time studying what you already know. Most people have a tendency to study areas that are of special interest to them or which they learn easily. Concentrate on the areas in which you are *weakest*.

4. Don't procrastinate. It's easy to find reasons that may seem important at the time not to study. Schedule specific hours and don't allow anything to interfere with your plans. If you're married, have a family meeting. Explain what you're doing and your plan to accomplish it. Ask for your family's support and try to involve them as much as possible in your goals.

5. During the week before your written test, rent a room in a quality hotel and move in for a couple of days to culminate your study efforts. I've done this before every promotional test I've taken and found it to be very beneficial. Schedule your time by allowing for several hours of intensive study followed by a break. During your breaks, eat, go for a swim, take a walk, whatever you find enjoyable. Then come back and hit the books again! The following is a suggested study schedule.

HOTEL STUDY SCHEDULE

Day 1

Time – A.M.	Activity
8:00-9:00	Breakfast
9:00-11:00	Study
11:00-11:30	Walk
11:30-12:30 P.M.	Lunch

Time – P.M.	Activity
12:30-2:30	Study
2:30-3:30	Exercise
3:30-5:00	Study
5:00-6:00	Break
6:00-7:00	Study
7:00-8:00	Dinner
8:00-10:00	Study

Day 2

Time – A.M.	Activity
8:00-9:00	Breakfast
9:00-12:00	Take Multiple-Choice Practice Test 1

Time – P.M.	Activity
12:00-1:00	Lunch
1:00-1:30	Walk
1:30-2:00	Correct Practice Test 1
2:00-3:30	Study areas of weakness as determined by Practice Test 1
3:30-4:30	Exercise
4:30-7:30	Take Multiple-Choice Practice Test 2
7:30-8:30	Dinner
8:30-9:00	Correct Practice Test 2
9:00-10:30	Study areas of weakness as determined by Practice Test 2

Note: While this schedule is a good, workable one, you may find that another arrangement works better for you. So don't treat it as the only appropriate way to use your study time. For example, you may find that taking Practice Test 1 a week or two before your hotel stay and basing more study time on its result would be most helpful to you. What is important is that you have a schedule that suits you and that you stick to it.

If this seems like a lot of work to you, you're absolutely right. The rank of sergeant is the most difficult to achieve because there are so many competitors vying for a limited number of vacancies. Lawyers studying for the bar exam can take their test again six months or a year later if they fail. You may have to wait three years or longer for another chance, so maximize your potential by doing everything necessary to ensure peak performance on test day.

> *You have to want it bad. You can find geniuses on any skid row and average intellects as presidents of banks. It's what pushes you from inside.*
>
> —CHARLEY WINNER

Reading Comprehension

Your ability to fully understand what you read is a required skill in test-taking. More police officers fail promotional exams because they don't understand the question or the answer selections than for any other reason.

Textbooks contain two types of words, *ordinary* words and *important* words. Authors use ordinary words just as you and I would if we were having a conversation. The prepositions, conjunctions, articles, and most of the adjectives and verbs are the skeletons on which the meaty key concepts (the *important* words) hang. The very fact that a word, or series of words, is not ordinary should alert you to the fact that you should be spending time looking the word up and reflecting on its meaning. Writers of instructional textbooks often give clues to what they feel is important by using bold type, italics, quotation marks, underlining, or a discussion of a term's definition. Being able to communicate your understanding in written or oral form will give you the high grades that can separate you from the pack.

Practicing Test-Taking

People who frequently take written examinations do better (all other factors excluded) than those who don't. If it's been several years since you last took a written test, practice as much as possible as part of your study routine. The sample tests provided will prove invaluable to you. Creating tests is easier than you may think. By this time, you should be able to make up some of your own questions and answers. Creating your own test is an effective way to study. Just make sure that you're positive of the right answer.

> *At the narrow passage, there is no brother and no friend.*
>
> —ARABIAN PROVERB

Taking the Multiple-Choice Test

Bring the following items with you on test day:

- box of paper clips
- several No. 2 pencils
- durable eraser
- large pad of paper
- watch

(These items are suggested, make sure to check your local policy as to what you are allowed to bring on test day.)

Your Physical Condition

Get a good night's rest before taking the test. This is one of the most important days of your career. Don't make the mistake of staying up late the night before the exam. If you wear glasses, don't forget to bring them. Dress comfortably. You won't be graded for your appearance on the written examination.

The Directions

When you arrive at the test site, choose a seat in the front row where you can hear the test directions better and where you'll have fewer distractions. Listen carefully to the test proctor. Sometimes the "rules" are changed at the last minute and suddenly announced on test day, particularly in matters relating to the grading of the test or the relative weights of test sections. If the method is different from that listed in the examination announcement, and you don't feel the change is beneficial to *you,* immediately notify the exam proctor and file an objection. Silence means acceptance! The test won't be stopped just because you file a protest, but you will have established the groundwork for later appeals.

Time

You'll be told exactly how much time you have in which to take the test. Quickly review all parts of the test to estimate how much time it will take you to complete it. A minute and a half per question on a 100-question, multiple-choice exam would take 150 minutes (two and a half hours). In a three-hour test, that would leave only 30 minutes for review. Check the time frequently to be sure that you're on schedule.

The Test Booklet and Answer Sheet

Read the instructions in the test booklet carefully. If there's something you don't understand, ask! Be sure that you have all the test materials indicated in the oral and written instructions. Usually, computer-type answer sheets, similar to those included in this book, are used for promotional examinations. Follow the oral and written directions, and use the type of pencil indicated by the exam proctor. Fill in your answers completely, and don't make any notations or marks on the answer sheet that might confuse the computer into taking points away from you.

Understanding Questions and Answers

Before you begin your written test, ask the exam proctor if you're allowed to mark on the test booklet. If you are, use this procedure to increase your comprehension of the questions and answer selections:

1. Carefully read the question and circle each word you don't know the definition of or are confused about. You can usually get a good idea of what the word means through reading the entire question.
2. Go back to the word you circled and substitute another word that you feel more comfortable with. Use this same process for the selection choices. An example:

Test Question: The sergeant's ability to apply the concept of "lost-time management" is important when conducting performance evaluations for which of the following reasons?

The key words in this question are *lost-time management* and *performance evaluations*. Circle *lost-time management* and write above it *sick time, injured time, absent without leave, etc.* Then mentally change the question to read "As a sergeant, why is my understanding of officers' use of sick time, injured time, and being away from work without authorization important when I call them in to do their performance evaluations?"

If the test monitor will *not* allow writing on the exam booklet, which sometimes is the case, write the confusing terms on a separate piece of paper.

Marking Questions and Answers

When taking the test, if you're allowed to write in the test booklet, highlight or underline key words in both the question and answer selections. If you come to a question that you're not sure of, skip it, but do one of two things so that you can quickly return to the question later.

1. Put a paper clip alongside the number of the question on both the test booklet and the answer sheet.
2. Put a check mark next to the number of the question on both the test booklet and the answer sheet. If you use this method, *be sure that you completely erase all the check marks from the answer sheet* before time is called so that the computer doesn't identify them as wrong answers.

In almost every police examination, someone skips a question and then gets his or her answer sheet out of sequence, resulting in a very low score. Using the paper clips or check marks will help you avoid this disaster.

As you read the question, circle the correct answer in the booklet and then transfer your selection to the answer sheet. Most multiple-choice tests provide either four or five answer selections per question. You can usually eliminate two of the answers as being obviously wrong; if it's allowed, cross them out in the examination booklet. In a four-question selection spread, you've increased your odds, if randomly selecting the answer, from one in four to one in two. You now only have to select the best answer of the remaining two selections, which are often very similar. Read the question again and then read the answers. Make sure you're certain what the question is asking. Many answer selections contain words called *specific determiners*. Specific determiners that are too broad often indicate the wrong choice. Examples of broad specific determiners are

only, all, never, nothing, everyone, no, always, none, must

Words that often indicate the *right* answer are

could, might, can, usually, sometimes, any, often, generally, occasionally, frequently, possibly, rarely, normally, seldom, may

Above all, make sure that you don't get "stuck" on any question. Remember, all the questions count the same, so if you hit a question that seems very complex or very difficult, mark it, fill in a "guess" answer, and move on. There's no point in agonizing over it and wasting your valuable test time or letting it throw you so completely that you lose concentration on following questions.

Returning to Unanswered Questions

Never leave questions unanswered unless the oral or written instructions indicate that you don't lose credit for questions left blank. Often, as you're taking the test, another question will refresh your memory about one of the questions that you've taken a guess on. Then you need merely to go back to the questions you've paper clipped or checked and select the right answer. If this isn't the case, carefully reread the question, circling key words and phrases and substituting your own words in questions and answers. The most difficult questions often leave you with two answer alternatives, which are often in direct conflict with one another (an either/or situation), yet both seem somehow to be correct. If you're still stuck, stay with your best guess.

Changing Answers

It seems that every time I've taken a test and changed an answer, I invariably changed a right answer to a wrong one. Test-taking statistics indicate that this is most often the case. Unless you're positive, don't change your answers. Trust your initial instincts. If you *do* change an answer, make sure that you completely erase the original answer mark. If you have time at the end of the test, review all of your answers, making sure that you haven't carelessly filled in a wrong answer choice even though you know the right answer. It can happen, so double-check.

3 Language Along the Path

Oral Tests

Understanding the Process

Receiving a high score on the oral examination for the rank of police sergeant is largely dependent on three things:

1. your understanding of the framework involved in constructing and conducting oral examinations
2. how well you prepare and what method you use to prepare for the test
3. your performance on test day

Many police officers believe in what I call "magical thinking." They think the fact that they are outstanding "street cops" will somehow magically translate into a high score on test day. Nothing could be further from the truth. Frankly, it just doesn't matter what you have or haven't done (in street performance) before walking into the test room. As in the world of sports, it's what you do in today's competition that counts. The number of felony arrests you've made or the community service projects you've worked on won't matter if you don't know the answers to the test questions.

All of us in the police profession know of officers who are promoted to sergeant, lieutenant, and above who really aren't good field police officers. However, they are good test-takers. The reason they receive such high marks is that they understand the system, practice, and most important, don't choke on test day.

The oral examination is used by most police departments and central personnel agencies for the selection and promotion of police officers. There are many types in use today. In fact, oral tests are used more often than any other evaluation instrument to "predict" the "future ability" of officers trying for promotion. It's also the type of test that police officers spend the least amount of time preparing for, even though they have the most personal control over its outcome.

> *Learning is like rowing upstream; not to advance is to drop back.*
> —CHINESE PROVERB

The Difference Between Oral and Written Tests

A *test is* a systematic procedure in which the individuals tested are presented with a set of constructed questions to which they respond; the response enables the tester to assign numbers or sets of numbers from which predictions can be made about a person's possession of whatever the test is supposed to measure. Both written and oral examinations and various combinations of each fall within this working definition.

Remember, the written test measures present proficiency, mastery, and understanding of general (generic) and specific (procedural) job knowledge. If written promotion tests are properly constructed and meet the standards of reliability and validity, they are fairly objective. They are *achievement* tests in that they measure present competence as well as predict future competence. They are designed to measure your proficiency and knowledge

in a small number of selected areas. What they lack is the ability to accurately evaluate your intrinsic or intangible qualities—such as leadership potential or organizational integrity. Written tests are incapable of recognizing "doing traits," such as verbal communication skills or appearance. This failing is one of the reasons oral examinations are given. Another reason is that oral tests are more cost-effective than other testing procedures and, if correctly created and administered, can add validity to the testing process.

The oral examination is *not* designed to further measure/evaluate a candidate's specific job knowledge. That would accomplish no more than giving the written test twice. Ideally, the oral interview evaluates the "doing behaviors." Doing behaviors are a combination of verbal responses, body language, gestures, and appearance factors that are observable to those administering the examination. Oral tests provide the tester the opportunity to

- ask questions which investigate the content of and reasoning behind a candidate's answers.
- provide for face-to-face, interpersonal role situations in which open-ended questions can be asked.
- ascertain a candidate's beliefs, attitudes, and intentions (in an oral examination the questions can have more depth).
- determine a candidate's lack of knowledge or confusion in specific areas.
- observe whether a candidate does or does not possess a wide range of "qualities" (for example, stable behavior).
- On the other hand, you can also exercise a great deal of control over your scores on oral boards. Knowing how these tests are constructed and how they work will help you prepare for your examination.

The Oral Board

Traditional Oral

An oral board is a testing process used to assess and rank order candidates according to abilities which have been predetermined to be necessary for successful job performance. Promotional examinations have been heavily litigated resulting in an acute awareness of the need for objectivity. To avoid claims of personal bias—and favoritism —experts from outside your police department serve as panelists on your oral board. Your chief of police or the head of your central personnel division contacts counterparts in other towns who select appropriate people from their agencies to be examiners at your test. Typical oral boards have three panel members. There's an increasing trend toward naming civilian police analysts, police psychologists, or other nonsworn personnel to be panelists along with police representatives. Oral boards testing officers for the rank of sergeant are normally made up of lieutenants and occasionally captains. Some departments even go out of state to obtain panelists in order to ensure objectivity.

The oral panel can convene in any facility large enough to accommodate a long conference table and four or five chairs. The proceedings should not be located in your own police department. The panel often convenes at city hall, a local high school or college, or another government building in your community. Candidates who successfully complete the written phase of the examination process (the passing score is usually 70%) are notified by mail of their mark and the date, time, and location of their appearance before the oral board. Some cities allow everyone who took the written test to go forward in the process and take the oral exam. The letter announcing your oral board date usually contains a number or coded device that you're required to bring with you to the exam.

Technical Oral

In a *nontraditional* (technical) oral exam, several oral panels may be convened. In this process, you'll go through up to three different oral tests, either in one day or over a series of days. Each panel examines your knowledge in different areas of policing, each usually narrower in scope than those covered in traditional oral boards. This procedure is much more difficult, both for the overall test administrator and for the applicants.

Other Types of Oral Examinations

Previously, we discussed that for a test to be *valid* there must be a distinct relationship between test questions and the tasks or behaviors necessary to perform a job successfully over time. This concept is as true for oral examinations as it is for written tests. To increase the job relevance of the oral exam and decrease subjectivity in grading, some cities and towns are taking a more structured approach to the oral examination by linking the test directly to the job task analysis. This has resulted in the creation of several different types of oral examinations that are more complex than either traditional or technical oral board tests. Examples of these types of oral examinations follow.

Mini In-Basket Scenario Followed by Oral Board

In a mini in-basket scenario followed by an oral board, candidates are presented with a packet of materials, similar to but on a smaller scale than the packet used in the assessment center in-basket examinations discussed later in this text. You'll be informed that you have a specific amount of time (ten minutes, for example) to review the information in the packet. The information instructs you to assume that you are a police sergeant and presents a scenario that you must resolve, such as a disciplinary problem with a subordinate, a sexual harassment complaint, or an internal investigation of an officer suspected of a criminal act. At the conclusion of the review period, you'll have a specified length of time (five minutes, for example) to make a presentation to the board explaining how you would handle the matter and why. After the presentation, the panelists (who are sometimes called "assessors") will ask you a series of questions regarding the scenario topic. In this type of oral examination, you and several other candidates can review the material at the same time and then report individually to different oral panels located in rooms throughout the building, thus allowing relatively large numbers of candidates to be tested simultaneously.

Video Presentation Followed by Oral Board

An exam consisting of a video presentation followed by an oral board begins with candidates watching a video depicting a scenario similar to those described for the mini in-basket scenario exercise. After viewing the video, you'll have about five minutes to prepare a presentation for the oral panel describing how you would handle the matter as a police sergeant. As with the mini in-basket exercise, after you make your presentation, the panel members will ask you questions regarding the video's topic. This type of oral examination also lends itself to four or five candidates viewing the video at the same time and then reporting separately to different panels.

Situational Exercise Followed by Oral Board

In a situational exercise, candidates assume the role of a police sergeant and role-play with one or more actors in a situation requiring supervisory action, such as a meeting with a subordinate who is continually late for work or who has asked to see the sergeant about a personal problem. You will be given an information packet typically containing background information about the employee, departmental procedures, and a copy of the labor/management agreement. You'll have about five minutes to review the information, after which the panel will call the subordinate into the room and you will handle the situation. In almost every case, the person playing the subordinate will bring up something not mentioned in your information packet, perhaps by making a statement such as, "Sometimes I think about shooting myself." During this exercise, the panel members are in the room but are not to be communicated with until they tell you that the situational part of the examination is completed. Following the exercise, the panelists win ask you a series of predetermined questions related to the topic(s) addressed in the situation.

More About Your Panelists

The chiefs of police who receive letters from another city requesting that one of their lieutenants or captains serve on an oral panel take the invitation seriously. Those selected represent both their cities and their police departments. The chiefs carefully choose people in whom they have full confidence because promotional tests will eventually be given in their towns too, and they'll expect any town they assist to reciprocate.

The people selected to serve on your oral panel may have a great deal of or very little experience in serving on oral boards. Once chosen, the panelists have several weeks lead-time before traveling to your city for the test. During this time, they receive material from the test administrator containing the following information:

- the dimensions of the job position
- an organizational chart of your police department
- the method (procedure) used to conduct the oral exam
- interviewing techniques and restrictions
- rating instructions

Additionally, the test administrator may ask the panelists to attend a training session several days before the scheduled examination, especially if the examination includes a mini in-basket scenario, video presentation, or situational exercise. During the training session, panelists practice grading candidates by viewing videos of previous examinations in which these types of exercises were used or by watching a role-player acting the part of a candidate. The objective is to train the panelists to grade candidates on observable behavior and what the candidates say as opposed to more subjective criteria, such as appearance and organization.

The Dimensions of the Job

The duties and responsibilities of a police sergeant are different in each organization. Panelists are given information about job tasks a sergeant performs in your city so that they have a common understanding of the scope of the position. An example of a "job task description" is illustrated on the next page.

Panelists use the job task description" as a guide in formulating the questions they'll ask you at the oral board. They want to make sure that the questions created are both appropriate and related to the jobs performed by a sergeant in your organization.

The Organizational Chart

The panelists receive a diagram illustrating the job tasks and levels of authority from the chief down to the patrol officer in what is termed a pyramid of authority. This information is important to panelists because it shows graphically exactly where sergeants fit in the organization and the types of supervisory responsibilities they routinely carry out.

POLICE SERGEANT

NATURE OF WORK

This is supervisory police work in directing an assigned squad of patrol officers in protecting life and property and in enforcing criminal and traffic laws and local ordinances. Work involves responsibility for the efficient and prompt performance of patrol officers performing the tasks of booking, transmitting, and/or receiving duties at the police desk; supervising prisoners within booking facilities and preparing written reports relative to their cases; supervising and participating in detective work when personnel of this class are on special assignment; and supervising officers in the field and responding to calls for service. All work is performed in accordance with department rules and regulations. General instructions regarding assignments and procedures are received from superior officers, and work is carried on under their supervision.

ILLUSTRATIVE EXAMPLES OF WORK

Inspects equipment and personal appearance of subordinates at roll call and ensures their readiness for duty; patrols assigned areas; checks patrol officers in the performance of their duties and gives advice and assistance when necessary; and books prisoners and ensures that correct charges are placed against them and that they are processed in accordance with departmental procedures.

In the traffic division, supervises traffic officers and assigns duties for special traffic conditions; personally supervises control of traffic in emergency situations; and inspects traffic control equipment to ensure proper functioning.

When assigned to investigative duties, visits scenes of crimes; searches for and preserves physical evidence; and investigates cases and supervises officers in their investigations.

Performs related work as required.

DESIRABLE KNOWLEDGE, SKILLS, AND ABILITIES

Working knowledge of the principles, methods, practices, and techniques of police work.

Working knowledge of the methods of preserving evidence and what constitutes admissible evidence.

Working knowledge of state statutes and local ordinances.

Ability to plan, control, assign, organize, and supervise the work of others. Ability to react quickly and calmly in emergency situations.

Ability to express oneself clearly and concisely both orally and in writing. Skill in the use and care of firearms.

Good physical strength and agility.

DESIRABLE EXPERIENCE AND TRAINING

A minimum of _____ years of experience as a (name of town) police officer. Graduation from high school and possession of a valid State of _____ driver's license.

Conducting the Traditional Oral

If a training session for panelists has not been given, on the day of the test (several hours before the first candidates arrive), the three people who have been selected to serve on your oral panel receive a briefing on the oral examination procedure used by your city. The meeting is conducted by the central personnel analyst assigned to oversee the administration of the test. During this time, the panelists get to know one another and review the questions they'll ask the candidates at the oral. Most cities allow panelists to construct their own test questions, although the city reviews them to make sure they are both appropriate and job-related. Inappropriate or illegal questions are discarded. Areas that must be avoided include race, color, national origin, ancestry, marital status, political party membership or activities, and religious affiliation or church attendance. In addition to the legal ramifications is an awareness that candidates might be upgraded or downgraded because of a panelist's personal bias. For this reason, some cities create their own mandatory and optional, questions and divide them among the panelists to ask candidates at the interviews.

The questions are designed to *impartially* and *objectively* evaluate the *knowledge, skill,* and *aptitude* of each candidate and to rank the applicants in the order of their competence. It's the panelists' responsibility to evaluate the candidates' responses and rate them objectively.

Because the board has only a short time to spend with each candidate (from 20 to 45 minutes, depending on how many officers are interviewed), they can ask only a limited number of questions. Each panelist selects two or three questions, which then become *mandatory* questions. Each candidate must be asked the mandatory questions; however, the panelists are free to ask optional or follow-up questions and frequently choose to do so.

During this preliminary meeting, the panelists are asked to review a list containing the names and addresses of each candidate to make sure that they know none of the candidates personally. If a panelist does know an individual on the list, the test administrator excuses that board member from interviewing that particular candidate and fills in for the panelist.

During the meeting, one of the panelists is selected to greet each candidate and introduce him or her to the others. Some cities elect to have a representative from the personnel department perform this task. Either a panel member or the test administrator will record the session. The third panelist often acts as a timekeeper to ensure that each candidate has approximately the same amount of time with the oral board.

Grading

Since the purpose of the oral exam is to measure a candidate's intrinsic qualities, which the written test can't adequately evaluate, a concern about these rating devices is that they may provide such a wide range of rater response that the test is not valid or reliable. Although grading forms vary, the *concept of* the mechanism remains relatively consistent.

Following are samples of two rating forms commonly used to evaluate candidates in oral exams:

RATING FACTORS

1. Overall Impression
General appearance, enthusiasm, speech, vocabulary, mannerisms, communication skills, clarity of expression.

| 40 | 50 | 60 | 70 | 80 | 90 | 100 |

2. Alertness, Self-Confidence
Readiness in grasping the meaning of questions, self-confidence, surety of answers.

| 40 | 50 | 60 | 70 | 80 | 90 | 100 |

3. Interest, Attitude
rest in the position sought, positive attitude about the functions of the job.

| 40 | 50 | 60 | 70 | 80 | 90 | 100 |

4. Judgment/Problem Solving, Presenting Ideas
Ability to exercise good judgment, make decisions, be dependable and consistent, use logic, get to the root of the problem, weigh alternatives, analyze situations, make conclusions.

| 40 | 50 | 60 | 70 | 80 | 90 | 100 |

5. Responsibility, Maturity
Possession of maturity necessary to handle the responsibilities of the position sought, integrity required of the job, awareness of the seriousness of the position.

| 40 | 50 | 60 | 70 | 80 | 90 | 100 |

6. Working Relationships, Ability to Perform
Ability to meet stress, promote worker cooperation, and handle the public relations requirements of the position sought.

| 40 | 50 | 60 | 70 | 80 | 90 | 100 |

7. Job Knowledge
Understanding of the duties, necessary abilities, methods, and practices of the position and ability to use skills in the execution of duties.

| 40 | 50 | 60 | 70 | 80 | 90 | 100 |

RATING FACTORS

1. Interpersonal Skills	_____	4. Candidate Impact	_____
2. Reasoning	_____	5. Judgment	_____
3. Comprehension	_____	6. Job Concept	_____

Fair			**Good**		**Excellent**		
70	75	80	**85**	90	95	100

The criteria established in the preliminary interview, the rating form used by your city, and the predetermined questions selected to be used on the oral examination comprise the test process by which candidates are evaluated.

During the interview, the panelists take notes on the officer's performance. Immediately after the candidate leaves the room, the panelists review their notes and, without discussing the candidate with other examiners, assign a numerical rating on each of the categories. After the individual ratings are completed, the group discusses any "significant differences" in the scoring on the individual categories. One or more of the examiners may have observed performance, positive or negative, that was overlooked by another board member. The board doesn't have to reach a consensus, however. In fact, ratings should not be changed unless a board member is convinced that the preliminary score given to a candidate doesn't truly reflect the level of competence.

After the board members have thoroughly reviewed and considered the ratings of a candidate, each panelist totals and averages scores on the individual criteria and assigns a final score. The three final scores are averaged to arrive at the candidate's final oral examination mark.

> *Whoever wants to reach a distant goal must take many small steps.*
> —HELMUT SCHMIDT

Conducting the Technical Oral

The technical oral is radically different from the traditional oral. It's intended to measure more than a candidate's intrinsic qualities. Some scoring may reflect traditional criteria, such as "appearance" and "oral communication skills," but the primary purpose of the board is to *evaluate a candidate's knowledge.* In a sense, it's similar to the written test, except the questions are a bit broader and obviously are oral. The process is set up like an oral board, but instead of one panel, there are two or even three in separate parts of the same building. The candidate appears before each board on the same day or over a series of days. The three panels examine different aspects of the candidate's knowledge and skills. Here's an example of what each board might test a candidate on:

Panel 1: Tests a candidate's broad-based knowledge of supervisory practices and skills.

Panel 2: Determines a candidate's knowledge of department procedures, training, manuals, or other technical supervisory data.

Panel 3: Examines a candidate's knowledge of state statutes, municipal ordinances, etc.

This type of test is difficult to administer. In order to have three separate boards, nine panelists must be selected, and three additional test monitors are needed. Managing the rotational flow of candidates through the various orals is awkward and time-consuming.

Grading

The validity of this type of test instrument is often questionable. An example of a rating form used on a technical oral follows:

RATING FORM		
Technical Oral Examination		
(10, 20, 40)		Job Knowledge
(6, 8, 10)		Comprehension and Alertness
(6, 8, 10)		Decision-Making Ability
(6, 8, 10)		Resourcefulness
(4, 5, 6)		Judgment
(4, 5, 6)		Poise and Appearance
(4, 5, 6)		Maturity
(4, 5, 6)		Personality and Speech
(4, 5, 6)		Interest and Initiative

The numbers in parentheses are used as evaluation guidelines. The first number is the lowest and the last number is the highest score a candidate can receive. The total of the numbers determines the officer's final score.

> *Let no man presume to give advice to others that he has not first given counsel to himself.*
> —SENECA

Conducting Oral Exams That Include Mini In-Basket Scenarios, Video Presentations, or Situational Exercises

Many of the same criteria used to evaluate candidates appearing before traditional and technical oral boards are also used to assess candidates when scenarios, video presentations, or situational exercises are incorporated into the process. The primary difference is that in the latter three, specific and observable behaviors expected of a successful candidate for the position have been predetermined and are often placed on a checklist that panelists use in the grading process. Although candidates' answers to panelists' questions still count toward their grades, those answers may be secondary to the candidates' displaying that they can actually translate knowledge into action. Because each of these oral tests allows panelists to observe the candidates reacting to or presenting a solution to a situation, panelists can more readily determine whether candidates can use their knowledge, skills, and abilities in actually doing the job, as opposed to merely knowing about how to do it. Many police administrators have complained that traditional oral testing produces high-scoring candidates who are "good test-takers" but lack the "doing" types of skills, such as leadership, judgment, and the ability to deal with a diverse mixture of people. Using these types of oral tests is an effort to incorporate more job relevance into the testing process without going to the time and expense of having candidates participate in a full-blown assessment center.

Following are examples of actual examinations that show you what to expect in your information packet if your oral examination consists of scenarios, video presentations, or situational exercises. The first examination is an example of a mini in-basket scenario, which requires the candidate to make a presentation to the oral board.

The City of Newburg Police Sergeant Examination
Oral Examination: Training

Directions:

For the purpose of this examination, you are to assume the role of a police sergeant. You have ten minutes from the time you open your examination packet to review the following question. At the end of ten minutes, you are to report to Room 204, at which time you will make a five-minute presentation to an oral panel explaining how you would handle this matter as a police sergeant. At the completion of your five-minute presentation, the panel members will ask you questions.

Oral Examination Question:

As a sergeant, one of your principle duties will be the training of subordinates. Assume that you are a police sergeant assigned to the Patrol Division. Officer John Smith has just graduated from the police academy and has been assigned to the Patrol Division under your supervision, beginning today. Explain in detail how you would determine what training Officer Smith should receive; the objectives, types, and amount of training to be given; and who would be directly responsible for seeing that Officer Smith is properly trained.

Your answer should also include the type of diagnostic and/or evaluation instrument you would recommend and how you would ensure the training is effective and efficient.

Some oral examinations, however, will require you to participate in a situational exercise. Here is an example of such an exercise.

The City of Newburg Police Sergeant Examination
Supervisor/Subordinate Counseling Examination

DIRECTIONS FOR TAKING THIS EXAMINATION

You are responsible for budgeting your time during this examination. You have a total of **40 minutes** to complete the entire examination process.

Officer James Jennings is outside of this room waiting for you to call him in. As soon as you open this examination packet, you have **20 minutes** to read the enclosed "Background and Facts" and "The Problem" sections and to call Officer Jennings in to take whatever action you deem necessary as a police sergeant to resolve the situation outlined in the scenario.

At the completion of the first 20 minutes of the examination process (or earlier should you determine you are finished), you will be asked questions by two panelists, who will be in the room observing the entire supervisor/subordinate examination.

Background and Facts

You are Sergeant Pat Andrews, currently assigned to the Patrol Division of the Newburg Police Department. Officer James Jennings, a 24-year veteran of the department, is a desk officer under your direct supervision. During the past six months, Officer Jennings's job performance has deteriorated significantly. He has become argumentative and is often late to work. He has failed to submit written reports in a timely fashion, and the reports he does complete contain glaring errors and must be rewritten. Additionally, in the past six months the officer's appearance has deteriorated. He has lost more than 25 pounds, has difficulty moving from point to point, and his uniform doesn't fit properly and is often dirty. He has used five sick days in the past two weeks. You suspect he may be a functional alcoholic.

Two weeks ago, you had a meeting with Officer Jennings to discuss his job performance. Officer Jennings informed you that he was having "family problems" and would "shape up." He also reminded you of his excellent past record and that he "broke you in" when you came into the department.

The Problem

Officer James Jennings is on duty at the front desk today and has been pacing back and forth, muttering to himself. He was 30 minutes late for work, is not in uniform, and his breath smells of alcohol.

Officer Jennings is currently outside this room waiting to see you. Call him in and take whatever action you deem necessary as a police sergeant to resolve the situation.

As a candidate, you would not see the following script that would be used by the role-player, but it is provided here to enhance your understanding of how the process works.

Script for Role-Player—Officer James Jennings

You are Officer James Jennings, a 24-year veteran of the Newburg Police Department. Your current assignment is as front desk officer working under the direct supervision of Patrol Sergeant Pat Andrews.

You are a functional alcoholic. Six months ago, your wife left you because of your drinking problem. During the past six months, you have become argumentative and have often been late to work. At work, you have failed to submit written reports in a timely fashion, and the reports that you have completed contain glaring errors and must be rewritten. Your appearance has also deteriorated. In the past six months, you have lost more than 25 pounds. Your uniform doesn't fit properly and is often dirty. Due to lack of food and too much alcohol, you are sick and have difficulty moving from point to point. You have used five sick days in the past two weeks.

Two weeks ago, Sergeant Andrews called you in to discuss your job performance. You told him that you were having "family problems" and would "shape up." You also reminded Sergeant Andrews of your excellent past record and that you "broke him in" when he came into the department.

Yesterday, after being served with divorce papers by your wife's attorney, you went on an all-night drinking binge. Although you managed to come to work today, you were 30 minutes late and forgot your uniform. You are wearing civilian clothes at the front desk and are pacing back and forth, muttering to yourself. When you are first called in by the candidate acting as Sergeant Andrews, you are hostile and demand to see a union steward. Then you put your head in your hands and begin crying.

Here's another example of an oral board situational exercise.

The City of Newburg Police Sergeant Examination
Employee Conflict-Resolution Examination

DIRECTIONS FOR TAKING THIS EXAMINATION

You are responsible for budgeting your time during this examination. You have a total of **40 minutes** to complete the entire examination process.

You are to read the "Background and Facts" and "The Problem" sections of this examination before entering the examination room. You have a maximum of **20 minutes** from the time you open this examination packet to read the materials and take whatever action you deem necessary as a police sergeant to resolve the situation outlined in the scenario.

After reading the "Background and Facts" and "The Problem" sections, you will enter the examination room where civilian Police Records Division employee Barbara Johnson is waiting to meet with you. Officer Tony Martin will be outside the examination room while you are speaking to Ms. Johnson. He will knock on the examination door for his scheduled appointment with you.

At the completion of the first 20 minutes of the examination process (or earlier should you determine you are finished), the panelists will halt the role-play and ask you questions regarding the scenario.

Background and Facts

You are Sergeant John Jones. Your current assignment is supervising the activities and personnel of the Patrol Division of the Newburg Police Department, and your normal hours of work are from 1530-2330.

Officer Tony Martin works directly for you as a front desk officer. Officer Martin was recently the subject of a sexual harassment investigation that concluded that he had made inappropriate remarks to Ms. Barbara Johnson, a civilian Records Division employee of the department. As part of a negotiated settlement, Officer Martin was given a three-day suspension without pay and was ordered to receive training on the department's policy on sexual harassment in the workplace. The training is to be given on the first day Officer Martin returns to work and prior to his assuming his duties at the front desk.

The Problem

Barbara Johnson is in your office waiting to talk to you and is very upset about something. Officer Martin is scheduled to return to work today and has an appointment with you. You are to call him in when he knocks on the door and take whatever action you deem necessary as a police sergeant to resolve the situation.

Included in this package is the Newburg Police Department's order on sexual harassment.

Once again, you would not be shown the following scripts for either the female or male role-player, but they are provided here to enhance your understanding of how the process works.

Script for Role-Player—Ms. Barbara Johnson

You are Ms. Barbara Johnson, a civilian employee of the department working in the Records Division. You filed a sexual harassment complaint against Officer Tony Martin, resulting in his being suspended by the department for three days without pay. As part of a negotiated settlement with the city, Officer Martin is required to receive sexual harassment training prior to returning to work and is to work a different shift than you.

You just learned that Officer Martin is returning to work today on the same shift you are working. You saw Officer Martin in the hallway, and he walked over to you and said, "Thanks for the vacation. You can run, but you can't hide."

You're very upset. You had an affair with Officer Martin but broke it off a year ago. He has refused to leave you alone. You are getting hang-up calls at home and suspect Officer Martin of making the calls. You're in the sergeant's office. When the candidate comes in, tell him or her that Officer Martin wasn't supposed to be working the same hours as you and relate the remarks Officer Martin just made and that you suspect he has been making harassing telephone calls to your home. Declare that you can't take any more of this and that you feel ill and are going home. Leave the office and slam the door.

Script for Role-Player—Officer Tony Martin

You are Officer Tony Martin. Married, with two children, you are a 14-year veteran of the department and your normal assignment is that of desk officer in the Patrol Division. Recently, civilian Police Records Division employee Barbara Johnson filed a sexual harassment complaint against you, which resulted in your being suspended by the department for three days without pay. As part of a negotiated settlement with the city, you are required to receive sexual harassment training prior to returning to work and are to work a different shift than Ms. Johnson. Although you were found "guilty" in the investigation, you refuse to accept its results and have consistently denied the charges. Furthermore, you did not have an "affair" with Barbara Johnson, nor did you see her in the hallway today or make any remarks to her. You think Barbara Johnson is paranoid and needs psychiatric treatment.

You are meeting with Sergeant Jones in his office prior to beginning work and have not had a chance to put your uniform on yet. You are a little hostile and angry about this charge being a part of your official department record.

Grading

Examples of two rating forms—one on oral communication and the other on supervisory control—that are used for these types of oral examinations follow.

Oral Examination—Newburg Police Sergeant

Candidate #:   Panel #: _____ Rater #: _____ Date#: _____ Time#: _____

DIMENSION 1: ORAL COMMUNICATION

To what extent did the candidate: Done Well   Acceptable   Not Done
1. Speak with clear, concise statements.
2. Maintain good eye contact with employees.
3. Give appropriate nonverbal messages.
4. Ask questions to clarify points.
5. Listen attentively.
6. Choose appropriate language to fit the situation.

DIMENSION 1: ORAL COMMUNICATION

POOR	NOT ACCEPTABLE	ACCEPTIBLE	GOOD	VERY GOOD
1	2	3	4	5

Oral Examination—Newburg Police Sergeant

Candidate #:   Panel #: _____ Rater #: _____ Date#: _____ Time#: _____

DIMENSION 2: SUPERVISORY CONTROL

To what extent did the candidate:	Done Well	Acceptable	Not Done
1. Display skill in telling subordinate when job performance/behavior was not acceptable..			
2. Display skill in establishing a course of action to resolve employee conflict(s).			
3. Display skill in referring an employee to counseling or other resources in a tactful manner.			
4. Display skill in using flexibility and discretion in handling employee grievances.			
5. Take action indicating support for and maintenance of department standards, goals, and ethics.			

DIMENSION 2: SUPERVISORY CONTROL

POOR	NOT ACCEPTABLE	ACCEPTIBLE	GOOD	VERY GOOD
1	2	3	4	5

Preparing for Your Oral Test

Now that you have a basic understanding of the oral board system, you can form your own study plan.

In most departments, it takes from three to six weeks to correct and analyze the written exam and announce the results to the candidates. Several more weeks may pass before the oral exam. Many police officers don't use the time between the written and oral test to their best advantage. They make the mistake of waiting to receive their written test score before they begin to study for the oral exam. Others fall prey to the psychological "head games" of their peers who also took the written exam and boast about scoring 100%. Keep in mind, as Benjamin Franklin so nicely put it, "Great talkers are little doers." Some officers spread rumors that an "injunction" has been filed against the test and it may be months before the oral exam, so "there's no use in studying." Often, someone who has unofficially "rank ordered" the officers who took the written test puts a promotion list on the bulletin board that's based on how officers "say" they did. Waiting for test results produces a great deal of anxiety and stress. After months of studying, you're tempted to fall back into your regular routine and ignore the idea of studying for promotion. It's simpler to just say, "When I find out what my written test score is, then I'll decide what to do."

If you listen to the rumor mill, take a defeatist attitude, and leave everything in a state of limbo, someone else will be wearing sergeant's stripes, not you! You've got to start studying again the day after the written test and continue until the moment before you walk in to take your oral exam. If others aren't doing the same, fine. So much the better for you. The oral examination counts for a large percentage of your final overall mark and separates the new sergeants from the also-rans.

To achieve a high score in any oral interview, you must have *excellent verbal communication* skills. Clear and effective communication (including body language) is the conduit through which you transmit information to the panelists.

Knowing is not enough in an oral exam. You must orally communicate what you know and explain how you will use that knowledge as a police sergeant. The test questions are designed to place you in hypothetical situations in which you must make a decision to

- take a particular course of action as a supervisor
- direct a subordinate to accomplish a task (delegate)
- commit a group of people under your supervision to a plan of action in order to accomplish a specific goal or series of goals

POSDCORB

The acronym POSDCORB, coined by Luther Gulick in 1937, is often a key component in promotional exams. It stands for "planning, organizing, staffing, directing, coordinating, reporting, and budgeting"—all skills expected of a sergeant and areas that you should concentrate on in your studies.

Planning and Organizing

Study resource material that deals with establishing short, intermediate, and long-range plans and designing and implementing those plans to achieve department goals and objectives. The material should cover these topics: proper planning of specific job tasks for subordinates and the allocation of resources to reach organizational goals; proper organization of time, material, and human resources in order to complete job tasks; and planning and implementing field operations under normal and emergency conditions. In other words, knowing what needs to be done and deciding who's going to do it.

Staffing

Study resource material that deals with establishing priorities: identifying and analyzing potential staffing problems and recommending courses of action; properly allocating physical and human resources in day-to-day operations as well as under emergency conditions; and planning the training, education, and career development of personnel.

Directing

Study resource material that deals with methodologies useful in guiding subordinates towards task accomplishment; monitoring and inspecting systems and activities, including the behavior of subordinates; positive, progressive, and negative discipline; motivation techniques and leadership styles and skills; readiness to make decisions, commit oneself or subordinates to a course of action, and take responsibility for failure; efficiently and effectively delegating to subordinates and using department resources.

Coordinating

Study resource material that deals with supervisory coordination of patrol and investigative personnel; coordination of line and staff functions to accomplish department objectives; basic principles such as unity of command and span of control; and coordination of outside resources.

Reporting and Budgeting

Study resource material that deals with analyzing and reviewing officer's reports; what is required in a proper report; what should be passed on to superior officers; sifting through facts and determining what is and is not important; the inspection process and the use of administrative, personnel, and field reporting systems; and the department's budget system and the supervisor's role in budget recommendations and implementation.

Answering Questions

One reason that officers fail to score highly on oral examinations is their tendency to answer the questions at the officer rather than the supervisory level. Questions relating to the following areas require responses based on *organizational integrity,* not comradeship.

- Officers drinking on duty
- Intoxication
- Sleeping on duty
- Use of narcotics or other controlled substances
- Employee theft
- Male officer versus female officer
- Training
- Discipline
- Protected classes
- Performance evaluations
- Sexual harassment

In an oral board on which I was a panelist, an otherwise excellent candidate would not recommend negative discipline regardless of the supervisory situation in which the board placed him. The candidate continually talked about "counseling," "retraining," and finally "reassignment," rather than proposing the negative discipline that wasobviously called for. Apparently, this candidate could not envision himself documenting improper employee conduct through the progressive-discipline procedure and recommending negative discipline. It was obvious to the board that the applicant was probably a good "street cop"—intelligent, loyal, motivated, and trustworthy—but he had not yet made the transition in his thinking past the personal to the organizational level. The notations on his oral board rating form contained such comments as "does not yet see the larger picture" and "this candidate is still thinking at the individual (self) level as opposed to considering what is good for his organization." He did not fare well.

In studying for the oral test, you must know the terms, concepts, and specific processes associated with both *generic* and *procedural* supervision in your department—flawlessly! When studying for the written examination, you read the reference material several times, highlighted areas, wrote out the subject matter on legal pads and index cards, and committed the information to memory. The process of studying for the oral test is similar. However, because the exam responses will be oral, to prepare effectively you must practice speaking these concepts and definitions *out loud*. Knowing all of the material is not enough; you must be able to communicate that knowledge in a clear, concise, and understandable manner, to the panelists. If the information remains locked in your head and never comes out of your mouth, or does so haltingly, you've lost the opportunity to tell the board what you know. Use these techniques to improve your oral-communication skills:

1. Review the major topic areas, job tasks, supervisory dimensions, concepts, and subjects you placed on your index cards for the written examination.
2. Correlate these with the Glossary of Key Terms, included in this book.
3. Begin creating your own oral board questions on a new set of index cards and follow each with the correct response (which you derive from your resource material).

For instance, in making up your questions, you might develop one like this: "Understanding the concept of vicarious liability is important for a police sergeant. Please tell this board what you know about vicarious liability and what mechanisms you will use as a police supervisor to protect your organization from civil litigation?"

The panel assumes that the majority of candidates know the book definition of vicarious liability, but remember, the board isn't judging you on technical job knowledge, but on such criteria as communication skills, attitude, judgment, maturity, reasoning ability, and interpersonal skills. Your index cards should reflect your personal ability to use this question to showcase the skills for which you are being tested. Yes, show the board that you know what the academic definition is, but also give specific, real-life examples of vicarious-liability situations. Explain how you would use leadership, motivational, interpersonal, and supervisory skills to successfully handle the vicarious-liability situation you've outlined for the board. Don't just say that you would ensure that your subordinates are properly trained and would document the training so your organization can defend itself in civil litigation. Illustrate how you will teach and *coach your subordinates* concerning vicarious liability and use the principles of motivation and leadership to gain willing compliance from your officers. Reading your index cards out loud will give you an opportunity to eliminate any "street lingo" or slang from your vocabulary. It will also improve your pronunciation and delivery.

> *Handle them carefully, for words have more*
> *power than atom bombs.*
> —PEARL STEPCHAN

Creating Your Own Mock Oral Board

Pretend that you're actually at the oral board, and using your video recorder, practice answering the questions you develop. Play the recording back and put yourself in the place of a panelist judging your answer. Does your answer show knowledge and understanding beyond the basic question? Does it illustrate your understanding of the underlying issues involved? Does it show your ability to apply supervisory concepts? How would you rate your communication skills? Are your thoughts well-organized? Do they flow easily, or are your main points disjointed and confused with *uh's* and *ah's* and gaps between ideas? Do you say "you know" over and over again?

Next, create an oral board in your own home. Record ten or fifteen of the questions you created. Space the questions with approximately five minutes of blank space between them. Get a table and place three chairs behind it. Put a pad and a pencil in front of each of the three chairs. Put the large stuffed animals you bought (a lion, a tiger, and a bear) in the three chairs. They are now your oral board panel. Set a fourth chair in front of the table facing your three stuffed animals, and put your recording on the table in front of it. Practice entering the room, smiling at your stuffed animal panelists as you shake their hands (maintaining proper eye contact, of course) and seating yourself in front of the panel. Turn on the recording and begin with the first test question.

A typical first question might be "Before we begin to ask you the specific questions on your oral examination, would you please tell the board a little about yourself?" Answer the question exactly as you would at a real oral board. Continue through all of the questions and repeat this exercise until you get it perfect. If you can do this with three stuffed animals, you can do it with three police lieutenants from out of town!

Another technique is to have your spouse, a friend, or a family member ask you the questions so you can practice your responses. If you can, use a video camera to record your practice sessions so you can see yourself as others see you. Ask yourself the following questions:

- What do I look like?
- What do I sound like?
- Am I sitting properly?
- Are my facial expressions and gestures appropriate for an oral test?
- Do I make eye contact with all three panel members when answering the questions?

You may be surprised, after reviewing the video, to discover that you have more weak points than you realized. Seeing yourself as others see you and adjusting for weaknesses is a very positive practice tool. At first, you may feel awkward answering questions at your mock oral board, but you'll very quickly see a vast improvement in your performance. Be sure to make use of all the oral exam practice material included in this book, following these same techniques. However you choose to practice, practice you must, or you won't score as highly as you're capable of in your oral test.

> *Mistakes are their own instructors.*
> —HORACE

Achieving High Scores on Oral Exams that Include Mini In-Basket Scenarios, Video Presentations, or Situational Exercises

All of the preparation techniques suggested to assist you in achieving high scores in traditional and technical oral examinations are also important for exams that require you to give a presentation or participate in a situational exercise. However, a slightly different approach must be taken with these types of oral examinations to receive high scores. First, take a look at examinations in which you give a presentation to the oral panel.

Oral Presentations

You won't be told in advance what type of oral examination you will be participating in. However, if you're instructed to enter a room along with four or five other candidates, the test will most likely be in three parts. First, you will review written materials describing a scenario that requires supervisory intervention, or you will watch a video that re-creates such a situation. You will then be advised that you have a short amount of time to prepare a five-minute presentation to a panel explaining how you would handle the situation as a police sergeant. Finally, the test administrator will instruct you and the other candidates to report to separate rooms to give your presentations, after which you will be asked a series of questions by the oral panel members.

Listen carefully to the test administrator's instructions. If the first part of the exam consists of reviewing written materials, it will also probably have written instructions. You're not being graded by anyone yet, so this is the time to ask questions if you're confused about what you are to do. Quickly scan the material and look for the *issue, problem, or need for supervisory intervention*, which is what you are to resolve in your presentation to the oral board. Paper will almost certainly be provided (you should have a pen and pocket notebook just in case it's not), and you should begin writing an outline of the major points that you want to address in your presentation to the panel.

If the first part of the examination consists of watching a video, immediately begin taking notes while viewing the video unless specifically instructed not to do so by the test administrator. When the video ends, begin making your outline of the major points that you want to present to the panel.

The techniques discussed for making a good first and last impression are very important in giving an oral presentation. Unless you're told that you are not to have contact with the panel members until your presentation is concluded, you should also follow the steps included in the section "Appearing Before the Oral Board." Approach each panelist and shake hands upon entering the room, and remember—at this point, you are in charge! Tell the panel members that you have reviewed the material (information packet or video) and have prepared a short outline of the presentation you are about to give them. If there is a blackboard or flip chart in the room, use it (your final score will be higher if you do), but before doing so, inform the panel that you are going to quickly jot down the major topics you want to highlight in your presentation. Three or four topic headings are all that are needed. For example, if the topic is training Officer Smith, then these might by your headings (while writing the topic headings on the blackboard or flip chart, say them out loud to the panel so there won't be an awkward silence as you're writing).

Training Program: Officer Smith

- Types of Training Officer Smith Will Receive
- Determining Training Objectives
- Assigning Responsibility for Training
- Following Up to Determine if Officer Is Meeting Training Objectives

Once the topic headings are on the blackboard or flip chart, it's much easier to cover each of them during your presentation.

The key here is that you have five minutes of uninterrupted time to dazzle the board with your superior communication skills and knowledge. Take full advantage of all five minutes. Although that may seem like a long time to speak on a single subject—especially if you'd rather be in a dentist's chair than speak in front of a group—if you use the communication skills you've developed as a police officer, you'll do fine. This is one of the reasons why I recommend you teach or take a presentation course before your promotional examination. The more practice you have speaking in front of a group, the more comfortable you'll be and the more professional your presentation will be.

When your presentation is finished, tell the panel you are done by saying, "This ends my presentation. Do you have any questions?" You will be directed to a seat, and the panelists will begin to ask you questions. You are now in the same position as you would be in a traditional or technical oral exam. Use the same tips recommended in the "Appearing Before the Oral Board" section, and you'll ace the exam.

The primary difference in the questioning at this type of test versus a traditional oral exam is that the panelist may ask "Why?" more often (for example, "Why did you delegate part of Officer Smith's training to a senior patrol officer?"). Don't allow "why" questions to put you on the defensive. View them instead as a great opportunity to discuss your department's training programs and whether these programs may be state-mandated for the officer's certification or a departmental initiative.

Situational Exercises as Part of Oral Exams

Assessment center kinds of exercises are beginning to be used more often in oral examinations. Assessment centers are covered in detail in "The Assessment Center" chapter, and you may want to study that material in detail before reviewing this oral exam section again. Let's use the sample supervisor/subordinate situational exercise involving Officer James Jennings to demonstrate how a situational exercise would work in an oral board examination and to discuss how you could achieve a high score if this type of exercise is used.

First, notice that the directions indicate time management is important by using bold print to communicate that "**You** are responsible for budgeting your time during this examination. You have a total of **40 minutes** to complete the entire examination process." Out of those 40 minutes, the directions inform you that "as soon as you open this examination packet, you have **20 minutes** to read the enclosed "Background and Facts" and "The Problem" sections and to call Officer Jennings in to take whatever action you deem necessary as a police sergeant to resolve the situation outlined in the scenario."

As you can see from the directions, the first part of the examination involves reading the material and the second part focuses on handling the problem. With the panelists in the room watching your every move, you have 20 minutes to review, call the role-player in, and resolve the situation. To use your time well, first read the material and, on a separate sheet of paper, jot down three or four things you want to cover in your meeting with Officer Jennings. The panelists will see you making an outline and you will receive extra points for "planning and organizing." Next, as recommended under the Supervisor/Subordinate Exercise, quickly re-arrange the furniture in the room for the type of interview the situation calls for. Place the chairs in front of or next to the desk in a manner that will put you in better control of the interview. Arrange all of your materials for ready reference before the interview begins. All of this preparation will be observed by the panelists. Most important, remember that you are no longer a patrol officer. You are playing the role of a police sergeant. Act the part!

Achieving a high score for this type of exercise is covered in detail in "The Assessment Center" chapter, but remember that handling the situation itself is only part of the oral examination. After it is concluded and "Officer Jennings" leaves the room, the panel members will ask you a series of questions during the remaining 20 minutes about the situation you just participated in. All of the tips covered in the "Oral Tests" chapter about achieving high scores on oral examinations apply here. Because the example exercise was a supervisor/subordinate problem, a wide range of questions on basic supervision could be asked in addition to why you did or did not take a specific action during the role-play. These questions might touch on the disciplinary process, referral of employees to an employee assistance program, leadership and/or supervisory styles, and performance evaluations. Questions asked following other types of situational exercises are covered in the chapter on assessment centers.

Other Significant Factors in Your Test Score

In addition to thorough knowledge of the resource material and excellent verbal communications ability, many other factors weigh heavily in oral examinations.

From the moment the panelist comes out to the waiting room to get you, you're being judged. Your facial expressions, gestures, hairstyle, clothing, and how you walk, smile, and talk all have an impact on what your final grade will be. Oral examinations are very subjective. The panelists have about 30 minutes to make a decision that will affect your entire career, so leave nothing to chance. Board members will consciously or subconsciously judge you based on many of the following:

Hair—Get a haircut just before the oral exam. Your hair should be neat and well-trimmed, and its length should conform to any requirements outlined in your department's rules and regulations. Female officers should style their hair to reflect department standards.

Facial Hair—Even if your department permits beards, shave yours off. The officers on your oral panel have been working for many years in a semi military profession, and most won't see a beard as a positive attribute. The oral board isn't the place to assert your independence. Mustaches and sideburns must also conform to your department's regulations.

Earrings—Under no circumstances should a male officer wear an earring to an oral test. If you usually do wear an earring, allow enough time for the hole to be unnoticeable before the oral board. Females should make sure their earrings are small and appropriate for work; dangling earrings call attention to themselves, not to your responses to the questions.

Fingernails—Your fingernails should be clean and trimmed. Females should avoid colored nail polish; use a clear gloss instead.

Rings—If you have a college ring, by all means wear it. If you're married, wear your wedding band. Don't wear more than one ring on each hand. Pinky rings are not appropriate.

Gold Chains—Don't wear them.

The Police Uniform—In most cases, you'll be required to wear your police uniform to the test. Bring an extra uniform in your car on the day of the test. If you get a flat tire driving to the exam, spill coffee on yourself (or one of your competitors accidently or intentionally spills coffee on you), or have some other unfortunate mishap, you can change into a fresh uniform. It's also a good idea to bring a sticky lint roller with you and a handkerchief or diaper to touch up the shine on your shoes just before you go in for the test.

The Police Hat—If you're appearing before the oral board in uniform, have your hat with you. If yours is soiled or has lost its shape, get a new one. Shine both the hat's bill and its shield to a high gloss. If it's a winter hat, make sure it's free of lint. Wear your hat when you enter the room, salute if appropriate, take the hat off and put it under your left arm before you sit down, and then place it beneath your chair. This maneuver takes a little practice before it's smooth and military. When the exam is over, your panelists will all rise and offer to shake your hand. Shake hands firmly; then put your hat back on before you leave. The panelists will be looking at your back as you exit, so square your shoulders and walk erectly.

The Police Shield—Polish it.

Name Tag—Unless you're instructed otherwise, wear your name tag in accordance with your department's regulations.

Union Pins—I recommend that you don't wear union insignia.

Medals—If you've received a department citation or been awarded a medal, wear it.

Insignias—Official department insignias (firearms expert, etc.) may be worn, but never "pig pins" or other such devices. I was recently a panelist at an oral board where a candidate came in wearing firearms instructor and range master insignia, but he didn't wear his service revolver. One of the other panelists asked him how he had gotten to the oral exam that morning. He replied that he had driven and parked his car in front of city hall. The panelist then remarked on his insignia and asked what he would have done without his service revolver (especially since he was in full uniform) if a robbery had occurred in front of him. The candidate was so unnerved after this that his performance was affected. Don't let this happen to you.

Sam Browne Belt—Unless your gun belt is already highly polished and free of cracks, buy a new one—and polish it up, paying particular attention to the buckle. Shine your holster, too. If it's showing signs of wear, get a replacement. If your service revolver has wooden grips, polish them as well, and clean the weapon itself, especially the part that protrudes from the holster. Clean your handcuffs and wear them as your department requires (in a case or hanging by a strap). If you're allowed to use a case, do so to avoid having them rattle when you enter the room, sit down, and leave. Don't bring your radio case or nightstick with you, and obviously, don't bring any unauthorized devices.

Uniform Shirt—Unless you're required to, don't wear a uniform coat or jacket; they're bulky and prevent freedom of movement. Whether you're in long sleeves or short, make sure all of the little threads are removed from around the buttons of your uniform shirt pockets. The shirt should be spotless, have a noticeable crease along the sleeve, and be completely free of lint both front and back. If military creases are not sewn in, ask your cleaners to iron them in. Display your shield, name tag, issued insignia, and medals according to your department's guidelines.

Tie—Wear the authorized uniform tie. It must be clean, wrinkle and lint-free. Its clasp should be department issue and properly placed.

Trousers—Make sure that your police trousers fit properly, especially at the shoe line, and that they have a razor-sharp, military crease. If your uniform pants are dark but have white pocket liners, be sure the pocket liners are clean. The front and back of the pants must be free of lint. Don't put anything in your pockets—remove your wallet, keys, and loose change. You don't want to jingle when you enter and leave the room or have any unnecessary bulges that take away from a streamlined, military appearance.

Shaving—Make sure that you're cleanly shaved.

Shoes—Don't wear the sneaker type running shoes that have become fashionable among street cops. Wear laced black shoes that can be shined to a high gloss, including the heels and the edge of the soles.

Socks—Wear new, black socks.

Civilian Clothing—Some oral boards require all candidates, or at least those in investigative assignments, to wear civilian clothing to the test. If so, a suit is preferable to a sport jacket and tie, although a blue blazer and gray slacks are always appropriate. Whichever you choose, your overall appearance should be businesslike and conservative. Pay particular attention to your shirt collar. Make sure it's well starched and not frayed or soiled. Your tie should be perfectly knotted and appropriate for your suit or jacket and slacks. Police tie clasps are permissible, but don't wear any with a political or religious connotation. Naturally, your coat and slacks should appear to have just come from the cleaners. Your shoes should be highly shined, and your belt and socks should match your overall attire. As with the police uniform, bring a change of clothing with you, just in case. Female officers should follow these same general guidelines and wear clothing appropriate for attending a business meeting.

> *It is quality rather than quantity that matters.*
> —SENECA

Tips

- When you find out where your oral board will be located, drive over and see what the parking situation is. Will you have to walk several blocks? You'll have to allow time for that. What if it rains or snows and makes a mess of your uniform? Plan for that too; be sure you have an extra uniform to leave in your car, and bring an umbrella along with your change of clothes.

- Pack a shaving case with a hairbrush, lint roller, baby's diaper or handkerchief, and nail file. Put it into a gym bag along with your hat and polished shoes and bring it with you. Find a bathroom and make certain you're squared away before your name or number is called.

- Try not to allow other candidates who may be present to "psych" you out. Mentally get yourself ready.

- You'll probably be required to check in with a test administrator, who will ask for your number or other such device that's been sent to you in the mail. Don't be surprised if you're told that the board is running late and your time has been moved back. This often happens at oral tests. Self-confidence is important especially at this stage of the process. Don't allow petty inconveniences to disrupt your concentration. Whatever means you use to get yourself up, now is the time to do it.

Checklists

Post the following checklists at home, and make sure you've taken care of each item before you leave for the test.

FEMALE CHECKLIST

- ❏ attendance letter or code
- ❏ college ring
- ❏ comb
- ❏ diaper or handkerchief (for shoes and leather gear)
- ❏ earrings (if desired—appropriate for a business meeting)
- ❏ fingernails (clean, clear polish)
- ❏ gas (fill up car)
- ❏ gym bag or carrying case
- ❏ hair (style appropriate for a business meeting)
- ❏ hairbrush
- ❏ know what time the test is
- ❏ know where to go
- ❏ know where to park
- ❏ leave early
- ❏ lipstick (appropriate for a business meeting)
- ❏ lint roller
- ❏ make-up (appropriate for a business meeting)
- ❏ money
- ❏ nail file

MALE CHECKLIST

- ❏ attendance letter or code
- ❏ beard (shave)
- ❏ college ring
- ❏ comb
- ❏ diaper or handkerchief (for shoes or leather gear)
- ❏ earrings (leave home)
- ❏ fingernails (clean and trim)
- ❏ gas (fill up car)
- ❏ gold chains (leave home)
- ❏ gym bag or carrying case
- ❏ hairbrush
- ❏ haircut
- ❏ know what time the test is
- ❏ know where to go
- ❏ know where to park
- ❏ leave early
- ❏ lint roller
- ❏ mustache (trim to department regulations)
- ❏ money
- ❏ nail file
- ❏ sideburns (trim to department regulations)

POLICE UNIFORM CHECKLIST
(Male or Female)

❏ badge (shine)

❏ blackjack (leave home)

❏ day billy (leave home)

❏ extra uniform (take with you)

❏ gun (clean, polish wooden grips)

❏ gun belt and holster (shine)

❏ hat (shine bill, lint free)

❏ name tag (wear unless instructed otherwise)

❏ official insignia (wear)

❏ shirt (trim threads, military creases, lint free)

❏ shoes (laced, black, highly polished)

❏ socks (new, black)

❏ tie (authorized, clean, wrinkle and lint free)

❏ tie clasp (department issue, properly placed)

❏ trousers (military creases, clean pocket liners,

❏ empty pockets, lint free)

❏ union pins (leave home)

Appearing Before the Oral Board

Remember, after the candidate who goes in before you leaves the testing room, it's normally ten or fifteen minutes before you're called in. The panelists are human, too, and they often come out to get coffee or use the bathroom. This isn't the time for one of them to see you slouched against the wall or pacing nervously up and down the corridor. You're supposed to be a leader, so behave professionally.

When it's your turn to take the test, one of the panelists or the test monitor comes out to get you. A panelist introduces himself or herself and leads you into the room. A test administrator may ask you to go in alone or may enter to introduce you to the board. Occasionally, the test monitor stays in the room to record or to observe the testing process. Expect to see people other than the panelists in the room: The board members rise as you enter the room in order to be introduced or introduce themselves to you.

It's show time from the minute you enter the room until you leave. You're onstage. Make immediate eye contact with each of the panelists. Smile. Extend your hand and give each a firm handshake. If you could do it with your stuffed animals, you can do it with the people around this table. Don't be surprised to see a laptop, folders, or rating forms on the table in front of the panel. Usually, one of them asks you to sit down. Courtesy counts. Say, "Thank you, sir" or "ma'am." Pull your chair directly up to the table. Sit erectly. Clasp your hands together on the table in front of you (prominently displaying your college ring, if you have one), and make eye contact with each of the panelists. One of the board members, usually the one sitting in the middle, has been assigned to begin the examination with an explanation of the procedure to be used or by asking a question designed to be an icebreaker. The question "Would you tell the panel a little about yourself?" is the sort of icebreaker designed to put you at ease.

You may see panelists smoking. They may ask you if you'd like to smoke. Don't! There's nothing quite so appalling as having candidates blow smoke in your face as they answer your questions. Obviously, chewing gum is also inappropriate. If paper clips, pencils, pads, or other items have been placed in front of you, don't nervously play with them as you're answering a question. Appear relaxed, confident, and sure of yourself. Don't slouch or lean back in the chair. Oral board members like to see plenty of teeth at interviews, so give them your best smile whenever it's appropriate.

> *A bad beginning makes a bad ending.*
> —EURIPIDES

Resumes

Some cities require candidates to submit a resume as part of the promotion process. Your resume is submitted to the oral board by the test administrator. Each member of the panel reviews it before you enter the room. A concern associated with using resumes as part of the testing process is that the panel may be unfairly influenced by its contents. Points should be given to candidates only for qualifications that apply directly to the criteria established on the test announcement. Resumes are sometimes included as one of the scoring criteria and receive a mark which is averaged in on the overall rating. Give careful attention to submitting a professional-looking, content-specific, resume. Following is a model resume for promotional examinations.

COVER PAGE

Presentation of Qualifications
Robert P. Simons
129 Sagebrush Road
Hartford, Connecticut 06102
Home: (860) 555-1392
Duty: (860) 555-2300

FIRST INSIDE PAGE

Robert P. Simoni
129 Sagebrush Road
Hartford, Connecticut

SUMMARY

The applicant, has nine years of experience with the City of Hartford Police Department and currently holds the rank of patrol officer. The officer has combined academic and professional skills which uniquely qualify him for promotion to the rank of police sergeant. The applicant is a highly motivated, goal-oriented achiever who believes that leadership is the key to effective supervision.

EDUCATION

University of Connecticut, Storrs, Connecticut
Bachelor Degree
Major: Criminal Justice
Minor: Business Management
Graduated: 19—, Honors with Distinction
Manchester Community College, Manchester, Connecticut
Associate in Science degree in Criminal Justice
Graduated: 19—
Hartford Public High School, Hartford, Connecticut
Graduated: 19—

SPECIALIZED TRAINING/EDUCATION

State Certified Police Instructor	State of Connecticut M.P.T.C.
Decision Making/Problem. Solving	Aetna Insurance Company
Supervisor Training Program	Hartford Police Academy
State's Attorney Law Enforcement	U.S. Justice Department
Medical Response Technician Program	Hartford Police Academy
In-Service Training Program	
Basic Narcotics Investigators School	State of Connecticut M.P.T.C.
Basic Recruit Training	Hartford Police Academy

SPECIAL BOARD ASSIGNMENTS

Cochairman Job Enhancement Committee	Union Steward Hardford Police Union
Labor Representative, Employee Assistance Committee	

COMMUNITY ACTIVITIES

Hartford Youth Baseball League Coach	Member, Lions Club
Police Athletic League Basketball Coach	Knights of Columbus, St. Mary's Church

EMPLOYMENT

City of Hartford Police Department	April 3, 20—, to present

If a resume is used as part of your oral test, it will be the first item the oral panel discusses with you. This is your opportunity to point out your strengths: college degrees, career-related training and education, superior job performance, awards, medals, community activities, and any other factors which may have prepared you for the position of police sergeant. Make the most of it.

First Impression/Last Impression

The impression you make with the oral board in the first few minutes is critical. The oral test provides you with an opportunity to "sell yourself." From the moment you enter the room, the panelists will be influenced, either positively or negatively, by many different qualities. Among these are

- how you walk into and out of the room
- what you look like
- your speech and its tonal qualities
- your body movements and gestures
- the words you choose and how you say them
- your facial expressions and the amount and intensity of eye contact with the panel

As a police officer, you use these same techniques in gathering impressions of others. Over the years, you've made rapid decisions about other people based on your "police instincts" (first impression). The oral board will be doing the same thing from the moment they see you.

The Panelists' Viewpoint

Let's review exactly what's taking place from the viewpoint of the people who hold your career in their hands—the panelists. They've each traveled from another city and are in an unfamiliar environment. Most are senior police officers who've come up through the ranks and who've probably gone through the same process you're now experiencing. They are achievers, people who take themselves and their responsibilities seriously. It's a safe bet that they are traditional in their thinking, values, and belief systems. After many years of supervising and managing, they are likely to ask questions, which have answers, that they consider basic. Depending on the number of candidates, you may be the first person they interview or the 53rd.

Anyone who's served on an oral board will attest to the fact that it's mentally and physically draining. Every 30 minutes or so another candidate comes through the door and is asked exactly the same questions in the same sequence. When large numbers of candidates are involved in the process, fatigue and the uniformity and tediousness of the procedure begin to take their toll. Regardless of their personal motivation and qualities, panelists are inevitably affected.

So, when you walk into the room, what makes you better than the 18 officers who may have come before you? You have to make it happen. Even though job knowledge is important here, remember, you're conducting a performance. Sitting there with a blank expression and answering the questions (even if the answer is correct) in a monotone is asking for a low score. You're trying to convince the panel that you have supervisory and leadership qualities, but if your voice is timid and your body language and gestures confirm that you aren't a leader, you won't succeed. If your voice, facial expressions, and deportment are harsh, that's how the panel thinks of you as an individual. Most accomplished speakers spend hours practicing before they get up in front of an audience. The more you rehearse, the better you'll perform on test day. If your appearance, body language, and mannerisms are appropriate, the panel is more apt to concentrate on **what** you say rather than on how you say it.

> *Your expression is the most important thing you can wear.*
>
> —SIR ASCHER

A Flash to the Future

Let's pretend that this is the day of your oral examination and walk through the process together. You, Officer Robert P. Simoni, have been studying consistently for several months. After the written test, you take a couple of days off and then hit the books again using the procedures outlined. For the past several weeks, you've been anxiously checking your mail for the results of your written test. One day you open your mailbox and see an official-looking envelope—a letter from your personnel department.

You rip it open and discover that "your score on the written examination for the position of police sergeant is 92%, and your rank order through this part of the process is sixth." You jump for joy, run into the house, and tell anyone who'll listen. You've already mentally calculated that there are nine current vacancies for sergeant. You've got it made! You're in!

Then you realize that the written test counts for only 50% of your final score, seniority 10%, your performance evaluation 5%, and the oral exam 35%. You dig out your "test announcement" and read that points for seniority and performance evaluation will be averaged in after the written and oral examinations are completed. You take another look at the personnel department's letter, which states

> Your oral examination will be held on December 14, 20—, at 11:30 a.m. at city hall, Room 203. Your exam number is 21076. Please bring this letter with you for admittance to the examination process.

Today is December 3, which gives you 11 more days to study and worry.

You're very familiar with city hall but the next day you decide to take a ride over there and check it out anyway. You find that the closest place to park your own car, rather than your police cruiser, at around eleven in the morning is a parking garage about a block away. You figure that it will probably be sleeting on packed snow the morning you're scheduled to take the test. Investigating the actual test site, you discover that Room 203 is a small conference room on the second floor next to the personnel office. It's dreary looking. The receptionist doesn't seem to share your enthusiasm. Well, at least you know where you're supposed to be, and it's lucky you checked on the parking situation so you won't be late for your test.

You apply to have both the day before and the day of the exam off from work so you can properly get ready. Your day off before the test is denied (everyone else wants the day off, too), and you have to work the evening shift the night before the exam. Everyone you work with wants to talk about the oral and tells you that, even though you have a high mark on the written exam, you'll probably "choke" on the oral. You manage to wrangle a couple of hours comp time from your sergeant, who's been on the job 28 years and has failed the lieutenant's test so many times he's stopped trying. His parting words of advice to you are "Good luck, kid."

You finally get home only to find that the washing machine has continuously been running on "fill," and now your basement is full of water. Your wife is highly irritated, and your kid came home from school with his third detention in the last two weeks. Your mother is coming for a "visit" tomorrow, and you're supposed to pick up your daughter at the dentist and return her to school "right after your little test." Oh, by the way, your wife's car wouldn't start and she had to leave it at work. She thinks she parked it in a lot she wasn't supposed to be in and it "got towed." Knowing that you'll do better on the oral if you get a good night's sleep, you go right to bed. Naturally, you can't sleep because all you can think about is the test tomorrow.

The next morning you awaken to find the house empty. Your wife has gone to work, and the kids are off to school. A note is on the table wishing you "luck." "Well, I'll have a good breakfast" you say, "to energize myself for the test." You open the refrigerator only to find that there aren't any eggs, milk, or juice. However, things do start to brighten up. Your uniform is back from the cleaners; you've clipped all the little threads from around the pockets; and you remembered to pack your case with a lint roller, comb, nail file, and diaper. All your uniform equipment is polished and shining. You've already stashed an extra uniform in the car and now note that it is sleeting heavily and the weather reporter is cheerily announcing that "commuter traffic is backed up at least 30 minutes, with numerous minor accidents." You review your index cards one last time over a cup of coffee and then say to yourself, "If I don't know it by now, I never will." You toss them onto the table hoping never to see them again.

Out to the car and ready to go. While driving, you keep mentally going over the key points you want to get across to the oral board and rehearse for the millionth time what you'll say if they ask you to "tell us a little about yourself."

About halfway there, you pull over to the side of the road and begin the internal process of psyching yourself up. Remember who you are, who you represent (mother, father, sister, brother, family, wife, children, friend, etc.).

"Why can't I be No. 1? The only person who can beat me, is me. Hell, it's a shame that they would even have the nerve to put me through this process. I know as much about police work, supervision, and management as they do and probably more! I've survived shootouts, drug raids, domestic battles, bar fights, investigations, court suits, and the whole nine yards. I can do this, no problem."

When you finally arrive at the parking garage, it's nearly full and you have to park on the fifth level. It's sleeting even heavier now, and you have to walk through the icy rain and slush to get to city hall. Luckily, you thought to bring an umbrella and a gym bag into which you put your police hat, shoes, and gun belt so they wouldn't get wet. Taking the elevator up to the second floor of city hall, you see that a table's been set up in the hallway adjacent to Room 203; two people are sitting behind it.

Walking up to the table, you, say, "Good morning, I'm Officer Simoni. I'm here to take my oral test."

The woman behind the table looks up with a confused expression and says, "What's your name?"

"Simoni, Robert P," you reply.

She begins leafing through a roster while the man behind the table stares at you, tapping a pencil on the table. She puts a check by something on the form and says, "I need your exam number. It's on the bottom of the letter we sent you."

You hand her the letter, and she compares it with her roster saying, "The oral panel is running a little behind. You were scheduled to go in at 11:30, but another candidate just went in. They may not want to take you until after lunch. Have a seat."

Naturally, you're already thoroughly irritated. Not only are you still damp from your walk to city hall and nervous about your test, you also don't know what the protocol here is. You're out of your element. This clerk and her silent partner, who's still staring at you but not saying anything, are not making the experience any easier. You don't know whether to sit down or find a bathroom and get squared away before the test. You decide to sit down. By 11:15, you're starting to get really nervous. You want a cigarette, but you left them in the car. Neither of the clerks at the table has moved since you arrived, and the other candidate still hasn't come out of the room. You go back over to the table again. Both civilians give you the kind of look that means you're bothering them. You try a smile and ask, "Am I supposed to go in at 11:30, or will the board be taking me after lunch?"

The woman says blankly, "What?"

You try to be diplomatic, smile some more, and ask, "When do I go in?"

The other clerk, the one still tapping his pencil, says, "There's a candidate in with the board right now. When he comes out, we'll ask the panel if they want to interview you then or wait until after lunch. We can't interrupt them in the middle of the test."

You walk away deciding you'd better change and get ready for the oral. It's now 11:20. Finding the bathroom at the end of the hall, you put on all your gear and run a diaper over the top of your shoes, hat bill, and leather. You're running the lint roller over your uniform when the door bursts open and in walks Officer "Big" (big as in "Big Henry") Sullivan. Big Henry flashes a wide grin and says, "Yo, they're looking for you out in the hallway. I'm supposed to go in after you get done."

Big Henry is as cheerful and calm as a person can be and apparently hasn't the least bit of anxiety about taking the test. You feel like you're going to throw up. You thank "Big Henry" and, while walking back to the table, see Officer Gary Johnson walking toward you. You figure he must have just come out from the oral board. "Hi, Gary, how'd it go?"

Gary's not a happy camper. "This test is a bunch of crap! Nothing they asked me had anything to do with being a sergeant. I'm going to see my lawyer right now!"

As he's storming off, you notice that the female clerk is waving her arm at you frantically. Now she's in a hurry? You walk over to the table.

"We've spoken to the board, and they'll interview you in about five minutes," she says smugly.

Sitting back down again, you start psyching yourself up one last time.

The door to the conference room opens, and a man dressed in a business suit speaks to the two clerks at the table. All three look in your direction, and you stand up, realizing that this is one of the panelists. He walks directly over to you, smiles, and extends his hand saying, "Good morning officer, I'm Captain West. Follow me and I'll introduce you to the rest of the people on the board."

You give Captain West a firm handshake, look him straight in the eyes, smile, and say, "Good morning, Captain West. I've been looking forward to this for a long time."

Following the captain into the room, you see a large conference table with three people sitting behind it—a male and two females. The woman on the far left-hand side of the table has a laptop in front of her. The other two people behind the table begin rising as you enter the room. The woman with the laptop remains seated.

Captain West says, "I'd like to introduce you to Lieutenant Phillips from the Springfield, Massachusetts, police department and Dr. Carmen Torrez, who works with the city of New Haven's police department."

As he's talking, Captain West moves behind the table and stands in the middle, between Lieutenant Phillips and Dr. Torrez. No one bothers to introduce the woman with the laptop, and you assume she's from the personnel unit. You salute as you approach the table, remove your uniform hat, and put it under your left arm. Smiling, you extend your hand to Dr. Torrez. She returns your smile and shakes your hand. "Good morning Dr. Torrez." You take a step to the right, "Captain West," you nod, while shaking his hand and making special eye contact with him. "Good morning lieutenant." The lieutenant's only response is a nod. Apparently he's been chosen to play the part of the "bad guy."

Captain West says, "Please have a seat, officer."

You note that each of the panelists has some forms, a legal pad, and pencils in front of them. Glasses and a water decanter are also on the table, along with an ice bucket next to the woman with the laptop. In front of the chair you'll be sitting in is an empty glass, an ash tray, a pad of paper, two pencils, and some paper clips. Your chair has been placed about two feet too far back from the table. You move it to the correct position, sit down and put your police cap under it. Sitting straight and folding your hands on the table, you make eye contact with each panel member. Your college ring is prominently displayed on your right hand. You're giving the board every indication that you're ready and actually looking forward to being tested. *You're selling yourself*

Captain West says, "As you know, you're here to take your oral test for the position of police sergeant. We realize that you're nervous. We want you to try to relax as much as possible. The panel will be asking you a series of questions. Answer them to the best of your ability. The three of us have sat on your side of the table and know what you're going through. You smile and nod to indicate you understand as the captain is talking. "Now, before the board begins the more structured part of the oral exam, could you tell us a little about yourself?"

You notice that the other two panel members have their pencils ready and are looking at you expectantly and that Captain West had picked up his pencil and adjusted his legal pad in front of him while he was talking.

"Certainly, sir." You smile and make eye contact from left to right as you're speaking. "Immediately upon graduating from high school, I enlisted in the Army and served as a military police officer for three years. During that time, I received extensive police training, which helped build the framework for my career as a police officer here in Hartford. While in the service, I got married, and my wife and I had two children. Toward the end of my enlistment, I began researching police departments in the state and chose Hartford because it was one of the largest in Connecticut and had an excellent reputation in policing. In 19—, I entered a special program that allowed me to leave the service two months early to join the Hartford Police Department. I graduated from the police academy third in a class of 42 and missed coming out number one by two tenths of a percent (a smile here). Upon graduation from the police academy, I was assigned to the patrol division, where I've spent the majority of my career. While I was in the service, I took some college courses, and once I completed my probationary period here in Hartford, I enrolled at Manchester Community College and received an Associate Degree in Criminal Justice. During that time, I gained a great deal of police experience and worked every assignment in the patrol division. I was fortunate to have served under a commander who believed that police officers should be able to perform every function in the police department, so I was regularly rotated through records, communications, booking, beats, and cruisers my first few years on the job, an experience that helped me gain a unique understanding of the police department components. I feel that that will be of great assistance to me when I'm promoted to sergeant.

"I've taken advantage of all the career development courses offered by our training division, and I've taken many specialized courses in investigations and some in supervision. I was chosen by the patrol commander to be a field training officer, responsible for training officers in patrol techniques when they graduate from the police academy. I've received numerous letters of commendation from the public and recently was awarded the department's Merit Award for Valor for rescuing a child in a burning building."

"As I gained more experience, I realized that further academic education would enable me to be a more effective police officer. I went back to school and recently received my B.A. from the University of Connecticut, where I graduated with honors. I've had special assignments in the crime suppression unit and the narcotics division. I'm also a member of the police academy's adjunct faculty for recruit and in-service training. I graduated from the Municipal Police Training Academy's Instructor Development Program. I serve as a union steward and have spent a great deal of time handling officer grievances. I'm the co-chair of the department's job enhancement committee and the labor representative to the department's employee assistance committee."

"I missed being eligible for the last sergeant's exam by two months and was very disappointed. I know that my training, education, and experience have prepared me to be a police sergeant. More than that, I believe that policing isn't just a job, it's a way of life. I'm very active in the community and a basketball coach for our Police Athletic League. I'm also a member of the Lion's Club and the Knights of Columbus, which does volunteer work for the homeless. I'm happily married, and my wife and I enjoy taking our family camping and canoeing. I know, if given the opportunity, I'll make an excellent police sergeant. This board can be assured that I will never embarrass either my organization or policing."

Back to the Present

As you can see, Officer Simoni got off to a good start (first impression) at his oral board. He went on to receive a high score and was promoted to the rank of police sergeant in the first group of candidates. The scene you've just read illustrates some of the intangible factors, which will affect your grade. They may have little to do with the test itself, but they directly relate to your ability to *perform* on test day. Some of the factors that affected Officer Simoni are

- being denied the day off before the test
- his colleagues' remarks about "choking" on the oral
- the basement filling with water
- the untimely visit from Mom
- his kid's detention
- his wife's car being towed
- a sleepless night
- nothing good for breakfast
- sleeting on test day
- having to park his car away from the test site
- disinterested personnel who are part of the testing process
- poor coordination in scheduling candidates
- being out of cigarettes
- Big Henry Sullivan's carefree attitude
- Johnson's sour grapes

Officer Simoni possessed enough self-confidence and motivational drive to allow him to perform, regardless of these negative outside influences. Will you?

Be aware of what's going on around you and the effect it's having on your ability to reach your peak level of performance. Take appropriate steps to counter negative influences. Plan for the unexpected.

Questions Frequently Asked on Oral Boards

The questions asked on oral examinations for the position of police sergeant are often keyed to local matters of specific interest. For instance, let's assume there have been a number of labor disputes in your area resulting in unruly picket lines. The police have had to make many arrests, resulting in a great deal of print, radio, and TV coverage. Citizen complaints and civil lawsuits against police officers have been made, and several officers and citizens have been injured. Given this scenario, there's an excellent chance there will be a question on the oral test dealing with the role of a police supervisor at the scene of a labor/management dispute. The following questions represent broad subject areas and principles of policing that frequently appear on oral examinations, and you may have to adjust the answer to suit your organization's circumstances.

1. **You are a sergeant assigned to the patrol division. One of the officers under your supervision (who has previously been an excellent employee) seems to have lost interest in the job. He has begun reporting late for duty; his response time on calls is below average; his appearance is becoming below standard; and a pattern of abuse of sick time is forming. How would you handle this situation?**

Possible response:

As this officer's immediate supervisor, I would have intervened earlier through the use of communication and counseling techniques. Reporting late for work and being below standard in appearance should result in immediate supervisory intervention. The second two performance factors you mention, below-average response time and abuse of sick time, are patterns that take longer to form. Our department has a computerized reporting system that allows supervisors to closely monitor these two factors.

Having worked with the officer, I would know what our specific supervisor/ subordinate relationship was (different techniques are used depending on the individual) and which technique had the best chance to succeed. I'd begin by sitting down with the officer over a cup of coffee and pointing out exactly what was lacking in the officer's work performance. I would solicit feedback to determine the reason for its decline. It's been my experience that the symptoms you mentioned often point to a problem off the job. I would do my best to discuss this with him and offer job-related assistance (counseling, some time off, a referral to the Employee Assistance Program, etc.) to make sure that he understood his value to our organization. Naturally, I would develop a specific plan, with input from the officer, to restore his work performance to at least a satisfactory level. I would also be sure that he understood the consequences of any future failure to perform at that level and would develop a schedule to inspect and monitor the officer's performance at regular intervals. I would also document our session so that I'd have a record in the event negative discipline was required in the future.

Supervisory principles covered in this response:

Communication, counseling techniques, knowledge of departmental systems, motivation techniques, employee incentives, planning, inspection, monitoring, documentation, the discipline process (positive, negative, and progressive), employee assistance programs.

2. **You are a sergeant in the patrol division assigned to the evening shift. One of your newer officers receives a dispatch to respond to an active bar fight. A more seasoned officer is sent as backup. You respond, and find that the inexperienced officer has a prisoner handcuffed and placed in the back seat of his cruiser. Upon investigating, you discover that the officer had absolutely no probable cause to effect the arrest. The arrest was made prior to the second officer's arrival. What would you do?**

Possible response:

If, after investigating, I determined that an officer under my supervision had made an arrest without probable cause, and that the arrest was therefore invalid, I would advise the officer of my findings and release the prisoner. I would then ascertain if the arrestee needed medical care and, if so, assist him in acquiring it. I would explain that further investigation had revealed insufficient evidence to proceed further in the arrest process and that he was free to go. If the individual wished to lodge a complaint, I would explain the department's citizen-complaint process to him.

Obviously, since I made the decision to release the prisoner, I would have concluded that the officer erred in effecting the arrest. I'd require the officer to submit a police report and endorse it through channels to the court so they would be aware of what had occurred. I would also sit down with the officer and, based on my initial investigation, any accompanying statements at the scene, the officer's oral feedback, and his police report, determine whether to recommend discipline, retraining, or a combination of both.

This is a potential vicarious-liability situation. I would orally and in writing make my supervisor aware of what had transpired and my recommendation concerning the officer.

Supervisory principles covered in this response:

State law, probable cause, investigative procedures, decision-making ability, department policy, supervisory notification responsibilities, counseling, feedback, communication, discipline, training, vicarious liability, organizational integrity.

3. **You are a newly appointed police sergeant at the scene of an emergency situation. A senior patrol officer clearly begins subverting your authority. How would you handle this situation?**

Possible response:

In an emergency situation, lives are often at stake. I would immediately order the officer to leave the scene and to report back to headquarters to await my arrival. This type of behavior can't be permitted but also shouldn't be dealt with either in the public view or in front of the officer's peers unless absolutely necessary. Once the emergency situation was over, I would go to police headquarters and advise the officer exactly what he had done wrong and that, due to the seriousness of his misconduct, I would recommend that he be formally disciplined.

The majority of subordinate behavior problems can be handled through counseling, motivational techniques, and monitoring. However, due to the seriousness of this particular case, I would recommend immediate punitive action.

Supervisory principles covered in this response:

Emergency situations, command presence, decision-making ability, counseling, motivation, monitoring, discipline, and department policy.

4. **While on patrol, you are in a long line of traffic approaching a major city intersection. When you arrive at the intersection, you observe a patrolman, whom you assigned to traffic duty, standing on the sidewalk. His tie is off (clipped to his shirt pocket), he is not wearing his police hat (hanging on the butt of his gun), and he is smoking a cigarette and listening to a portable radio with attached earphones. What would you do?**

Possible response:

I would immediately instruct the officer to put on his hat and tie, put out the cigarette, and remove the radio. I would advise him that all four behaviors are in violation of the department's rules and regulations and that he was displaying poor judgment, not only in the obvious departmental rule violations, but also in the image he was portraying of our police department to the public.

I would ask him why he wasn't directing traffic. If his response was unsatisfactory, I would so advise him. I would instruct him to submit a report concerning the incident and tell him that I would recommend that appropriate charges be brought against him through the department's disciplinary process. I would make sure that he got out into the street and performed his job assignment and would monitor his performance to ensure compliance.

In addition, I would be concerned why the officer was exhibiting this behavior. At a later date, I would sit down with him and determine if this was an isolated incident or if the officer had concerns on or off the job which were affecting his work performance. If so, I would do my best to assist him, or, if it was a problem that I couldn't handle at my level, refer him to the department's Employee Assistance Program.

Supervisory principles covered in this response:

Supervisory skills, discipline, decision-making skills, inspection, monitoring, report systems, counseling, motivation, employee assistance mechanisms.

5. **You are a sergeant assigned to the narcotics squad. While off duty, you are at a local restaurant with some friends who are not police officers. You observe a male you know to be a police officer, in plain clothes, in a booth at the rear of the restaurant, accompanied by two females. As you walk by them, you observe a quantity of white powder on the table and the officer snorting it up his nose with the cut half of a straw. What would you do?**

Possible response:

Based on the information contained in this question, I would have probable cause to believe that a crime was being committed in my presence. I would immediately notify headquarters. I'd ask for a backup unit and a supervisor to be sent to the scene. I would then return to the table, properly identify myself, and place all three persons under arrest. I would confiscate all evidence and appropriately search all three parties—both for my protection and to locate further contraband. I would then turn the evidence over to the responding supervisor and submit a complete report.

Follow-up question:

You would arrest a fellow police officer?

Possible response:

Yes, sir.

Second follow-up question:

What if, after you took the time to make the telephone call, all the cocaine was gone?

Possible response:

The original question indicated there was white powder on the table and that the officer was snorting it up his nose with a cut straw. I don't have positive proof that the white powder is cocaine. However, the totality of circumstances would establish probable cause that a crime was being committed. I could legally make the arrest based on that probable cause. It would be unlikely that some residue would not be found, even if all the observable powder had been consumed. In all probability, the snorting straw would be located and have residue inside it.

My duty is clearly to effect the arrest, search, and obtain evidence. It's up to a court to decide the guilt or innocence of the three persons. I believe that, given the circumstances, my actions would be appropriate, required, and reasonable.

Third follow-up question:

How would you search the females?

Possible response:

I would begin by immobilizing all three people who were under arrest as completely as possible. I would search the area immediately under their control and any handbags adjacent to where the women were sitting. I would wait for a female officer before conducting a further search, unless I felt either female prisoner had a weapon secreted on her person or contraband that was likely to be destroyed. If that was the case, I'd limit my search to that specific area. Depending on the circumstances, I might have a female patron of the restaurant search the women prisoners. My actions would be reasonable but would depend on the exact situation as it unfolded.

Supervisory principles covered in this response:

Decision-making skills, organizational integrity, department procedure, investigative procedures, narcotics, search and seizure, rules of evidence, arrest procedures, probable cause, searching females.

6. **You are a sergeant conducting roll-call inspection. During the inspection, you observe an officer behaving strangely and smell a strong odor of alcohol on his breath. What would you do?**

Possible response:

My first step would be to remove the officer from roll call. If he was intoxicated, I wouldn't allow him to go out on the street. I would advise my lieutenant of the situation, and the officer would be relieved of duty. Arrangements would be made to have the officer taken home. His service revolver would be confiscated. I would document what had occurred and recommend disciplinary action.

I would very closely monitor the officer upon his return to work. In addition to using the formal disciplinary process, I would discuss this incident with the officer to try to determine if his behavior was a symptom of a substance-abuse problem or just a one-time occurrence. I'd counsel the officer and refer him to the Employee Assistance Program.

Supervisory principles covered in this response:

Sensitivity, decision-making ability, supervisory communications, chain of command, reports, discipline process, inspection, monitoring, counseling, substance abuse, employee assistance programs.

7. **A female officer approaches you after roll call. She states that all of the male officers use excessive profanity just before roll-call inspection. She finds this situation distressing and wants action taken. What would you do?**

Possible response:

I would ask the officer to document the complaint with specifics as to the who, what, when, and where of these occurrences. I would advise the officer that an investigation would be conducted and that she would be apprised of the results. I'd inform my immediate supervisor of the complaint and forward the officer's report for his review. If then assigned to conduct the investigation, I would determine if the condition alleged in the complaint did, in fact, exist. If so, I would warn those involved to stop exhibiting this behavior. I would institute roll-call training concerning sexual harassment in the workplace.

I would document my actions and advise the complaining officer of my investigation concerning her complaint. I'd also monitor the situation, conduct follow-up inspections, and take appropriate action if the condition persisted.

Supervisory principles covered in this response:

Sensitivity, organizational integrity, complaint and investigative procedure, chain of command, reporting systems, discipline, sexual harassment, training, monitoring, and inspection.

8. **Crime analysis is a vital function in police departments. You are named as the supervisor in charge of a newly formed crime analysis unit. What would be the basic objectives of such a unit?**

Possible response:

Before making such a determination, I would confer with my immediate supervisor to find out the chief of police's expectations for the unit. I would also do research on crime analysis units by checking with other police departments that have such systems and reading resource material in the field. Depending on the equipment available, I would develop a program that was task specific to the objectives of my department. One of the primary objectives of crime analysis units generally is for the identification of crime patterns through modus operandi correlations. This is especially helpful in preventing crime and increasing the awareness of field officers to enable them to make earlier interventions. Another basic objective is to provide department command staff statistical information on areas of increased criminal activity so personnel can be efficiently assigned. The crime analysis unit, through correlation of data, also furnishes leads to investigators by providing information on suspects whose modus profile matches those of current offenders. The unit can also be very useful in measuring crime and evaluating the results of crime-specific departmental programs.

Supervisory principles covered in this response:

Planning, research, training, goal setting, crime patterns, modus operandi, statistics, evaluation techniques, measurement techniques, and coordination of activities.

9. You are a sergeant assigned to the patrol division. You're advised by your immediate supervisor of a new Supreme Court decision affecting police personnel. He instructs you to conduct training concerning this court decision for the 60 officers assigned to your squad. How would you accomplish this?

Possible response:

I would review the Supreme Court decision with both our training staff and legal counsel. After obtaining their input, I'd develop a lesson plan, handouts, and implementation schedule for roll-call training. After review and approval by my supervisor, I would administer the training and document the names of the officers who had received it.

As this board knows, training is one of the most effective affirmative defenses to vicarious-liability claims. In the case of a Supreme Court decision, I would recommend that all police personnel in the department receive instruction concerning it, using the lesson plan I developed as a model.

Supervisory principles covered in this response:

Planning, research, training, communication, documentation, vicarious liability, organizational integrity, scheduling.

10. As a sergeant assigned to the field, what supervisory techniques would you use to ensure that your subordinates are properly performing their assignments?

Possible response:

In my opinion, before you can hold subordinates accountable, you have to be certain they understand what level of performance is acceptable. I believe that communication is one of the keys to effective supervision. I would invest the time necessary to ensure that each of my subordinates understands exactly what level of performance is expected in his or her specific job assignment. I'd also ensure that each officer is properly trained and has appropriate equipment to accomplish the job tasks that are required to perform the assignment.

Once I had established this supervisory framework, I could use a variety of mechanisms to monitor officers. On the statistical level, I would review the computerized information on calls for service, which would tell me the types of calls officers are responding to, their response times, their time off on calls, and the total time they spend off the line. I would also monitor their citizen-complaint profiles and lost-time management reports. All of this information would give me a great deal of data on employee performance.

As a field sergeant, I would consistently monitor the radio and respond to calls to observe my subordinates' performance. A sergeant's duties include coaching, motivating, and inspecting personnel. Depending on my span of control, I would meet frequently with each subordinate to discuss ways to improve the efficiency and effectiveness of delivering police services to the community. As a first-line supervisor, I would be the channel through which upward and downward communications flow and would attempt to lead each subordinate to his or her optimum level of job performance.

Supervisory principles covered in this response:

Performance criteria, evaluation techniques, equipping personnel, training, monitoring, inspecting, communications, reporting systems, leadership, motivation of personnel.

4 Crossroads Along the Path

The Assessment Center

Understanding the Process

An assessment center is not a place to go to take a test. An assessment center offers a testing *process*. Promotional testing is intended to "predict" whether (and to what degree) a candidate has the traits needed to become an effective supervisor. The use of assessment center testing is a direct reflection of a loss of confidence in the prediction ability and validity of traditional police testing devices (written and oral tests, seniority, performance evaluations, etc.). Traditional testing for promotion has been heavily litigated in recent years, resulting in court decisions which have found promotional examinations to be "discriminatory," "not valid," "unfair," and "bearing little relationship to objective guidelines."

Police administrators and central personnel testing specialists began searching for an alternative, which would not only increase test validity, but also ensure the career development of police officers. Traditional police promotional examinations are one-dimensional, resulting only in filling vacancies. A way was sought to test candidates for promotion that would also determine strengths and weaknesses so further professional development could be planned. The assessment center testing procedure meets these objectives.

The assessment center is a *process in which candidates participate in a series of systematic, job-related, real-life situations while being observed and evaluated by experts in policing, supervision, and management.* Trained evaluators, called "assessors," observe candidates, individually and in groups, performing exercises/scenarios that simulate conditions and situations a sergeant would encounter in real life. It's this attempt to simulate actual working conditions that separates assessment center testing from the academics of written exams and the subjectivity of oral tests. However, many police executives have serious reservations concerning assessment center testing and view the process as nothing more than a "super oral exam." You'll find the preparation techniques for the oral examinations very helpful in preparing for assessment center testing as well.

History of Assessment Centers

Assessment center testing was originally developed during World War II. The agents of the Office of Strategic Services (OSS) knew that pure academic training and education were not adequately preparing their operatives for real-life situations in wartime. Their people scored well on academic tests but sometimes didn't perform well under pressure and were unable to apply academic principles to real people, places, and things. We face this same concern in police recruit and in-service training. For example, a recruit who scores 100% on a written test on "handcuffing techniques" can't necessarily place a prisoner in handcuffs.

The OSS developed a series of situational tests that placed operatives into situations that required specific performance behaviors to successfully perform under the conditions they would face while on actual assignment. This combination of a written curriculum with situational exercises produced superior personnel. In the private sector, American Telephone and Telegraph has been using assessment centers since 1956. In the past decade, many companies began using the process, not only for promotional testing, but also for selection, career development, and training. The use of situational testing techniques may be new to American policing, but they have been used by the police in England for many years. While the process still has many detractors, it is gaining support in police departments across the United States.

How Situational Exercises Are Developed

The primary method of developing the simulated exercises (mini-tests) is similar to that used in constructing written promotional examinations—it begins with the completion of a job task analysis. The specific skills, behaviors, and characteristics important to being a sergeant in your police department must be determined. After these "critical work behaviors" are established, exercises are developed which evaluate whether a candidate has the traits required for successful job performance. In assessment center testing, these are known as "critical success factors" or "dimensions." They are the criteria against which you will be evaluated and tested. Following are some of these dimensions. These will, of course, vary from city to city.

DIMENSIONS FOR THE POSITION OF POLICE SERGEANT

1. **Oral Communication**

   Clear and effective oral expression of ideas to individuals and groups. Includes body language, facial expressions, and gestures.

2. **Written Communication**

   Clear and effective organization and presentation of concepts in writing. Includes style, vocabulary, grammar, and format.

3. **Planning and Organizing**

   Ability to formulate a plan of action for self and others. Skill in determining how to accomplish a job task with finite resources and documentation of appropriate records.

4. **Controlling**

   Inspecting, monitoring, evaluating, and correcting subordinates. Includes establishment of acceptable performance levels, application of corrective techniques, and skill in recognizing and working with an employee who has a personal problem.

5. **Environmental Awareness**

   The gathering and use of information about situations and events inside and outside the police department to identify possible concerns and opportunities. Includes the recognition of potential crisis situations, the recognition of symptoms of good and bad morale, and the ability to adapt to change.

6. **Organizational Integrity**

Behavior that indicates active support for the objectives and standards of the police department. Includes willingness to accept and project the policies of the department as your own, ability to put personal feeling aside for the good of the organization, ability to maintain good media relations, ability to foster interpersonal cooperation, and ability to maintain confidentiality.

7. **Interpersonal Sensitivity**

Behavior that indicates a caring attitude toward the feelings, needs, and values of others. Includes communication skills (listening, feedback, etc.) and a sensitivity to cross-cultural needs.

8. **Leadership**

The motivational techniques and styles necessary to guide individuals and groups toward organizational goals. Includes ability to delegate to and empower individuals, still in obtaining the active participation of others, ability to maintain spirit de corps and morale, and ability to give direction and accept responsibility for decisions.

9. **Judgment**

Ability to develop a specific, goal-oriented course of action based on information and observations. Includes analytical thinking, recognizing and understanding the underlying issues of a problem, problem-solving skills, and ability to make decisions and accept responsibility under pressure.

10. **Meeting Management**

Skill in meeting with individuals and groups to accomplish departmental objectives. Includes communication ability, group dynamics, and effective meeting management techniques.

11. **Professionalism**

Specific behaviors, actions, and attitudes which display the highest standards of the police profession. Includes personal appearance; professional demeanor under s tress; ability to display confidence, leadership, and authority; ability to receive constructive criticism; and projecting a positive, professional image.

12. **Technical and Professional Knowledge**

Knowledge and understanding of the concepts associated with technical and professional police information. Includes knowledge of federal, state, and local laws; budgets and the budgetary process; rules, regulations, and procedures of the police department; labor contracts and personnel rules and procedures; information systems in the police department and city government; investigative principles and procedures; and court decisions that relate to policing.

After completing the job task analysis and formulating dimensions, the test analyst devises a mechanism to grade the examination. Usually, the analyst meets with the chief of police and his command staff, along with a sampling of lieutenants and sergeants, to determine the relative 'weighting" of each of the dimensions (such as the 12 listed earlier). The test analyst, along with the committee, determines the relative importance of each of these dimensions by comparing one to the other and assigning a numerical score to each (weighting) based on how important that trait is in performing the job of sergeant. For example, "organizational integrity" might be given first priority and weight of five, while 'meeting management" may receive only a weight of one. So the highest mark a candidate could receive in the dimension "organizational integrity" would be five points, and in "meeting management" one point. Such weighting is done so that proper emphasis is placed on the skills most important in performing the job. This helps to establish the validity of the testing process.

Situational exercises are developed in which candidates must display these traits (dimensions) to perform the exercise in a manner acceptable for a sergeant in your organization. Since in real life there are many ways to handle a situation and still be "correct," assessors are chosen who have expertise in policing/supervision and are given specialized training in the assessment center process. The more dimensions included in the exercise, the more job-related the testing criteria is. Using the list of 12 dimensions as a guide, a test specialist would create a real-life scenario that included as many of these dimensions as possible. The goal would be to include all 12 in each exercise; however, a minimum of 8 meets the requirement of job-relatedness in the example illustrated. The more overlapping the dimensions, the greater the ability of the exercise to reflect the skills required to perform the duties of a sergeant and the better the assessment center exercise will be.

How Assessment Centers Work

One of the problems with assessment centers is managing large number of candidates. It's expensive and time-consuming when compared to traditional testing. Each candidate goes through from four to eight individual or group exercises, with a minimum of two assessors evaluating each (except for the exercise known as the "in-basket," in which there is generally only one). Because assessment centers often use four "role-players" as part of the exercises, more people are needed. The higher the rank the procedure is testing for (lieutenant, captain, assistant chief, chief), the lower the number of candidates and the more manageable the testing process becomes.

A location large enough to have different rooms for the exercises, role-players, test monitors, assessors, and candidates are required. It must also be free from day-to-day business interruptions. Often, an assessment center is held at a business closed for the weekend, a hotel that has individual conference rooms, local high schools or colleges, etc. As is the case in traditional testing, a promotional testing announcement is posted and the normal application procedure must be followed. In order to limit the number of candidates going through the assessment center process, cities often first give written, oral, and/or other traditional tests. Only those officers who successfully pass these exams go on to the assessment center.

Test consultants hired to administer assessment centers invest a great deal of time to ensure not only that the exam is job-related and fair, but also that candidates understand the process and how it works. Usually, the job task analysis and related job dimensions are handed out to candidates, along with written material explaining the process and the procedures that will be used. Meetings are held with candidates to further explain the procedure and answer questions about the test. It's important to the chief of police and your city to make sure that candidates for promotion perceive the test to be fair, appropriate, and valid. As with traditional oral and written examinations, the date, time, and location that you're scheduled to take the assessment center examination is usually sent to you by the personnel department. Depending on the number of candidates and type of exercises, the test may last up to two full days. You're told whether to appear in uniform or in civilian clothes. The same standards mentioned as important in traditional testing apply to assessment centers. Upon arrival, you're given a written schedule that has the times and locations of your individual tests.

Preparing for the Assessment Center

The exercises most often used in assessment centers for the rank of sergeant, along with the appropriate dimensions and tips on how to receive high scores in this type of testing, are illustrated below. Read each of the exercises, suggested responses, and tips carefully. If you're going to be involved in assessment center testing, you'll also want to carefully review the Assessment Center Practice Test included in this book. Even if you're taking only the traditional oral exam, you should make use of the assessment center practice materials, since both exams cover similar principles, if in different formats.

> *To be a champ, you have to believe in your-self when nobody else will.*
> —SUGAR RAY ROBINSON

The In-Basket Exercise

A police sergeant often deals with memorandums, written and oral complaints, investigative reports, internal documents, letters, and telephone calls in day-to-day work. In this exercise, you and the other candidates (depending on the number, this is sometimes done in groups) are seated together in a room at desks or conference tables. The test monitor places a large manila envelope in front of each candidate, containing the "in-basket" (day-to-day paperwork) of a typical sergeant in your department. The directions for completing the questions are in writing, and the test monitor doesn't answer any questions concerning taking the test. You're told exactly when the test will begin (and end), the manila envelopes can be opened, and the written directions may be read individually by each candidate. When time is up, each candidate puts all the material back in the manila envelope and turns it in to the test monitor. All of the in-basket responses must be in writing.

The written directions will explain the role you are to assume for the completion of this particular exercise. For example, you might be assigned the position of desk sergeant, booking room supervisor, communications supervisor, or patrol sergeant. The objective is

to have you handle the in-basket exactly as you would if you were a real-life sergeant in one of these assignments. If the written instructions specify that you are a patrol sergeant, for example, your in-basket might include the following:

PATROL SERGEANT'S IN-BASKET
TODAY'S DATE 4/28

Item 1—A note from your lieutenant directing you to complete an investigation relative to a citizen complaint against an officer under your supervision. It is on department stationery, typed or in ink, as illustrated below

To: Sergeant Brown
From: Lieutenant Phillips
Take appropriate action and reply by 5/10

Attached to it is a citizen's complaint package.

Item 2—An interdepartmental memorandum from Captain Adams concerning high-speed pursuits to be read at today's roll calls.

Item 3—A telephone message for you to call city councilman Thompson about a parking ticket he received.

Item 4—A management report detailing the calls for service for officers under your direct supervision for the month of March with a written note on the bottom stating, "Take appropriate action and reply to me by 4/30, Lieutenant Phillips."

Item 5—A request for a preapproved day off from one of your subordinates to attend a wedding three weeks from now.

Item 6—An arrest report submitted to the court, completed by one of your officers. There is a note from Lieutenant Phillips attached to it stating that the report was reviewed by another sergeant (on your day off) and the charge against the accused was "omitted." The note further states, "Take appropriate action and return directly to me prior to leaving the building today. I have to make a separate report out on this."

Item 7—Another memorandum from Lieutenant Phillips directing you to prepare a recommendation on roll-call training on the department's "Firearms Guidelines" in light of a new federal court ruling, which is attached. Your recommendation is due 5/8.

As you can see, because of all of the written material attached to these memos, a candidate appears to have to do a lot of reading. But if you actually take the time to read each sentence, you'll never finish the exercise. Part of the test is to see how well you plan and organize your time. The test directions require you to say in writing how you would handle each of these tasks, as if you actually were a sergeant in that role. In Item 5, for instance, you write, on the day-off request, a reply to the officer saying, "Please resubmit directly to me one week prior to the day you want off, and I'll consider your request at that time."

You sign it, "Sergeant Brown" because that's the role you're assuming in this exercise. You also note on the bottom, "1 would place the day-off request in the officer's mail slot and, if possible, see him to explain that I can't project days off that far in advance." This procedure would give you "points" with your assessor for the following dimensions:

- written communications skills
- planning and organizing

- interpersonal sensitivity
- professionalism
- technical and professional knowledge

The time limit is purposely short because the objective is to place you under considerable pressure to complete all of the tasks contained in the in-basket within the time allotted. You must, therefore, prioritize your work from most to least important. Added pressure is applied by having a laptop recording your session in the room. At the beginning of the process, the test monitor explains that, while candidates are completing their in-baskets, they may hear a prerecorded message on the laptop to be interpreted as they would in real life should they receive such a message as a sergeant in the role they are assuming. If this does happen, candidates are required to write out how they would handle it.

For example, while you're completing your in-basket, the recording is turned on by the test monitor and all candidates hear the sound of a telephone ringing. When the ringing stops, a voice says, "This is Sergeant Mahoney in communications. Two of your units were just dispatched to an active holdup of a gas station located at 113 Huntington Street. An employee of the station has been shot. An ambulance is on the way." The recorder then shuts off. The candidates are now required to write what they would do. Obviously, if you write that you would immediately respond to the scene and include all of the supervisory things you would do prior to and upon arrival, it would consume a great deal of the time allotted for the exercise, although this may be the correct way to handle the test, especially if you've already completed the more important items in your in-basket. Make certain to include a statement saying that the items listed that had due dates of today (4/28) would be completed, even if you had to remain at work on your own time. This will give you added points for organizational integrity.

The in-basket exercise is a pressure-packed, mentally fatiguing, problem-solving dilemma. The criteria normally associated with in-basket exercises are

- decision-making
- sensitivity
- planning and organizing
- delegation
- written communications
- judgment
- problem analysis
- organizational integrity
- stress tolerance
- leadership

How to Receive a High Score

Time and ability to organize your work are important components of the in-basket exercise. As mentioned earlier, the clock is used to put candidates under pressure, so use it to your best advantage. Read the instructions thoroughly. Make certain you know what role you're playing. What are the duties and responsibilities of a sergeant in that role? What authority do you possess? Who are your subordinates and superiors? Prioritize your work. Briefly glance through all of the paperwork in your in-basket and **rearrange it from top to bottom from most to least important.** Look for due dates and other indicators that work needs immediate attention. Complete the exercise with the goals of the department in mind, not of individuals. The seven items in our mock in-basket would be prioritized, beginning with the *most important,* as follows:

First Item—Item 2, the memo from the captain concerning high-speed pursuits to be read at roll call.

Reason: Regardless of what else happens during your tour of duty, officers report for work and attend roll call. Obviously, if the captain has written a memorandum on high-speed pursuits, it indicates that *present policy is not being followed or new policy has been created.* From an organizational-integrity viewpoint, this item should be placed first.

Possible written response: To: Lieutenant Phillips. Memo read at roll call on 4/28. See attached roster of officers present. Sergeant Brown.

Second Item—Item 3, the phone message from the city councilman about the parking ticket.

Reason: What's the underlying issue? Is the chief going to receive a phone call from the city manager because the city councilman complained that you didn't return his call? Would your failure to act cause the chief to speak to the captain, resulting in a memo written to your lieutenant? Would the lieutenant then endorse the memo to you? City council members are important people in government. A phone call could prevent all of these problems. Also, it's quick to handle and requires only a few lines.

Possible written response: Telephoned councilman 4/28. Explained the department's policy on protesting parking tickets. Arranged to mail him a Parking Ticket Protest Form. Separate memo to Lieutenant Phillips regarding phone call and action taken. Sergeant Brown.

Third Item—Item 6, the incomplete arrest report to the court which Lieutenant Phillips instructed you to handle "prior to leaving the building."

Reason: Your immediate supervisor wants it done right away. This particular in-basket item would include information informing you that the officer who originally submitted the report is readily available.

Possible written response: Meet with officer. Have the officer complete the report. Counsel the officer for failure to submit a proper report. Document. Write a memo to Lieutenant Phillips.

To: Lieutenant Phillips, Date: April 28, 20–
From: Sergeant Brown, Copy to: File
Subject: Arrest Report Re: Officer Paul Jones

The undersigned instructed Officer Jones to complete the attached report. The officer was counseled relative to his failure to complete the "charges" section of the report. His arrest reports will be closely monitored in the future. Please see the attached report for forwarding to the court.

Fourth Item—Item 5, the request from your subordinate for a preapproved day off three weeks from now.

Reason: The remaining three items are more time consuming and have due dates in the future. This one is quicker and easy.

Possible written response: Write it on the actual request as discussed earlier.

Fifth Item—Item 4, the calls for service report on officers under your supervision. Reason: It's the next logical item left that doesn't require additional information.

Possible written response: Review for any obvious negative patterns requiring immediate attention. Place in my tickler file for 4/29 for more comprehensive review and analysis. Work on, later today if time permits.

Sixth Item—Item 1, the complaint against the officer.

Reason: By this time you've received the "phone call" and indicated your response to the robbery. By the time you had read the instructions, scanned the items, prioritized your in-basket, and completed from three to five of the items, the recorded message would have played.

Possible written response: Read. Tickler file for 4/29.

Seventh Item—Item 7, roll-call training on the "Firearms Guidelines" due 5/8.

Reason: It's complicated and requires extensive work. The test is designed so that you're not able to complete this item.

Possible written response: Read. Confer with Lieutenant Phillips to schedule time to accomplish. Place in tickler file for 4/29.

Your in-basket will also contain other items designed to be fillers. These may include maps, graphs, department orders, etc. Some may be pertinent, while others are designed to be time-consuming if read in their entirety. Scan and prioritize. Separate the important from the unimportant.

Meeting with Your Assessor

Usually, this is the only exercise at the assessment center in which you will meet face to face with your assessor to discuss your answers. Because your responses have to be reviewed in depth by your assessor prior to that meeting, this interview is scheduled toward the latter part of the assessment center process. The reason for the meeting is to determine the thought process you used to complete the exercise. Why did you work on some items and not others? What was your reasoning for handling a situation in a particular way? In every other assessment center exercise, the assessors can see, hear, and evaluate whether or not you're exhibiting a behavior characteristic that falls within one of the predetermined dimensions. The in-basket exercise reduces everything to writing. What you wrote and the manner in which you prioritized may differ from the handling of other candidates yet still be valid depending on your explanation to the assessor. In order to make sense out of this exercise, the assessor must review your written responses with you. During this interview, all of the methods previously recommended for use in an oral examination are important. Appearance, oral communication ability, demeanor, eye contact, body language, etc., will directly affect your assessor's perception of you. Even though assessors are trained not to allow anything but the pre-established criteria to enter into their scoring, it's almost impossible not to. A good "first impression" and the use of interpersonal skills will increase your in-basket rating. The methods suggested to excel in oral exams are important in the remaining exercises.

The test that follows your in-basket exercise may be scheduled for ten minutes or up to an hour later. The in-basket exercise (which almost always comes first in the assessment center process) inevitably leaves you physically and mentally drained, and you probably won't have the faintest idea how well you did. Waiting too long before your next situational exercise can place you at a disadvantage. Use the time between exercises to check your uniform and to study your index cards. If the wait is extended, don't spend it with other candidates discussing the in-basket exercise. Turn the wait to your advantage by going somewhere alone, perhaps out to your car, to study.

The remaining assessment center exercises are monitored by a minimum of two assessors. One of the major mistakes officers make in the remaining exercises is *forgetting that this is a test!* Don't get so wrapped up in playing the role that you forget the assessors are monitoring everything that you do and say!

The Supervisor/Subordinate Exercise

This test is sometimes referred to as the "oral examination" in assessment centers. When you report to the assigned room, you'll find a desk with another manila envelope on it and two assessors seated unobtrusively in the room. They'll speak to you only to give you a specific time to open the envelope and follow the written instructions. In this exercise, you're given written information placing you in a specific, supervisory, police department role. The test creates a scenario in which a subordinate has a problem—for example, a discipline problem, personal concern, or poor work performance—which necessitates your interrelating with the officer as a supervisor. In this exercise, you must analyze the situation, develop a plan of action, and then interview one or more role players who are waiting outside the room for you to call them in. The role players are trained to react as an actual police officer would under the circumstances outlined in the situation. The role players are not from your department but are in police uniform. The objective is to simulate a real-life situation that you have to deal with. Since the assessors observe everything you say and do—from your facial expressions and command presence to your voice control and supervisory skills—all the dimensions listed on page 81 are important here. Here's an example of a typical supervisor/subordinate exercise:

SUPERVISOR/SUBORDINATE

You are a sergeant assigned to the evening shift in the department's patrol division. On December 12, 20—, Lieutenant Flynn calls you into his office and hands you a report written by two officers under your supervision. Both officers are assigned to a foot beat in one of the city's housing projects. The report reads as follows:

The undersigned officers have been assigned to the Parker Heights housing project since January of 20—. The officers did not volunteer for this assignment but were advised by Captain Johnson that they were selected because the area has a severe drug problem. Captain Johnson told the officers that if they cleaned up the area he would reassign them to cruisers and that the officers wouldn't have this assignment for any longer than six months. Captain Johnson has now been reassigned to the internal affairs division, and it has been eight months. The officers feel that they have done an excellent job in addressing the narcotics problem within the area and request they be reassigned to cruisers in areas with a more diversified population as soon as possible.

Officer Paul Fleming
Officer Kenneth Tyler

Lieutenant Flynn also informs you that he has spoken with Captain Johnson, who doesn't recall promising the officers anything. Lieutenant Flynn informs you that both officers and their union steward are standing by to discuss this situation. He instructs you to meet with the officers and "handle the matter."

Your time has already begun. You have 30 minutes from the time you entered this room to plan how you will handle the situation and to carry out that plan. Both officers and their union steward are outside of this room right now. Also included in this package is a brief synopsis of Officer Fleming and Officer Tyler's backgrounds, along with a copy of the current labor/management contract.

How to Receive a High Score

Once again, time is a critical factor. As you're reading through the various items in your test package, underline or highlight key material. Use a separate sheet of paper to outline exactly what your plan will be when you call the officers and their steward in for the interview. This will be noted by the assessor and give you extra points for "planning and organizing." In many assessment centers, all notes are turned in to the assessors.

Rearrange the environment appropriately for the type of interview the situation calls for. Place the chairs in front of or next to the desk in a manner that will put you in better control of the interview. Arrange all of your material for ready reference before the interview begins. The assessors will observe all of this preparation. *Remember, you're playing the role of a sergeant. You're no longer a patrol officer, Act the part!*

When you open the door, greet all three officers with a smile and a handshake, which will give you added points for professionalism and interpersonal sensitivity. During the interview, the assessors judge you on all of the dimensions that apply: oral communication, planning and organizing, controlling, organizational integrity, interpersonal sensitivity, professionalism, and technical and professional knowledge. Listen to the officers; let them air their feelings; act concerned; take notes while they're talking; smile when appropriate; show empathy; refer them to the section of the labor/ management contract that states, "Job assignments are not subject to the grievance process"; make it clear, in a friendly way, to their union steward that this really isn't a matter for union intervention; make no promises, but tell the officers you'll give every consideration to their request depending on the needs of the department;

praise them for their good work. Motivate! Lead! Supervise! When you're ready to end the interview, stand, shake the role-players' hands, smile, and walk them to the door.

In order to do well at assessment centers, you have to be a good actor. Proponents of this type of testing argue that candidates, when put under pressure, behave as they would in real life. That may be the case for officers who haven't read this book, but since you know in advance the behaviors that will fulfill the requirements of the grading dimensions, you'll add points to your final score. You're as much "onstage" in an assessment center as you are in the oral exam, so play the role, act the part, know the rules of the game!

The Leaderless Discussion Group Exercise

The objective of this exercise is to assess your reactions and behaviors when you interrelate with a group. You are seated with other candidates (usually five to seven) around a table. Technically, at least one assessor should be present for each candidate. In actuality, however, each assessor may monitor two or more officers. Each candidate is provided with background information on a specific problem—a problem that requires group discussion and decision. The written instructions usually state that the group must elect a spokesperson who will present their consensus to the role-player acting the part of the chief of police or another high ranking superior officer. An example of a typical leaderless discussion exercise follows:

LEADERLESS DISCUSSION

A major issue facing police departments today is "lost-time management." You are all police sergeants here as a committee appointed by the chief of police. Discuss methods of improving the department's "lost-time management" system. No one on this committee has been placed in charge. You have 40 minutes to prepare a recommendation and make a presentation to the chief of police.

How to Receive a High Score

Leadership, judgment, oral communication, organizational integrity, controlling, and meeting management skills are the dimensions directly related to this exercise. You need to immediately establish yourself by offering ideas for the group to respond to. The danger in this exercise is being such a good listener that time runs out without your having the opportunity to say anything. Be careful of what I call the "paralysis of analysis"—don't spend so much time thinking about what the group is saying that you're left out. Volunteer right away to be the group "recorder." Take notes on what everyone says and at the same time

become appropriately involved in the discussion. If you're the recorder and no one else is taking notes, then you'll very likely be the person to address the chief in the end. All assessors will then be concentrating on you! Also, suggest that someone in the group keep track of the time and allow five to eight minutes for the final presentation. Both of these tactics will add points to your score for planning, controlling, and meeting management.

The trick is to offer frequent ideas without appearing to have taken over the discussion. Knowing *when* to talk is as important as what you say. The assessor is looking for the ability to interrelate with people. Manners are important in this exercise. Don't interrupt when others are talking. If the meeting gets out of hand, be the one to take quiet, firm control. You might suggest brainstorming by going around the table and having each person relate ideas in ten words or less. If someone else is vying for the role of spokesperson, suggest that each of you highlight a different part of the group's suggestions. Praise other people at the table by saying "good idea, John," or "Donna has an interesting concept that I think the group should explore further." This will give you points for interpersonal sensitivity. Of course, if you think John or Donna has the intelligence of an amoeba and they've made an incredibly stupid comment, you don't want to be heard praising them, since the assessors may then think you haven't much sense either. But at the same time, you don't want to overtly attack and appear insensitive. Your best bet here may be to nod noncommittally, indicating only that you've heard the speaker.

If someone else in the group hasn't said anything, you might say, "Paul, what do you think about *this idea?*"; this tactic gives you the floor to explain your idea and, at the same time, puts Paul in position to speak next.

When giving the group's consensus and recommendations to the chief, be sure to begin with the fact that you represent the committee, not just yourself. Oral communication skills are very important here. Use this opportunity to your advantage. The same techniques you practiced for your oral board will score heavily in this segment. Smile, make eye contact, shake hands if appropriate, etc.

The Community Meeting Exercise

In this test, you enter a room, which is empty, except for your assessors. One assessor hands you written instructions, which might use a format similar to the following:

COMMUNITY MEETING

You are a sergeant assigned to the patrol division and detailed by your captain to attend a community meeting in your supervisory area. She advises you that the meeting was called by residents and businessmen to discuss adding additional "foot beats" to the neighborhood. They are expecting the chief of police to be present at the meeting. He's not coming. You are to attend the meeting in his place. You are not to commit any police resources at this meeting. The exercise will begin 5 minutes after you're handed these instructions and will terminate in 40 minutes.

How to Receive a High Score

This exercise tests a full range of dimension criteria. For this reason, it's an excellent test, but it's used infrequently because of the number of role players required. Shortly after you read the instructions, you will hear a commotion in the hallway outside the room. The role-players, acting the parts of angry residents and business owners, enter the room in an agitated state. The assessors evaluate your handling of the situation and organization of the meeting. Expect the role-players to ask you some of the following kinds of questions:

- Where's the chief?
- Why are you here?
- What authority do you have?
- Where's the captain? The lieutenant?
- Why can't we have more foot patrol in our neighborhood?
- When can you begin increasing the amount of patrol coverage in the neighborhood?
- Why did it take the police 40 minutes to get there when I called about that prowler last week?
- I got a parking ticket for double parking just for a minute while I helped my sick mother into a clinic. How come you people harass honest citizens and ignore the dope deals right out in the open on my street corner?

As you can see, this exercise lends itself to evaluating candidates as they are exposed to a variety of pressure-packed situations. Once again, it's very easy in the heat of discussion to forget this is a test! Possible techniques to use for this exercise are:

1. Rearrange the room as soon as you finish reading the instructions. Some assessment centers place a podium in the room with the written instructions for completing the exercise on it. Don't speak to the group from behind the shield of the podium. Set up a table and arrange chairs around it and sit down before the group comes in.
2. When the noisy crowd enters, stand up. Smile and tell the group that you're glad they could come. Offer them seats. Diffuse the situation.
3. Before the role-players can ask you anything, make an opening statement. Tell them who you are, why you're there (to bring their concerns back to the captain), and what the limits of your authority are.
4. Explain department policy and procedure, but don't get into arguments with the role-players about these rules. Remember, this is a test! Show the assessor that you possess organizational integrity and put your organization first in everything.
5. Communication, meeting management, interpersonal sensitivity, judgment, professionalism—all are vital components of this exercise. The techniques used to achieve high scores in oral exams can be used very effectively in the community meeting exercise.

The assessment center exercises used for your test may not be exactly the same as those discussed here. However, the *techniques* offered *will* work regardless of which variation of the test is administered. Many test analysts insist that you can't study for an assessment center because the exercises are "real-life situations" and you'll revert to the way you would actually handle it. Don't believe it! Not only can you study for assessment centers, you must! Although here you'll interrelate with people, you still must know supervisory principles and techniques in order to do well on the exercises. Study for an assessment center as you've learned to study for written and oral examinations.

> *It is by presence of mind in untried emergencies that the native mettle of a man is treated.*
>
> —Herman Melville

The Physical Examination

Understanding the Process

Most officers think that the testing process ends after they receive their final score from the personnel department. In many departments, that isn't the case. After the various components of the testing system are corrected and tabulated (written test, oral exam, seniority points, performance evaluation, etc.), officers are placed on an "eligible list." An eligible list is a numerical ranking, from highest to lowest, of all officers who have successfully passed the testing process. It's not a promotion list. To become a promotion list, the eligible list must be "certified." You can usually find the certification process in your city's personnel rules. Although the procedure varies, normally there is a minimum of two certification components: passing a physical examination and either the "rule of three" or the "rule of five."

If you're required to pass a physical, *it's as much a test as your written or oral exams*. This requirement is highly controversial. You took and passed a physical exam for initial employment as a police officer. The question is whether it is appropriate to require you to pass another physical to become a police sergeant. The rationale used by many central personnel agencies is that, in moving from one job classification to another, you're "applying" for a separate position in city government. To be "hired" for this new position, you must pass a physical exam. If you fail the physical, you may be denied promotion, but that failure won't necessarily affect your current status as a patrol officer because it's a different "job." The use of physical examinations as part of the promotion process has been the subject of labor/management negotiations in some departments resulting in contractual language prohibiting the use of such exams to exclude candidates for promotion. Court litigation in this area centers on whether the physical examination can reasonably be defended by the city as being job-related. For instance, if your physical reveals that you have high blood pressure, it makes little sense to eliminate you from being placed on the eligible list for sergeant while allowing you to go on the street every day and perform the more physically rigorous duties of a patrol officer. But whatever the legal questions involved, you don't want to fail the physical and wait five years while a civil court adjudicates your lawsuit.

Ideally, you should find out if you'll have to pass a physical even before the promotional test is announced. This forewarning may give you enough lead time to do something about the shape you're in. However, you must be careful who you ask and the language you use when you do. For example, if you were to call your personnel unit and ask whoever answered the phone whether a physical is part of the testing process for the rank of sergeant, here's what probably would happen: The person from personnel would tell you to "hold on" and then come back on the phone and say, "Nope, I checked with Mr. Nobody, who said it's not part of the test." The reason you might get this kind of response? The semantics are such that many personnel agencies don't consider the physical a test—they consider it a *requirement*, just as "length of service" may be a requirement for you to be eligible to take the promotional test.

Consider this scenario: Unaware of the intricacies of the system, Officer Jones receives a letter from the personnel unit advising him that his final score on the sergeant's exam is 95.2% and his rank is No. 1. Since there are three vacancies for sergeant, Officer Jones figures he'll be promoted. However, the last sentence on the letter from personnel advises him that all "eligibles" must pass a physical examination prior to appointment and includes a date and time for Officer Jones to report for his physical. Since he's found to be 55 pounds overweight and to have an elevated blood pressure, he is not "eligible" for promotion. The chief then promotes candidates two, three, and four, who did pass their physicals and were on the certified list supplied to him by the central personnel unit for promotion. Officer Jones's name didn't even appear on the certified list for promotion received by the chief. Officer Jones complains and is referred to the original test announcement, requirements section, which states, "and any other physical requirements to perform the job."

If your department has a union or affiliation that represents police officers, they are the people who should be asking these questions for you. If your department is unaffiliated, pursue the answers to these questions through written correspondence addressed to the person in charge of your city's personnel department.

> *Health alone is victory.*
>
> —THOMAS CARLYLE

Important Elements in the Physical Examination

There are two areas of special significance to police officers taking physical examinations for promotion:

1. height/weight ratio
2. blood pressure

In the absence of other major physical problems, being overweight and having high blood pressure are the primary reasons officers fail their physicals. Both of these conditions are usually treatable in the time between the announcement of the original test and the completion of the final eligible list. I strongly recommend that before doing anything else, you contact your own doctor and have a complete physical examination.

Height/Weight Ratio

Some central personnel agencies send their officers to a city-operated clinic to have their physical, while others contract with local doctors. In either case, determine if there is a height/weight criterion and what happens if you don't fall within the recommended guidelines. Some cities are still using insurance company life-expectancy charts as a standard for height/weight classification as illustrated on the next page:

HEIGHT AND WEIGHT TABLES
According to Frames, Ages 25-59
(weight in pounds, indoor clothing)

MEN

Height (in shoes)

Feet	Inches	Small Frame	Medium Frame	Large Frame
5	2	128–134	131–141	136–150
5	3	130–136	133–143	140–153
5	4	132–138	135–145	142–156
5	5	134–140	137–148	144–160
5	6	136–142	139–151	146–164
5	7	138–145	142–154	149–168
5	8	140–148	145–156	152–172
5	9	142–151	148–158	155–176
5	10	144–154	151–160	158–180
5	11	146–157	154–163	161–184
6	0	149–160	157–170	164–188
6	1	152–164	160–174	168–192
6	2	155–168	164–178	172–197
6	3	158–172	167–182	176–202
6	4	162–176	171–187	181–207

WOMEN

Height (in shoes)

Feet	Inches	Small Frame	Medium Frame	Large Frame
4	10	102–111	109–121	118–131
4	11	103–113	111–123	120–134
5	0	104–115	113–126	122–137
5	1	106–118	115–128	125–140
5	2	108–121	118–130	128–143
5	3	111–124	121–132	131–147
5	4	114–127	124–135	134–151
5	5	117–130	127–141	137–155
5	6	120–133	130–144	140–157
5	7	123–136	133–147	143–159
5	8	126–139	136–150	146–163
5	9	129–142	139–153	149–170
5	10	132–145	142–156	152–173
5	11	135–148	145–159	155–176
6	0	138–151	148–162	158–179

(indoor clothing weighing 5 pounds for men and 3 pounds for women; shoes with 1-inch heels)

If you anticipate a problem meeting the weight requirement, discuss the matter with your own physician to develop a plan to lose weight. Losing about two pounds per week in a supervised program is generally considered the safest way to lose weight. Unless you're severely overweight, you should have plenty of time to lose the pounds you need to.

High Blood Pressure

Due to the nature of our work, hypertension has become an occupational hazard in policing. High blood pressure can result from a number of causes, but the disease is treatable with a variety of methods including diet and drugs. The time to find out that you have high blood pressure is not when the city sends you for your physical. It may be too late by then. Find out early so that, if you do have a blood pressure problem, you can be put on a medically supervised program to bring it down before the department physical.

Certifying the Promotion List (Rules of Three and Five)

As mentioned earlier, after the final scores are announced, candidates are placed on an eligible list for promotion. The list may last up to three years. Vacancies are created when sergeants retire, resign, or are promoted to lieutenant. In some organizations, the actual vacancy doesn't occur until all of the time the retiring sergeant has on the "books" is used up. For example, Sergeant Brown might have a retirement party on May 1 and leave. However, his vacation time, accrued holidays, etc., may actually carry him on the payroll through July. The vacancy you're looking for so you can get promoted may not be filled until then.

However, let's assume that there are, in fact, four current vacancies for sergeants. Some departments go right down the list, promoting the top four people on the eligible list. Other agencies use what is known as the "rule of three." When a vacancy occurs, the department head (chief of police) requests that the vacant position(s) be filled. The central personnel agency provides the chief with the top three names from the certified list for each vacant position. If the chief is requesting that four vacancies be filled, he is then supplied with the top five names from the certified list. This system is illustrated by the following chart.

CERTIFIED LIST AND SELECTION OF FOUR VACANCIES

Vacancy 1			Vacancy 2		
1. Richard Brown	95.5%		1. Jeffrey Stone	92.0%	
2. Jeffrey Stone	92.0%		2. Enrique Gonzalez	89.5%	
3. Enrique Gonzalez	89.5%		3. Paul Johnson	89.0%	

Vacancy 3			Vacancy 4		
1. Enrique Gonzalez	89.5%		1 Paul Johnson	89.0%	
2. Paul Johnson	89.0%		2. Pamela Stone	88.5%	
3. Pamela Stone	88.5%		3. Anthony Lorenzeti	82.0%	
(*Chief* selects Gonzalez)			(*Chief* passes over *Johnson* and selects *Stone*)		

With the "rule of three" in effect, the chief of police has the right to choose any person from the list of three eligible candidates for each position (and need not take the top-ranked candidate). In this case, it means that Officer Johnson doesn't get promoted and Officer Stone does. The "rule of five" gives the chief of police an even wider selection spread. Officers are "passed over" for a wide variety of reasons: poor work record, abuse of sick or injured time, citizen complaint profile, to fulfill affirmative action goals, politics, etc. So, there's more to getting promoted than just doing well on your written and oral exams, and the more you know about the process the better you can prepare a plan to succeed.

5

Theory
and
Concept
Study Guide

Study Guide

Use the following study guide to assist you in preparing for your sergeant's examinations. The guide is not intended to be all inclusive, but rather to review the fundamental theories and concepts important in police supervision. Regardless of whether you'll be taking a written, oral, or assessment center exam, there are elements of supervision common to sergeants everywhere. Study the following eight areas as an adjunct to the reference books listed on your sergeant's promotional test announcement.

Leading

Getting things done through people is the primary responsibility of a police sergeant in any department. Test questions are designed to determine how you will go about fulfilling this responsibility. For example, what can a sergeant do so that police officers enjoy coming to work, perform at the highest level of which they are capable, and view the objectives of the police department as their own? Good sergeants accomplish this goal through *leading*. Others willingly adopt a leader's vision because they believe that the leader's objective is in their own best interest.

Leadership is not an intrinsic quality with which a person is born nor is it reserved for the upper police ranks. People such as General George Patton, John F. Kennedy, St. Francis of Assisi, Winston Churchill, and Mahatma Ghandi, to name just a few, were all great leaders. We remember them for their abilities, values, beliefs, and accomplishments. However, not one of them was born a leader. They became leaders through hard work, self-sacrifice, commitment, and the courage to stand up for what they believed in. History is full of exam-pies of both individuals and groups who overcame great odds and succeeded because of the special impact of a leader. Consider the fact that Spartacus inspired a handful of slaves to rout a Roman army. During the Civil War, a ragtag Southern army, battle-weary, hungry, and without shoes, marched double-time 14 miles to defend Sharpsbury under the leadership of Robert E. Lee. These leaders inspired their men to render services to others and to gain self-respect in a community of achievers. Police sergeants must strive to do the same.

In his book *Police Administration,* O.W. Wilson identifies, as many others have, leaders' common traits. He wrote that leaders "are usually above-average in intelligence, emotionally stable, and psychologically strong. While they might not all demonstrate enthusiastic, forceful, or outgoing personalities, many of them have considerable enthusiasm for their own ideas and great forcefulness or drive in setting and achieving goals."

Leaders possess self-discipline, poise, the courage of their convictions, and the ability to empower people to accomplish specific tasks toward an organizational objective. The mark of leaders is that they enable people to accomplish more than they thought possible. They lead people toward goals instead of driving them. They *empower* their subordinates by giving up some of their authority so that the subordinates have the opportunity to grow and reach their full potential, take pride in their work, and visualize organizational goals as their own. A leader makes people feel that what they are doing is important, replacing the *we versus they* (labor versus management) attitude, which is common in many police departments, with a more positive *us* working environment. Accomplished sergeants spend a great deal more time raising people up than putting them down.

In policing, leaders are created by providing a work climate where the pursuit of excellence is an established norm. Sergeants don't magically become leaders simply because they pass a test and sew three stripes on their uniforms—that grants them only formal authority. Leadership must be fought for and earned in the most difficult arena of all —through interrelating with people. This focus on people, rather than things, is the main difference between leading and managing. Managers are primarily concerned with things: the bureaucratic, machinelike running of the police organization—the budgets, paperwork, personnel reports, equipment, and rosters associated with policing. Leaders, on the other hand, are more concerned with *people.* They accomplish goals with and through people and understand that human resources are the most vital component of any organization.

Police sergeants are first-line supervisors. As such, they are closest in rank and personal contact with the people who perform the vast majority of the work in policing, police officers. The difficult part of being a sergeant is to balance the primary responsibility to implement the directives of management as if they were their own with an important secondary duty to communicate from labor to management the concerns of police officers, which may conflict with those very policies. This dual role is one of the reasons it's so important that sergeants develop leadership traits. Any knowledgeable police administrator will be the first to say that police sergeants are the key to running an effective and efficient police department.

Police sergeants are in a unique position to lead. It's the sergeants who respond to emergency calls for service (hostage situations, bank robberies, etc.), implement the day-to-day plans of the organization, give roll-call training, and are on the street every day with their officers. Since sergeants come into contact with more people than any other rank and have the largest span of control, they have more *opportunity* to lead in the true sense of the concept than other ranking officers do.

There are many definitions of leadership. Nathan Iannone, the author of *Supervision of Police Personnel,* defines leadership as "the art of influencing people by directing, guiding, and controlling in such a way as to obtain their willing obedience, confidence, respect, and loyal cooperation in accomplishment of an objective." To be leaders, sergeants must develop the following attributes:

- technical skill and competence
- a value and belief system based on self-discipline and integrity that will encourage others to have faith in them; setting the example for others to follow
- enthusiasm, vigor, self-confidence, and physical energy; seeking out responsibility and taking responsibility for their decisions and actions
- organizational integrity and a strong work motivation; the ability to sell the ideas of the organization to subordinates in such a manner that they willingly adopt them
- good communication skills and the ability to give employees constructive feedback on their behavior and work performance

Several key factors dealing both directly and indirectly with leadership and management often appear on promotional examinations. Study each of these in depth as they appear in the reference books listed on your test announcement. Some basic concepts are covered here.

Leadership Styles

The patterns of behavior used by leaders to influence subordinates are often classified under specific leadership or management styles.

Theory X and Theory Y Management Behavior

In 1960, Douglas McGregor described two classical behaviors in his Theory X and Theory Y Leadership Model. McGregor's Theory X manager is more concerned with output than with people. These individuals are often autocratic, overly work-oriented, short-tempered, and easily angered and lead by fear and intimidation. They feel that people dislike work and must be coerced, controlled, and constantly directed. They are task-masters, people who work best in structured environments that have a host of rules and regulations. Theory X managers may be quite successful in getting things done when short-term tasks are important to completing an overall objective and when a limited amount of time has been allotted.

Theory Y managers are the opposite of Theory X managers. They believe in participatory management, setting an example for others to follow. They want to be liked by their subordinates and believe that people generally like work, seek responsibility, and will get the job done if given the chance to do so.

Autocratic Leaders

Autocratic leaders are similar to Theory X managers. They make decisions without input and announce them to their subordinates. They don't empower people or share their authority with others. They are not concerned with allowing employees input into the decision-making process and are highly task-oriented. This type of leadership style is quite effective in policing during emergency situations where a great deal of control is needed but does not serve the organizational needs during day-to-day operations or over an extended period of time.

Free-Rein Leaders (Laissez-Faire)

Free-rein leaders turn over all decision-making authority to their subordinates after outlining a task to be performed and don't become directly involved unless requested to do so. Supervisors who use this style of leadership may believe that they are "developing" people; however, in reality, laissez-faire leadership works only for a short while with highly skilled, self-motivated employees. This leadership style is sometimes seen in investigative divisions that have highly competent personnel. However, in the semi military atmosphere of policing, free-rein leaders are short-lived.

Participative Leaders (Democratic)

Leaders who believe in participative management share overall decision-making with their subordinates. They encourage group discussion and consult with their subordinates before making a decision. However, they retain final decision-making authority.

Situational Leaders

There isn't a single leadership or management style that's most effective in police organizations. Creative sergeants recognize that people have individual needs, values, and belief systems. A leadership style that works with one person may not necessarily work with another. Circumstances and conditions (such as emergency situations) may require sergeants to adopt an autocratic style for short periods of time. Participative management doesn't work at homicide scenes or in controlling civil disorders. However, sergeants should probably use a participative management style for most day-to-day operations because it leads to more effective and efficient task accomplishment, high morale, and esprit de corps.

Following are characteristics of a participative management style.

Participative Managers

- are clearly aware of the organization's morale
- are approachable
- are effective communicators
- are thoughtful and considerate of others
- share decision making with subordinates
- inform subordinates of the true situation
- counsel, train, and develop subordinates
- support change
- allow errors
- acknowledge good work

There are many proponents of other leadership and management styles, such as adaptive management, charismatic leadership, the institutional manager, positional management, etc. However, careful analysis reveals that, for the most part, these are merely a combination or offshoot of the styles discussed here. The police sergeant's ability to become a leader is closely related to our next topic: the motivating of personnel.

> *The genius of a good leader is to leave behind him a situation which common sense, without the guise of genius, can deal with successfully.*
> —WALTER LIPPMAN II

Motivating

Sergeants' promotional examinations often include written and oral test questions on how to motivate police officers. Following is a discussion of the basic motivational theories and how first-line supervisors in the police profession apply them.

The police sergeant is responsible for ensuring that police officers properly perform job tasks that will accomplish the department's objectives. It is important that first-line supervisors motivate their subordinates because that motivation affects the efficient and effective delivery of police services to the public. Good motivation promotes the following results, among others:

- increased productivity and quality of work performance
- increased employee job satisfaction, morale, and esprit de corps
- decreased lost time due to employee illness, job stress, and burnout
- increased employee self-esteem and confidence
- decreased employee grievances
- increased employee retention

Many motivational theories that have a positive impact on private sector employees have little influence on police officers. Policing is a unique profession. Most of the duties performed by police officers are accomplished with a minimum of direct supervision and in a work environment completely alien to the average person's "normal" working conditions. The daily stresses of today's police officer are as debilitating as a combat soldier's. This fact, coupled with sergeants' inability to reward subordinates with traditional incentives common in the private sector (pay raises, bonuses, perks, etc.) places the police supervisor at a distinct disadvantage.

So what *can* sergeants do to motivate? They can begin by becoming students of human relations and motivational techniques. Before you take your promotional exam, you should understand the following basic motivational theories.

Motivational Theories

Maslow's Hierarchy of Needs

Abraham Maslow, a psychologist, developed a theory concerning how individuals satisfy basic needs. A need is a deficit that an individual seeks to fill. Maslow separated these needs into five categories:

1. physiological—the need for shelter, food, physical health, rest, sleep
2. safety—the need for freedom from physical and emotional threat, personal safety, and security
3. social—the need for friendship, love, and a sense of belonging
4. esteem—the need for self-esteem and recognition from others
5. self-actualization—the need for fulfillment of potential

TRADITIONAL HIERARCHY OF NEEDS

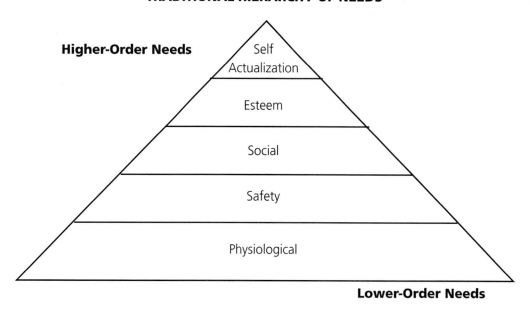

TRADITIONAL HIERARCHY OF NEEDS

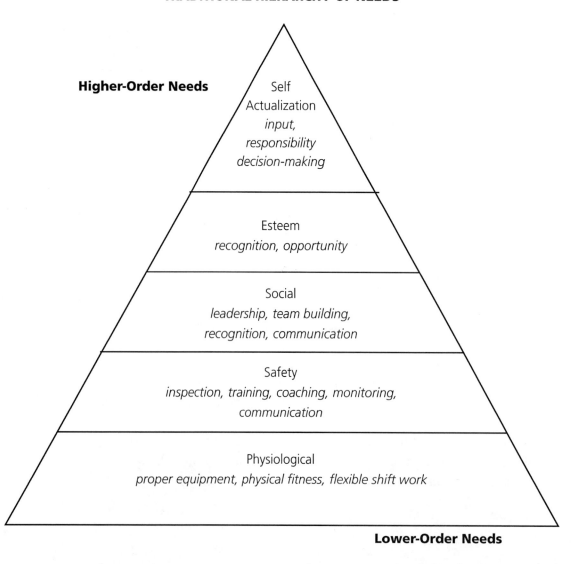

A police sergeant can help to satisfy the needs of police officers, using Maslow's theory as a model, in the following ways:

1. physiological—ensuring that officers have an opportunity for a meal break during their tours of duty, are properly equipped for inclement weather and emergency conditions, are physically fit, and have proper intervals between shifts
2. safety—providing frequent inspection (safety equipment, vests, revolvers, flashlights, etc.), training and education (situational exercises, coaching, communication, feedback), monitoring, and evaluation
3. social—engaging in modeling, team building, structured discipline, recognition, coaching, and personal contact
4. esteem—supplying formal and informal recognition, performance evaluation, and increasing responsibility and opportunity
5. self-actualization—allowing input to the decision-making process, initiation and implementation of projects, and increasing responsibility

Maslow suggests that a person will satisfy a lower-order need (physiological, safety) before progressing to satisfaction of a higher-order need. In policing, supervisors who use motivators designed to influence higher-order needs will not be successful if the officers' perception is that lower-order needs have not been satisfied.

Maslow's theory is a basis for thinking about police officers as individuals. What specifically can a sergeant do to motivate a police officer? Will one style work for most police officers, or must different techniques be used for every individual under the sergeant's supervision? A look at other motivational theories begins to answer these questions.

Herzberg's Two-Factor Theory

Frederick Herzberg, an industrial psychologist, developed a theory that offers two factors, which he calls "satisfiers" and "dissatisfiers," as motivators of people. Satisfiers, are those elements that can lead to job satisfaction and thus to higher motivation and productivity. Dissatisfiers don't necessarily cause dissatisfaction, but rather motivate employees only when the element is absent. For example, many of the benefits in police union contracts (pay, vacation time, sick leave, fringe benefits, etc.) cease to be factors in motivating people unless they are taken away. Here is a further illustration of Herzberg's theory:

Herzberg's Two-Factor Theory	
Satisfiers/Motivators	**Dissatisfiers**
Promotion	Money
increased Responsibility	Rules and Regulations
Recognition	Equipment
Individual Achievement	Job Status

Alderfer's ERG Theory

Alderfer's theory of motivation is similar to Maslow's. However, instead of five sets of hierarchical needs, Alderfer's concept contains only three:

1. existence—food, water, pay, and working conditions
2. relatedness—meaningful social and interpersonal relationships
3. growth—individual development and contributions to others

Alderfer's theory is especially applicable to police work because he suggests that if people are frustrated in an attempt to satisfy a higher-need (growth), they redirect their efforts to satisfy a lower-order need. This behavior is often observed in police officers who exhibit the symptoms of burnout. The sergeant must interrupt the cycle of idealism, reality, apathy, and burnout, so prevalent in policing today, in order to further stimulate employee growth.

A Comparison of Motivational Theories

Maslow's Hierarchy of Needs	Herzberg's Two-Factor Theory	Alderfer's ERG Theory
self-actualization	satisfiers	growth
esteem		
social		relatedness
safety		
physiological	dissatisfiers	existence

There are many other motivational theories (equity theory, expectancy theory, behavior modification, etc.) that attempt to explain why and how people are motivated. The three reviewed here are as helpful as any others in preparing for your promotional exam. The ideas fundamental to all three are as follows:

1. Motivation is individual and *intrinsic*. What motivates and is meaningful to one officer may not be important to another. Individuals bring different value systems, beliefs, perceptions, cultures, needs, abilities, and personal expectations with them to the organization.
2. The police supervisor can influence the motivation of subordinates by being sensitive to variations in their needs, abilities, and individual goals.
3. The police sergeant must become directly involved with police officers and use a variety of motivational techniques depending on the individual. The sergeant must coach and communicate, create an atmosphere of trust and commitment, set high expectations for performance, recognize and reward good work, and be consistently fair while respecting the group.
4. The effective police sergeant lowers barriers to growth through structured discipline, training, and education and by making it possible for police officers to become involved with activities that they feel are worthwhile.

Remember, from a supervisory viewpoint, positive motivation involves the use of techniques that will result in *willing* performance of job tasks that lead to organizational objectives. Coupling the needs of the individual officer with those of the department is the key to successful motivation.

How many times in your career have you discussed with your colleagues why the "administration" doesn't put the "right" officers in the "right" jobs? Why is one officer working a line car when she should be in narcotics or another officer assigned to a motorcycle when he should be in the police academy? Balancing individual needs and abilities with organizational goals is an important part of motivating your subordinates.

> *They are able because they think they are able.*
> —VIRGIL

Disciplining

Sergeant's exams often contain questions on how to handle subordinates who are not performing their job assignments satisfactorily, who violate a department rule, procedure, or guideline, or who are the subject of a citizen complaint or internal investigation. Once again, it's the sergeant who has the most direct contact, control, and influence over their behavior. There are three types of discipline in a police organization.

Types of Discipline

Positive Discipline

There is a natural tendency to interpret the word "discipline" as it is used conversationally—as "punishment." The word shares its root, however, with the word "disciple"—one who is taught or trained by another. "Positive discipline," as opposed to "negative discipline," is based on this more positive meaning. Positive discipline involves "constructively coaching and training subordinates as to the behaviors and performance factors which are acceptable or unacceptable and correcting minor mistakes without using punishment." The objective is to encourage subordinates toward self-discipline and train them in methods to improve their job performance, which not only increases the efficiency of the police department, but also creates a work environment where officers share in a cooperative spirit of pride in themselves and their organization and are in compliance with its policies.

Negative Discipline

Negative discipline should be used only when positive discipline has failed to influence a police officer to conform to departmental standards in behavior or job performance. Negative discipline is punishment, or punitive action, designed to discourage, correct, or reform a subordinate and deter others from similar actions. When using negative discipline, the sergeant must be certain

- to gather the facts and analyze all of the factors concerning both the situation and the subordinate
- to ensure that punishment is fairly applied and consistent with other penalties for like offenses, judging the case on its own merits
- that the punishment is certain (as a deterrent to others) and quickly follows the offense
- that the reprimand is in private
- that the incident is completely, accurately, and precisely documented

Progressive Discipline

The progressive disciplinary process is based on the principle that officers should have the opportunity to correct their mistakes before more stringent punishment is applied. Although each case should be judged on its own merits, repeated offenses should receive progressively stronger penalties. To be most effective, punishment should be administered as quickly as possible after the offense and increase in intensity and severity depending on the seriousness of the violation. Discipline should be consistent and uniform while still allowing for the weighing of extenuating circumstances. Generally, disciplinary action should follow this chronological progression:

1. oral warning
2. documented counseling
3. oral reprimand
4. written reprimand
5. suspension without pay
6. demotion
7. termination

Naturally, in cases of serious misconduct, the progression would begin at the higher ranges in this process.

> *Correction does much but encouragement does more.*
>
> —GOETHE

Communicating

A sergeant's most important skill is the ability to communicate with subordinates, peers, and superiors clearly and effectively. Human resources are the most important component of a police organization. Policing requires the coordinated activity of large numbers of people working together toward clearly defined organizational objectives. Effective communication provides for the flow of information in an organization so that it will function and make decisions effectively. Although there are many communication systems and distribution points in a police organization, the sergeant is in a key position to pass information downward to subordinates and upward to superior officers and managers.

What Is Communication?

Communication is the transfer of information, attitudes, and understanding between individuals or groups. The communication *process* is the *way* by which a sender communicates with a receiver. That may be oral, physical, written, or a combination of these. Oral communication involves the use of spoken language. Physical communication includes gestures, facial expressions, signs, and other kinetic body movements used in conjunction with the spoken word. Physical communication expresses attitudes and emotions and adds emphasis to oral communication. For example, the sergeant who tells a subordinate that he or she has done a good job, while at the same time smiling and making a sign with the circle of the thumb and forefinger, indicating A-OK, has used oral and physical to convey a message, and the physical portion of that message may well have been the stronger. In policing, written communication, also often referred to as "formal communication," takes the form of orders, procedures, rules and regulations, and memorandums.

Downward, Upward, and Horizontal Communication

Most police information moves from the top **downward** through face-to-face and/or written communication and may include roll calls, orders, memos, bulletins, computer printouts, meetings, training sessions, etc. The purpose of downward communication is to provide officers with the information they need to do their jobs, outline objectives, and obtain feedback to improve organizational efficiency and effectiveness. Communication from the sergeant to subordinates normally takes the form of instruction, information, indoctrination, controlling, reasoning, or feedback.

Upward communication is the flow of information from the bottom of the organization upward to the top. Without upward communication, police administrators would not have the information they need to plan for the future. Sergeants control the flow of information and feedback, upward and downward, between officers and those higher in the chain of command. The sergeant transfers information from subordinates to management concerning performance, morale, human and physical resource needs, tactics, grievances, and decision-making.

Horizontal communication takes place between people at the same organizational level, such as between officers or from sergeant to sergeant. This type of communication is used to coordinate people and equipment toward task accomplishment. It also fulfills social and group needs.

The Sergeant's Role in the Communication Process

Because the ability to communicate effectively is so important to being a good supervisor, sergeants should consistently upgrade that ability. You should be aware of the following concepts and guidelines, which often appear on written and oral sergeant's exams.

Formal Communication Channels

Formal communication channels provide organizational structure in a police department and consist of standard operating procedures, orders, correspondence, and other written messages that communicate the official "policy" of the department. This type of communication provides for the standardization of procedures, establishes a minimum level for acceptable performance, minimizes filtering and distortion of communication, and lessens vicarious liability by documenting its receipt by subordinates.

Informal Communication Channels

Informal communication channels develop when formal channels don't exist or fail to meet the needs of the officers. The police "grapevine" often distorts information, creating rumors. The "rumor mill" is further encouraged by time pressures and outside influences, unclearly communicated objectives, or undetermined facts of an incident (for example, an officer-involved shooting). Informal lines of communication are not necessarily negative; rumors often contain elements of the truth. Sergeants can use the grapevine to the advantage of the organization in certain circumstances but must remain aware that a distortion of communication will almost certainly occur as the message is filtered from one person to another. A sergeant involved in the informal communication process has an opportunity to apply motivational techniques, obtain feedback, handle informal grievances, and influence subordinates towards organizational values that are not specifically written down in orders and procedures.

Effective Communication

The communication process affects all aspects of police work. A sergeant's ability to transfer information, send and receive messages, assure that understanding has taken place, and remove barriers to effective communication is critical to the department's success. For sergeants, positive answers to the following basic questions are essential to communication between supervisor and subordinate:

- *Am I clear on precisely what I wish to communicate?*
  If a sergeant isn't certain exactly what message is to be communicated to officers, the officers almost certainly will not understand it.
- *Have I chosen the most effective communication method?*
  A sergeant must determine whether the message (communication) should be written, oral, or a combination of both, what effect the communication will have on

the subordinate(s), and the best time and place for effective communication to take place. For example, if the communication is negative, it is most effectively done in private; if it is positive, it is most effectively done in front of the officer's peers.

- *Does feedback indicate understanding?*
  If the officer does not understand the message, there has been no communication. A sergeant must be able to elicit and correctly interpret verbal or physical feedback from officers that affirms that understanding has taken place. A sergeant obtains such feedback by asking questions, conducting inspections, and reviewing reports.
- *Have I explained the purpose of the communication?*
  Acceptance and understanding will increase if the reasons new orders or policies have been created are explained to officers.

Barriers to Effective Communication

Because the communication process involves the sending of messages between people and groups of people with different perceptions, values, beliefs, and levels of experience, communication breakdowns often occur. A common barrier to effective communication is the failure of the sergeant to listen to subordinates. Sergeants who have developed the ability to be good listeners are often seen by their officers as good supervisors, interested in the officers' welfare. Good listening promotes good feedback and provides information with which to make informed decisions. Remember, you can't listen if you're talking.

The distortion or filtering of information as it travels upward or downward through the various communication channels is another common barrier to effective communication. The larger the number of people and the greater the distance a message has to travel, the more likely that it will be distorted. In police organizations, it's often true that only good news reaches the top and most of the bad news is filtered out before it reaches the executive level, a disadvantage to the organization because decisions will be made without all of the information available or with a distorted view of reality. Communication travels more easily downward in a police department than upward.

Other barriers to effective communication include the personal, the physical, and the semantic. *Personal* barriers are the most common, including emotions, values, motivation, and beliefs. A sergeant should take into consideration the differences among people when planning how to communicate. *Physical* barriers include noise, walls, and distance. For example, conducting roll call for 100 officers requires proper planning if effective communication is to take place. *Semantic* (language) barriers often occur when a sergeant uses terms, words, or jargon that officers don't understand—for example, a veteran sergeant who uses street jargon in addressing probationary police officers. Don't assume that officers know either technical or slang police terms.

Delegating

Delegation is the turning over or entrusting of one's work to a subordinate(s), while remaining accountable for its completion. All tasks in a police organization should be delegated downward to the lowest level that has the ability to effectively perform the assignment. While some matters can't be delegated, sergeants should delegate those tasks subordinates are capable of performing. Proper delegation has the following advantages:

- It frees sergeants from performing routine tasks so that they can use their time for more important matters.
- It is an effective way to get the job done. Work that can't be accomplished by one person is spread out to larger numbers of people.
- It increases morale, efficiency, and productivity by providing an opportunity for officers to upgrade their skills and take part in the decision-making process.
- Remember, sergeants can delegate work and the authority to complete job tasks but can't avoid the responsibility for seeing that the job gets done.

Roadblocks to Delegation

When a sergeant delegates a task to a subordinate there is always the risk that the job will not be performed well. Some supervisors feel a need to do the work themselves, fearing that poorly performed work by a subordinate will reflect on them. Good supervisors accept the fact that there is more than one way to perform a job properly and that officers will sometimes make mistakes requiring further training and coaching. Other supervisors won't delegate because they think the subordinates will then receive the credit for task accomplishment. But failure to properly delegate inevitably results in a loss of efficiency and productivity.

How to Delegate

In delegating work to subordinates, sergeants must clearly explain the parameters, guidelines, and authority under which a specific job task or series of job tasks leading to an objective is to be performed. The limits of the subordinates' authority and responsibility for completing the assignment must be thoroughly communicated and understood, as well as what specifically it is that the sergeant wants done. The sergeant and officer should have a clear understanding of the acceptable level of performance, the criteria used to measure successful completion of the assignment, and the time allotted for completion of the task.

A sergeant should establish a framework of control over the officer's work (through inspection, meetings, review of reports, etc.) so that a determination can be made that the work is being properly accomplished. Officers can't be held responsible for the accomplishment of assignments unless they have been delegated the authority necessary to accomplish them. Policing is unique because job performance carries the additional "responsibility" to act whether a supervisor is present or not.

Controlling

Sergeants are responsible for ensuring that subordinates properly perform their job assignments, comply with department policy, rules, and procedures, follow orders, and behave within the guidelines established by the organization. Because the majority of police work is performed without direct supervision and often under adverse conditions calling for split-second decisions, the willing conformity of officers is the ultimate goal. Control is the influencing and guiding of people toward organizational objectives. Sergeants control through visual observation, inspection, communication, modeling proper behavior, and reviewing records and reports.

Sergeants have the responsibility to communicate to subordinates acceptable levels of performance and behavior and to hold officers accountable for their actions or failure to act. Conducting day-to-day inspections is the primary method of control.

Supervising

The roots of the word *supervision* imply that a supervisor has *super* (over, above) *vision* and thus, is able to see more clearly than subordinates. It follows then that the sergeant should be a teacher, coach, and counselor showing others the "way" of policing.

During the last several decades, the role of the police has evolved from crime prevention and order maintenance to include a myriad of public service functions. Police departments have become large, complex organizations requiring officers and civilians to possess wide-ranging skills and abilities which were not thought to be necessary even ten years ago. Police technology, computer information systems, business management techniques, communications, unionization, and forensics, to name just a few, have undergone dramatic changes during the past several years. As police organizations became more complex, the skill, ability, and education level required of officers increased. As policing has changed, so has the role of the sergeant as a first-line supervisor. Modem police supervisory concepts have moved closer to the private sector and away from many of the traditional, semi military practices. The authoritarian supervisory style is costly in terms of loss of employees, dissatisfaction, lost time, and low productivity and efficiency. A more subtle supervisory approach aimed at voluntary compliance, motivating, advising, instructing, and leading is required of today's police sergeant,

The sergeant, more than any other rank, has the responsibility for the direct supervision of police officers. The primary role of the police sergeant is to *ensure that the job gets done properly* and to *advise subordinates of how to improve their work performance.* In policing, supervision can be defined in broad terms as "working with and through people to implement organizational objectives." Sergeants *direct, correct,* and *control* subordinates' work performance and develop subordinates' skills through training, suggesting, coaching, and monitoring. While remaining responsible for the implementation of policies and procedures developed by their superiors and communicating these to subordinates, sergeants are also responsible for the morale, conduct, and performance of subordinates and for representing their views to superiors. Sergeants are responsible for both the technical aspects of work performance (the methods and techniques necessary to properly perform the job) and for personnel (the human factors inherent in directing and controlling the work of others). Sergeants have a duty to routinely check the work of subordinates to ensure they are following department rules and procedures. A primary duty of sergeants is to support the policies of the police department. In all interactions with police officers, sergeants should give the impression that they fully support, endorse, and believe in the policies of the department. Supervisors who openly question such policies and procedures or who are critical of superior officers fail in their responsibilities.

What the Department Expects from Its Sergeants

- Knowledge and application of supervisory, leadership, and motivational techniques
- Ability to work with and through people to get the job done
- Planning, coordination, and delegation of work to achieve short-term, intermediate, and long-term goals efficiently and effectively with maximum productivity
- Establishment of an acceptable level of work performance for subordinates
- Development and enhancement of the skills of subordinates through training, instructing, modeling, monitoring, and coaching
- Ability to communicate effectively with subordinates, superiors, and the public
- Loyalty

Evaluating

A sergeant's primary job is to advise officers on how to improve their job performance. To accomplish this, an organization must have clearly defined standards as to what constitutes acceptable job performance. All performance evaluations seek to "evaluate and measure the quality and quantity of employee performance"—difficult to achieve in policing because law enforcement doesn't produce a tangible product which can easily be measured. A greater number of arrests, calls responded to, convictions, or parking tickets issued doesn't necessarily mean that one police officer is performing better than another. With the exception of clearly defined criteria, performance evaluations are subjective and rely on the individual sergeant's judgment as to whether an officer has performed properly.

Formal Evaluation Systems

Formal evaluations officially rate an officer's performance against preestablished criteria using a range of scores on a standardized form. To be effective, formal evaluations should be limited to clearly defined and observable behaviors essential to successful job performance. Evaluation systems using forms, which measure the personality traits of an officer, such as "commands respect from his peers," engender resentment and distrust, defeating the purpose of the evaluation, which is to develop the individual officer. Following are advantages of a formal evaluation system:

FORMAL PERFORMANCE EVALUATION SYSTEM ADVANTAGES	
Organizational	**Individual**
Provides a structured format to help make decisions concerning merit pay increases, special assignments, and promotions.	Gives officers a chance to express their feelings, concerns, and ambitions.
Provides documentation for disciplining, demoting, or terminating officers who are not meeting performance standards.	Identifies areas for self-improvement.
Enhances communication between the officer and supervisor.	Motivates officers by providing feedback on their job performance.
Informs officers of how to improve their job performance.	Gives recognition to officers who are performing above average.
Identifies areas in which officers need additional training.	

Rating Errors on Formal Evaluations

Police promotional examinations often contain questions on common errors made by sergeants in conducting formal performance evaluations. The following three rating errors are the most common.

The Halo Effect—Because performance evaluations ultimately depend on a sergeant's judgment, his or her personal preferences are difficult to eliminate from the process. The halo effect is a tendency of supervisors to rate subordinates on overall general impressions instead of on the criteria listed on the rating form. For example, a sergeant who personally looks favorably on a high arrest rate would have a tendency to give a higher rating to officers with high arrest rates even though the listed criteria are professionalism, job knowledge, and organizational integrity. And conversely, a sergeant who values a particular trait might assign lower ratings in the other criteria if the sergeant believes the valued trait is absent in the officer.

Leniency—Leniency is the most common rating error in making performance evaluations. This tendency of supervisors to rate officers higher than deserved has many causes. The most significant are the belief of the supervisor that other supervisors rate leniently, a desire to avoid an unpleasant confrontation with an officer when the evaluation interview is held, a lack of supervisory training in conducting performance evaluations leading to the belief that the performance evaluation system is without merit.

Error of Central Tendency—The error of central tendency is the inclination of supervisors to group all officers at the acceptable, or average, level. Often, performance evaluations require supervisors to explain or document the reasons for high or low marks, a requirement not present if the officer is "average." This tendency to give an average rating also may occur if the supervisor is not very familiar with the officer being evaluated.

Informal Evaluation Systems

An informal evaluation system is the mechanism used by the sergeant to evaluate and document officer performance on a day-to-day basis—a process that should be continuous and which may take the form of a daybook, diary, video recording, etc., of both good and bad officer performance. Visual observation should be accompanied by an inspection of reports submitted by the officer, lost-time management records, calls for service, personnel records, etc.

6 Multiple-Choice Practice Tests

◆ ◆ ◆

The content of the written examination for the rank of police sergeant varies from department to department across the country. However, the supervisory concepts involved remain constant. It doesn't matter whether you work in New York City or Dallas, Texas, when it comes to first-line supervision. The supervisory principles of a sergeant at a hostage situation or dealing with a subordinate who violates the department's rules and regulations are the same.

The multiple-choice tests contained in this guide are representative and deal with broad-based supervisory and management concepts, principles, and theory common to all police departments. The object of taking practice examinations is twofold—first, to enable you to assess your strengths and weaknesses so that you will know what areas to give further attention to; second, to increase your skill in test-taking. Officers who practice taking tests do better, all other factors excluded, on their examinations.

Before you take the practice multiple-choice examinations, read again the sections on improving your techniques for taking multiple-choice tests. Make the conditions in which you take the practice tests as realistic as possible.

Find a quiet place, free from interruptions. Follow the directions carefully. Use the standard computer-type answer sheet provided (the vast majority of written examinations use them). Take the entire exam in one sitting, and in the time allotted, without using any references. Don't look ahead to the answer key to see how you're doing. Manage your time and highlight key words in the question and answer selections. Don't read information into the question that is not there or change your answers unless you're positive. Experiment with the test booklet by marking out answer selections as they are eliminated, etc.

After finishing the test, compare your selections with the answer key immediately following the test. A Self-Evaluation Topic Chart is provided to assist you in identifying areas in which you need further work. Answers and analysis follow each practice test. Be sure to read *all* of these.

Good luck!

Answer Sheet for Multiple Choice Practice Test 1

Remove this sheet and use it to mark your answers.

Name: _____ Social Security Number: ____/____/____

1	(A)	(B)	(C)	(D)
2	(A)	(B)	(C)	(D)
3	(A)	(B)	(C)	(D)
4	(A)	(B)	(C)	(D)
5	(A)	(B)	(C)	(D)
6	(A)	(B)	(C)	(D)
7	(A)	(B)	(C)	(D)
8	(A)	(B)	(C)	(D)
9	(A)	(B)	(C)	(D)
10	(A)	(B)	(C)	(D)
11	(A)	(B)	(C)	(D)
12	(A)	(B)	(C)	(D)
13	(A)	(B)	(C)	(D)
14	(A)	(B)	(C)	(D)
15	(A)	(B)	(C)	(D)
16	(A)	(B)	(C)	(D)
17	(A)	(B)	(C)	(D)
18	(A)	(B)	(C)	(D)
19	(A)	(B)	(C)	(D)
20	(A)	(B)	(C)	(D)
21	(A)	(B)	(C)	(D)
22	(A)	(B)	(C)	(D)
23	(A)	(B)	(C)	(D)
24	(A)	(B)	(C)	(D)
25	(A)	(B)	(C)	(D)

26	(A)	(B)	(C)	(D)
27	(A)	(B)	(C)	(D)
28	(A)	(B)	(C)	(D)
29	(A)	(B)	(C)	(D)
30	(A)	(B)	(C)	(D)
31	(A)	(B)	(C)	(D)
32	(A)	(B)	(C)	(D)
33	(A)	(B)	(C)	(D)
34	(A)	(B)	(C)	(D)
35	(A)	(B)	(C)	(D)
36	(A)	(B)	(C)	(D)
37	(A)	(B)	(C)	(D)
38	(A)	(B)	(C)	(D)
39	(A)	(B)	(C)	(D)
40	(A)	(B)	(C)	(D)
41	(A)	(B)	(C)	(D)
42	(A)	(B)	(C)	(D)
43	(A)	(B)	(C)	(D)
44	(A)	(B)	(C)	(D)
45	(A)	(B)	(C)	(D)
46	(A)	(B)	(C)	(D)
47	(A)	(B)	(C)	(D)
48	(A)	(B)	(C)	(D)
49	(A)	(B)	(C)	(D)
50	(A)	(B)	(C)	(D)

51	(A)	(B)	(C)	(D)
52	(A)	(B)	(C)	(D)
53	(A)	(B)	(C)	(D)
54	(A)	(B)	(C)	(D)
55	(A)	(B)	(C)	(D)
56	(A)	(B)	(C)	(D)
57	(A)	(B)	(C)	(D)
58	(A)	(B)	(C)	(D)
59	(A)	(B)	(C)	(D)
60	(A)	(B)	(C)	(D)
61	(A)	(B)	(C)	(D)
62	(A)	(B)	(C)	(D)
63	(A)	(B)	(C)	(D)
64	(A)	(B)	(C)	(D)
65	(A)	(B)	(C)	(D)
66	(A)	(B)	(C)	(D)
67	(A)	(B)	(C)	(D)
68	(A)	(B)	(C)	(D)
69	(A)	(B)	(C)	(D)
70	(A)	(B)	(C)	(D)
71	(A)	(B)	(C)	(D)
72	(A)	(B)	(C)	(D)
73	(A)	(B)	(C)	(D)
74	(A)	(B)	(C)	(D)
75	(A)	(B)	(C)	(D)

76	(A)	(B)	(C)	(D)
77	(A)	(B)	(C)	(D)
78	(A)	(B)	(C)	(D)
79	(A)	(B)	(C)	(D)
80	(A)	(B)	(C)	(D)
81	(A)	(B)	(C)	(D)
82	(A)	(B)	(C)	(D)
83	(A)	(B)	(C)	(D)
84	(A)	(B)	(C)	(D)
85	(A)	(B)	(C)	(D)
86	(A)	(B)	(C)	(D)
87	(A)	(B)	(C)	(D)
88	(A)	(B)	(C)	(D)
89	(A)	(B)	(C)	(D)
90	(A)	(B)	(C)	(D)
91	(A)	(B)	(C)	(D)
92	(A)	(B)	(C)	(D)
93	(A)	(B)	(C)	(D)
94	(A)	(B)	(C)	(D)
95	(A)	(B)	(C)	(D)
96	(A)	(B)	(C)	(D)
97	(A)	(B)	(C)	(D)
98	(A)	(B)	(C)	(D)
99	(A)	(B)	(C)	(D)
100	(A)	(B)	(C)	(D)

Multiple-Choice Practice Test 1

Directions

This examination consists of 100 multiple-choice and true/false questions. Select the most correct answer. Use the answer sheet provided to record your responses. There is only one correct answer to each question.

Time: 3 hours

1. Repression of crime can best be described as the
   - (A) apprehension of offenders and recovery of stolen property
   - (B) discovery of conditions that create criminal activity
   - (C) elimination of the opportunity for the commission of criminal acts
   - (D) increased patrol in areas experiencing a high level of criminal activity

2. In conducting day-to-day inspections of officer performance, the sergeant should
   - (A) document each of the job tasks performed by an officer
   - (B) determine whether an established performance criteria is being met
   - (C) immediately complete a supervisory report detailing the results of the inspection
   - (D) inspect all officers performing similar job tasks each tour of duty

3. The principal role of a police sergeant is to
   - (A) advise officers on ways to improve their job performance
   - (B) inspect all officers within his or her span of control every shift
   - (C) communicate equipment needs up through the chain of command
   - (D) ensure that all assignments are filled

4. Of the following, which is a disadvantage of using foot patrols?
   - (A) They are not cost-effective
   - (B) They ineffectively provide police service
   - (C) They do not provide optimum mobility of personnel
   - (D) all of the above

5. The effectiveness of a police department is influenced least by which of the following?
   - (A) proper supervision
   - (B) progressive management techniques
   - (C) motivation of personnel
   - (D) the number of police officers in the department

6. Communication channels and lines of authority in a police department ensure all of the following except

    (A) delegation of authority

    (B) placing of responsibility

    (C) territorial functions

    (D) supervision of work

7. A supervisor's span of control is best described as

    (A) the number of subordinates that can effectively be supervised

    (B) the number of subordinates to whom work is delegated

    (C) a diagnostic evaluation correlation between numbers of supervisors and subordinates

    (D) the number of officers working in a district or area during a specific period of time

8. Sergeant Mahoney directs Officer Jennings to conduct an inspection of the on-street construction jobs within his patrol district. This is an example of

    (A) apprehension of authority

    (B) delegation of authority

    (C) the control point in an inspection process

    (D) the exception principle

9. The principle of unity of command can best be described by which of the following?

    (A) Each person within an organization should report to one supervisor

    (B) Each function within a police department must be classified and provided with a job description

    (C) Supervisors should communicate laterally with other supervisors

    (D) First-line supervisors should not conduct inspections of officers outside their span of control

10. Positive discipline most often takes the form of

    (A) progressive punishment

    (B) documented counseling

    (C) training

    (D) modeling techniques

11. Of the following, which is the least likely to be a barrier to effective communication?

    (A) filtering

    (B) distance

    (C) rumors

    (D) distortion

12. Lieutenant Fleming delegates an assignment to Sergeant Brown, which he completes in a satisfactory manner. This is an example of
    (A) completed staff work
    (B) the exception principle
    (C) inspection control
    (D) staff supervision

13. One of the roles of a police supervisor is to monitor the job performance of subordinates. The best time to correct improper performance is
    (A) when conducting the subordinate's performance evaluation
    (B) when the supervisor has a chance to speak with the subordinate alone
    (C) at the time that the improper job performance is observed
    (D) after reports relative to the incident are submitted

14. Sergeant Jennings calls for a volunteer to guard a prisoner at a local hospital. This method of assigning personnel
    (A) is proper if approved and negotiated through the union
    (B) should never be used by supervisory personnel
    (C) is up to the judgment of the sergeant's supervisor
    (D) is generally not an acceptable practice

15. The most significant cost in a police department budget is
    (A) physical resources
    (B) personnel
    (C) range equipment and qualification
    (D) vicarious-liability insurance

16. To be most effective, punishment should be administered
    (A) as a deterrent to others
    (B) immediately
    (C) as formal discipline
    (D) in every case which calls for it

17. Delegation of work is a vital component of the supervisory process. Which of the following terms is most closely related to this principle?
    (A) the exception principle
    (B) span of control
    (C) unity of command
    (D) completed staff work

18. Communication in a police department passes through channels known as
    (A) the communication process
    (B) grapevines
    (C) the communication net
    (D) filtering

19. Subordinates should not be criticized in front of
    (A) their peers
    (B) other supervisors
    (C) civilian personnel
    (D) (A) and (C), but not (B)
    (E) (A), (B), and (C)

20. Studies of police response time indicate that the likelihood of arrest is increased if officers' arrival time is within
    (A) three minutes after the crime
    (B) four minutes after the crime
    (C) five minutes after the crime
    (D) There is no correlation between arrest and response time

21. Spot maps are most useful
    (A) in justification of special line budget items
    (B) as a means to effectively combat crime
    (C) to indicate locations of criminal activity
    (D) to regulate supervisory spans of control.

22. The constitutional standard of particularity requires that search and seizure warrants specify
    (A) who is to be searched
    (B) what is to be searched.
    (C) what is to be seized
    (D) (A) and (C), but not (B)
    (E) (A), (B), and (C)

23. Justification for personnel increases must be supported by factual data. Which of the following is the most important justification for such an increase?
    (A) increased crime
    (B) increased calls for police service
    (C) comparing departments of similar size
    (D) increased number of businesses and residences

24. The greatest obstacle to effective communication is
    (A) improper feedback
    (B) distance
    (C) failure to listen properly
    (D) inconsistent body language

25. After giving an order, the sergeant has a responsibility to follow up to ensure compliance. This is accomplished by
    (A) inspecting
    (B) communicating
    (C) coordinating
    (D) supervising

26. When a sergeant is giving instructions to subordinates, the use of either slang or highly technical jargon should be
    (A) avoided
    (B) used only with the help of visual aids
    (C) used only when accompanied by handouts
    (D) used only with veteran officers

27. Sergeants have a responsibility to keep their superiors informed. This information is most often communicated
    (A) informally
    (B) in writing
    (C) orally and in writing
    (D) informal reports

28. Leadership is best described as
    (A) an intrinsic skill
    (B) an extrinsic behavior
    (C) a learned skill
    (D) an inherited trait

29. In emergency situations, the sergeant would be most likely to use
    (A) direct orders
    (B) indirect orders
    (C) delegated orders
    (D) implied orders

30. The most common error made by supervisors when rating subordinates is
    (A) the halo effect
    (B) leniency
    (C) error of central tendency
    (D) bias

31. Preventive patrol is most effective in preventing which of the following types of crimes?
    (A) burglary
    (B) auto theft
    (C) murder
    (D) sexual assault

32. A sergeant who is in the process of deciding who is to do what and when is
    (A) planning
    (B) implementing
    (C) coordinating
    (D) directing

33. The span of control in a police department is largest at the
    (A) administrative level
    (B) management level
    (C) supervisory level
    (D) detective level

34. Organizational systems and procedures serve to guide officers in the performance of their duties. Situations, which develop, that are beyond the control of officers could result from all but which of the following?
    (A) excessive training
    (B) a defective department S.O.P.
    (C) the absence of a procedural directive
    (D) improper supervision

35. Personnel assigned to detective or criminal investigation assignments require
    (A) less close supervision than patrol officers
    (B) close and continuous supervision
    (C) more supervision than patrol officers
    (D) only staff supervision

36. Increased police patrols within an area would generally be least successful in preventing the crime of
    (A) burglary
    (B) robber.
    (C) prostitution
    (D) murder

37. The most effective delivery of police services results from
    (A) frequent change of officers in their assignments
    (B) assignment of officers to areas for extended periods
    (C) overlapping of foot patrols
    (D) random patrol by two-officer units

38. The development of rumors in police departments is most likely to result from
    (A) shift work
    (B) decentralization
    (C) use of formal communication.
    (D) a lengthy chain of command

39. While patrolling your assigned area at approximately 1145 hours, you hear via radio one of your subordinates engaged in a high-speed chase with a motorist who has struck another vehicle and fled. Several more cruisers are heard to have joined in the chase, which is now approaching the downtown area. You should
    (A) radio the officers to proceed with caution
    (B) radio the officers and instruct them to cease pursuit of the vehicle
    (C) join in the pursuit of the vehicle in order to direct its apprehension
    (D) radio officers nearby to establish a roadblock

40. Which of the following is least important in being an effective police sergeant?
    (A) technical skill in all areas subordinates will handle
    (B) organizational integrity
    (C) human relations skills
    (D) communication skills

41. The best type of evidence in a criminal case is "physical evidence." Which of the following is a true statement?
    (A) Physical evidence is extremely reliable
    (B) Proper preserving of a crime scene increases the chance to obtain physical evidence
    (C) All physical evidence is admissible in court
    (D) (A) and (B), but not (C)

42. Upon observing a violation of department orders, the sergeant should
    (A) advise a superior officer prior to taking "official" action
    (B) take no action until a union steward is notified
    (C) take immediate action
    (D) none of the above

43. You respond to the scene of a barricaded person armed with a rifle. After designating a scene perimeter, you should set up your command post
    (A) within the perimeter in order to quickly direct operations
    (B) within the perimeter to facilitate a staging area
    (C) outside the perimeter in a safe-fire zone
    (D) as close to the barricaded person as possible

44. Which of the following terms has the same meaning as a police "regulation"?
    (A) rule
    (B) policy
    (C) procedure
    (D) goal

45. Planning is most closely related to
    (A) leading
    (B) controlling
    (C) staffing
    (D) organizing

46. People are most motivated toward goals through which of the following?
    (A) desires
    (B) self-motivation
    (C) wants
    (D) stimulus response

47. Most orders from a sergeant to a subordinate should take the form of a
    (A) written command
    (B) verbal command
    (C) suggestion
    (D) request

48. The objective of the discipline process is to punish officers who have violated department guidelines.
    (A) True
    (B) False

49. Sergeants from one unit or division should communicate directly with sergeants from other units or divisions when making routine decisions. This form of communication is
    (A) Lateral communication
    (B) Upward communication
    (C) Downward communication
    (D) The communication net

50. Which police rank plays the most important role in the training process?
    (A) Academy instructor
    (B) Field sergeant
    (C) Field training officer
    (D) Staff sergeant

51. Ideally, the span of control for a line sergeant should be
    (A) Three to five officers
    (B) Five to eight officers
    (C) Eight to ten officers
    (D) Ten to twelve officers

52. Maslow's hierarchy of needs suggests that the most basic need of people is
    (A) Physiological
    (B) Self-actualization
    (C) Achievement
    (D) Affiliation

53. A traffic division is a
    (A) Line function
    (B) Staff function
    (C) Line and staff function
    (D) None of the above

54. Commendation of officers is most effective when
    (A) Performed in public
    (B) Given to the officer in writing
    (C) It is a function of staff personnel
    (D) All of the above

55. The first step in the decision-making process is
    (A) Fact finding
    (B) Inspection of the problem
    (C) Determination of a need
    (D) Data analysis

56. A budget is the work of the police department described in monetary form.

    (A) True
    (B) False

57. You are sergeant in charge of the narcotics squad, and you obtain written consent to search an apartment. While you and your subordinates are doing so, the occupant advises you that she is withdrawing her consent. You must stop the search.

    (A) True
    (A) False

58. Which skill is considered to be most important in a good sergeant?

    (A) Communication
    (B) Directing
    (C) Controlling
    (D) Disciplining

59. The basic purpose of the patrol services is to

    (A) Serve the needs of the community by responding to calls for police service
    (B) Render assistance to victims of crimes of felony
    (C) Eliminate the opportunity for crimes to be committed
    (D) Patrol selected areas in a random manner to be effective

60. Police omnipresence is the arrest of criminal violators and the protection of life and property

    (A) True
    (B) False

61. The best indicator of effective performance at the detective level is

    (A) Case clearance rate
    (B) Percentage of cases resulting in arrest
    (C) Percentage of cases resulting in convictions
    (D) Number of cases resulting in recovery of property

62. A series of convenience stores have been robbed. In each case the suspect wore a ski mask, entered at closing time, and left a silver dollar on the counter. This is an example of

    (A) A corpus delicti
    (B) A modus operandi
    (C) A habeas corpus
    (D) Declaratory evidence

63. Of the following drugs, which is an opiate?

(A) Heroin

(B) Cocaine

(C) Marijuana

(D) Ethyl alcohol

64. The "suppression" of crime is primarily a duty of

(A) Narcotics detectives

(B) Tactical units

(C) Patrol officers

(D) SWAT units

65. The fact that no physical evidence was found at the scene of a homicide most likely means that

(A) The suspect wore plastic gloves

(B) The suspect cleaned the scene prior to leaving

(C) The police probably didn't conduct a thorough enough search

(D) There wasn't any physical evidence to be found

66. One of the primary duties of police officers is to prepare complete and accurate reports. Police reports are based on

(A) A complete investigation of every case

(B) A true representation of the facts as known to the officer

(C) Preparation of the report directly from the information available

(D) All of the above

67. The police sergeant has a responsibility to ensure that

(A) Upward communication is filtered prior to delivery

(B) Downward communication is filtered prior to delivery

(C) Upward communication is not filtered

(D) Downward communication is filtered

68. Which of the following statements would be admissible in court?

(A) A dying declaration

(B) Second-hand information given to a member of the clergy

(C) Rumor concerning a known organized-crime figure

(D) (A) and (B), but not (C)

69. As a sergeant in charge of the scene in a hostage situation, which of the following positions is appropriate for you to have your hostage negotiator take?

     (A) Promise the suspect anything as long as it buys time
     (B) Make no promises of any kind, but try to buy time
     (C) All issues are negotiable
     (D) Agree to no demands, but buy time

70. The case of *Mapp v. Ohio* had extraordinary effect on law enforcement because it

     (A) Reaffirmed the *Weeks v U.S.* case
     (B) Applied the federal exclusionary rule to state courts
     (C) Allowed for the search of containers in locked vehicles
     (D) None of the above

71. In a police department, the need for training officers is

     (A) Dependent upon their job classification
     (B) Dependent upon their rank
     (C) Requisite
     (D) Required only once each fiscal year

72. The Fourth Amendment to the U.S. Constitution deals with

     (A) Freedom of the press
     (B) Right to counsel
     (C) Freedom of religion
     (D) Search and seizure

73. Maintaining the chain of custody of physical evidence is important so that its "integrity" will be preserved. Which of the following procedures is most likely to maintain this integrity?

     (A) Ensuring that all evidence is submitted to a crime lab for analysis
     (B) Having a superior officer initial each piece of evidence along with the officer
     (C) Accounting for any person who has handled the evidence
     (D) Placing each piece of evidence in a marked container

74. The first role of the police sergeant, upon hearing via radio that several of his or her units are being dispatched to the scene of an active bank robbery, is to

     (A) Coordinate the response of the units
     (B) Play the area
     (C) Respond to the scene
     (D) Deploy personnel to handle other calls

75. A sergeant arriving at the scene of a sexual assault has a responsibility first to
    (A) Secure the crime scene
    (B) Ensure that the victim is tended to
    (C) Coordinate paramedic response
    (D) Inspect personnel in performing their duties

76. Of the following drugs, which is a stimulant?
    (A) Heroin
    (B) Cocaine
    (C) Alcohol
    (D) Marijuana

77. Tool impression would most likely be found on which of the following items?
    (A) The inside barrel of a revolver
    (B) The striker plate of a safe
    (C) A window sill
    (D) A car door

78. A sergeant who knows that a probationary officer is not performing his or her duties properly but takes no steps to correct the situation is guilty of
    (A) Negligent retention
    (B) Negligent supervision
    (C) Negligent training
    (D) All of the above
    (E) (B) and (C), but not (A)

79. A bank has been robbed in the downtown area. Two armed suspects have fled and, due to police intervention, run into a nearby store, where they have taken hostages. The command post should be set up directly at the scene so as to be able to control and direct personnel.
    (A) True
    (B) False

80. The system of fingerprint classification used by most police departments in the United States is
    (A) Herschel's papillary line patterns
    (B) Bertillon's measurements of lines
    (C) Henry's classification plan of five basic patterns
    (D) Inked impressions rolled from a suspect's fingers

81. Positive discipline can best be defined as the coaching or teaching of officers in ways to improve their job performance.

    (A) True

    (B) False

82. Personal use of which of the following drugs has the most negative effect on individual police officers?

    (A) Caffeine

    (B) Nicotine

    (C) Alcohol

    (D) Cocaine

83. Rigor mortis usually is observed

    (A) Immediately at the time of death

    (B) Just prior to muscular flaccidity

    (C) Three to six hours after death

    (D) Eight to ten hours after death

84. The police sergeant has a responsibility to conduct frequent inspections of personnel. Generally, inspections

    (A) Raise morale

    (B) Lower morale

    (C) Have no effect on morale

    (D) Are perceived as negative

85. The sergeant estimates work-force requirements

    (A) By a review of calls for police service

    (B) By a review of inspection reports from the previous shift

    (C) By projected workload requirements

    (D) As a result of the number of officers granted days off

86. Postmortem lividity appears

    (A) Black and appears first in the abdomen area

    (B) Greenish yellow and appears three to six hours after death

    (C) Purplish and appears first in the lower portion of the body

    (D) Black and appears on the front of the body

87. Sergeant Deniro wants to make sure that his subordinates are properly performing their job assignments. This can be accomplished

    (A) Through day-to-day inspections

    (B) Through review of crime-analysis data

    (C) By conducting performance valuations on personnel

    (D) By delegating routine tasks to subordinates

88. The United State Supreme Court decision in *Miranda v Arizona* reaffirmed what earlier decision?
    (A) *Brown v Mississippi*
    (B) *Escobedo v Illinois*
    (C) *Brown v Board of Education of Topeka*
    (D) None of the above

89. The best deterrent to misconduct is
    (A) Close supervision
    (B) Over-supervision
    (C) Certainty of punishment
    (D) Participative management

90. Burglary is considered to be one of the most dangerous crimes because
    (A) Burglary is a Part 1 crime
    (B) The loss of victims normally is from their homes
    (C) Burglars are often armed and use weapons to avoid capture
    (D) Of the intrusive nature of the crime

91. Which of the following is the least important factor in judging officer performance?
    (A) Peer leadership ability
    (B) Quality and quantity of work completed
    (C) Arrest rate
    (D) Ability to communicate well with the public

92. In a criminal trial, the primary role of the defense attorney is to
    (A) Cause the jury to doubt the guilt of his or her client
    (B) Discredit the testimony of police officers
    (C) Cause the jury to determine justice
    (D) See that the guilty are punished and the innocent go free

93. The primary reason for limiting the number of personnel who enter a crime scene is to preserve physical evidence.
    (A) True
    (B) False

94. A sergeant responding to the scene of a bomb threat at a school should first
    (A) Evacuate the school
    (B) Notify headquarters of the situation
    (C) Gather the pertinent facts
    (D) Deploy personnel

95. Given a limited number of personnel, the sergeant should assign officers according to areas

    (A) In which the most calls for service are likely to occur

    (B) Which have a high flow of vehicular and pedestrian traffic

    (C) In which police officers will be most observed

    (D) Which are centrally located

96. The best performance evaluation is that which rates officers against predetermined performance criteria.

    (A) True

    (B) Tales

97. The statement "The sergeant always has the best interest of the department in mind" is an example of

    (A) Motivation

    (B) Organization integrity

    (C) Esprit de corps

    (D) Self-discipline

98. Sergeants who allow their subordinates to have a voice in the decision-making process while reserving final decision-making authority for themselves are using

    (A) Situational leadership

    (B) Participative management

    (C) Autocratic leadership

    (D) Free-rein management

99. Most alcoholics work regular hours

    (A) True

    (B) False

100. Sergeants should delegate all tasks to subordinates so that they will have more time to train officers.

    (A) True

    (B) False

Scoring Multiple-Choice Practice Test 1— Answer Key

It's important to determine the areas in which you're weak so you can give them more attention while studying. The code in parentheses which immediately follows the correct answer to each question will assist you in filling out the Self-Evaluation Topic Chart to determine your areas of strength and weakness.

	Code		
Administration	A	Patrol Techniques	P
Communication	C	Supervision	S
Investigation	I		

1. C (P)	26. A (C)	51. B (S)	76. B (I)
2. B (S)	27. C (C)	52. A (S)	77. B (I)
3. A (S)	28. C (S)	53. B (A)	78. E (S)
4. D (P)	29. A (S)	54. A (S)	79. B (S)
5. D (A)	30. B (S)	55. C (S)	80. C (I)
6. C (C)	31. B (P)	56. A (A)	81. A (S)
7. A (S)	32. A (A)	57. A (I)	82. C (S)
8. B (S)	33. C (S)	58. A (C)	83. C (I)
9. A (A)	34. A (A)	59. C (P)	84. A (S)
10. C (S)	35. A (S)	60. B (P)	85. C (S)
11. C (C)	36. D (P)	61. A (I	86. C (I)
12. A (S)	37. B (A)	62. B (I)	87. A (S)
13. C (S)	38. D (S)	63. A (I)	88. B (I)
14. D (S)	39. B (P)	64 C (P)	89. C (S)
15. B (A)	40. A (S)	65. C (I)	90. C (I)
16. D (S)	41. D (I)	66. D (S)	91. C (S)
17. B (S)	42. C (S)	67. C (C)	92. A (I)
18. C (C)	43. C (P)	68. A (I)	93. A (I)
19. E (S)	44. A (A)	69. C (P)	94. C (S)
20. A (P)	45. D (S)	70. B (I)	95. A (S)
21. C (P)	46. B (S)	71. C (A)	96. A (S)
22. E (I)	47. D (S)	72. D (I)	97. B (S)
23. D (A)	48. B (S)	73. C (I)	98. B (S)
24. C (C)	49. A (C))	74. A (S)	99. A (S)
25. A (S)	50. B (S)	75. A (S)	100. B (S)

Self Evaluation Topic Chart

To assess your progress in each area, check the space marked "right" or "wrong" for each question, mark the total of the right answers in the space below, and compare your result with the evaluation given. Then fill out the Overall Score chart which follows to compute your final score. As you study, concentrate your efforts in those areas in which you are weakest.

ADMINISTRATION			COMMUNICATION			INVESTIGATION		
Question Number	Right	Wrong	Question Number	Right	Wrong	Question Number	Right	Wrong
5			6			22		
9			11			41		
15			18			57		
23			24			61		
32			26			62		
34			27			63		
37			49			65		
44			58			68		
53			67			70		
56						72		
71						73		
						76		
						77		
						80		
						83		
						86		
						88		
						90		
						92		
						93		

Number Right:
10-11 Excellent
9 Fair
8 Fair
Under 8 Poor

Number Right:
8-9 Excellent
7 Fair
6 Fair
Under 6 Poor

Number Right:
19-20 Excellent
17-18 Good
14-16 Fair
Under 14 Poor

PATROL TECHNIQUES			SUPERVISION					
Question Number	Right	Wrong	Question Number	Right	Wrong	Question Number	Right	Wrong
1			2			22		
4			3			41		
20			7			57		
21			8			61		
31			10			62		
36			12			63		
39			13			65		
43			14			68		
59			16			70		
60			17			72		
64			19			73		
69			25			76		
			28			77		
			29			80		
			30			83		
			33			86		
			35			88		
			38			90		
			40			92		
			42			93		
			45			98		
			46			99		
			47			100		
			48					
			50					

Number Right
11-12 Excellent
10 Good
9 Fair
Under 9 Poor

Number Right
45-48 Excellent
41-44 Good
37-40 Fair
Under 37 Poor

Overall Score
Administration
Communication
Investigation
Patrol Techniques
Supervision

Number Right
_____
_____
_____
_____

Final Score _____

Answers and Analysis for Multiple-Choice Practice Test 1

1. (C) The root of the word *repression* gives a clue to the answer. To *repress is to* stop or deter. Crime repression is the primary purpose of vehicular and foot patrol. Officers should be spending approximately 60% of their time on preventive patrol and 40% in responding to calls for service. The prevention of crime by eliminating the opportunity for its commission is a basic tenet of law enforcement.

2. (B) The objective of supervisory inspection is to ensure that officers are properly performing their jobs, a determination that can be made only if there are predetermined criteria a minimum standard—from which the sergeant can make an evaluation. Choice (D) implies that the sergeant must inspect *every* day, while (C) uses the word *immediately,* which makes the choice unrealistic. Choice (A) is not the role of a sergeant. For this question, you can deduce the correct answer through a process of elimination.

3. (A) Choices (B), (C), and (D) are all potentially correct answers. However, (B) uses the word *every,* making the response too restrictive, and (D) is a staffing function. Since (A) and (C) are both roles appropriate to a sergeant, you must choose the *most* correct answer by making sure you understand what the question is asking. The *principal* role of a police sergeant is to advise officers on ways to improve their job performance, choice (A).

4. (D) Read the question carefully. The word *disadvantages* is the key. Foot patrol is not cost-effective, efficient, or mobile when compared to vehicular patrol.

5. (D) Circle the word *least*. The phrasing of the question means that you must prioritize the answer choices from most to least important. Choice (D), the total number of officers in the department, is least important for departmental effectiveness. Each of the other three choices is more important than mere numbers of officers.

6. (C) You're looking for the one item that communication channels and lines of authority do *not* ensure; note the word *except* in the question. Choices (A), (B), and (D) *are* all ensured. (C) is the correct answer because territorial functions are those tasks specific to a particular beat or district and have nothing to do with communication channels or lines of authority.

7. (A) Choice (D) can be eliminated because officers may be working within a sergeant's area but not be under his or her span of control; this situation may occur with detectives, traffic officers, or other specialized units. Span of control is not a *diagnostic* or *evaluation* instrument as offered in choice (C). So you must choose between (A) and (B). The best answer is (A) because of the words *effectively supervises,* which is the basis of the principle of span of control.

8. (B) Note the use of the word *directs* in the question. In assigning Officer Jennings to conduct the inspection, Sergeant Mahoney is also giving him the formal authority to perform the job. To *delegate is* to give one's work to another. The authority comes from Sergeant Ma-

honey as a superior officer in the police department. The other choices have nothing to do with the delegation process.

9. (A) You can immediately eliminate choice (B) because it isn't within the scope of a sergeant's responsibility. Choice (C), while true, is incomplete because it doesn't explain *when* the communication should take place. (D) might be correct if it didn't use the words *should not*, which translate to *never* (A) is the *best* answer because it precisely defines unity of command, a basic principle of supervision in both the public and private sectors.

10. (C) Positive discipline is not punishment, nor is it documented counseling, so you should eliminate choices (A) and (B). Modeling techniques are normally used *prior to* the disciplinary process. The most common form of positive discipline is (C), training. If an officer makes a mistake in performing a job task, such as completing a traffic accident report, the sergeant should show (train or retrain) the officer how to do it correctly.

11. (C) Circle the words *least likely.* Choices (A), (B), and (D) (filtering, distance, and distortion) *are* definite barriers to effective communication. Choice (C) may at times cause concern in the communication process, but it's the *best* answer because it has the *least* effect on communication of the choices listed.

12. (A) Some test-takers would have a tendency to read more into this question than is there by seeing "satisfactory manner" as perhaps meaning "barely adequate," but there is nothing in the question to suggest that meaning. Sergeant Brown accomplishes the job task delegated by Lieutenant Fleming. This is an example of completed staff work. Choice (C) has nothing to do with what the question is asking. Choice (B), the exception principle, is a plausible answer. But it is not the *best* answer because the exception principle, which suggests that work should be completed at the lowest level possible, is applied *prior* to the delegation process, not after it, and because we have no information here that the sergeant's level was the lowest level possible for this particular task.

13. (C) The "hot stove" rule applies in this question. The sergeant should advise an officer of improper job performance immediately after it is observed, in the absence of other matters requiring immediate attention.

14. (D) Although this technique is frequently used by many supervisors to select officers for less-than-desirable job assignments, asking for volunteers gives the impression that the assignment isn't as important as others and leaves the sergeant in a poor supervisory position if no one volunteers. Thus, you can eliminate choices (A) and (C). Choice (B) is not the best answer because it contains the word *never,* and there may be *some* circumstances, such as in training probationary employees, in which the sergeant might want to use this technique.

15. (B) Although you might think that equipment is the most costly item in the police budget, human resources, or personnel (salaries and benefits), are by far the most significant in terms of cost.

16. (D) Every answer choice in this question is potentially correct. Remember, you're looking for the best answer. Prioritize. Punishment is a deterrent, choice (A), only if it is administered in every case that calls for it, choice (D). Punishment doesn't necessarily have to be

formal discipline, (C). It *should* be administered as soon after the infraction as possible but rarely *immediately* as offered in (B).

17. (B) A supervisor can't delegate work unless there are subordinates to delegate it to. Delegation occurs when sergeants turn over work for which they are responsible to others within their span of control, choice (B), the personnel working for and reporting to them.

18. (C) Choice (B), grapevines, and (D), filtering, are *barriers* to effective communication. (A) refers to the *process* by which communication passes from sender to receiver. A communication net, choice (C), correctly identifies the *channels* through which communication passes.

19. (E) Criticize in private; praise in public.

20. (A) Statistically, the faster the response time the greater the likelihood of arrest. The fastest response given is in choice (A), three minutes.

21. (C) Spot maps have nothing to do with budgets or span of control, which eliminates choices (A) and (D). In themselves, spot maps are not an effective way to combat crime, as offered in choice (B). As given in choice (C), spot maps are most useful in indicating locations of criminal activity.

22. (E) Even if you are not familiar with this constitutional standard, the use of the word *particularity* should give you a clue to the answer. In order to *search,* you must know *what* you're going to search, *who* you're going to search, and what it is that you're *looking for* (A), (B), and (C) should all be specified, so the correct answer is (E).

23. (D) Personnel increases mean more police officers. The tendency is to base increases in the number of police officers on increased crime, (A), or a larger workload, (B). However, the best justification for increased personnel is ratio of officers to population (residents).

24. (C) In order for communication to take place, there must be at least two people. (C) is the correct answer because if the receiver is not listening to the sender, communication is not taking place.

25. (A) The sergeant ensures that orders are followed by conducting frequent inspections of personnel. Choices (B) and (C) have little to do with ensuring compliance, and (D), supervising, is too broad.

26. (A) Instructions should be given in clear, concise language that will be understood. The use of slang or technical jargon should be avoided.

27. (C) Choice (B), in writing, and choice (D), in formal reports, are basically the same thing. Informally, (A), and the first part of choice (C), orally, are the same thing. Answer (C), orally and in writing, is the most complete, and therefore the best, answer. A sergeant keeps superiors informed both orally and in writing.

28. (C) It is a myth that people are born leaders, which eliminates choices (A) and (D). Leadership is more than just an extrinsic (outward) behavior as offered in (B). The best answer is that leadership is a learned skill.

29. (A) Circle the words *emergency situations*. In an emergency situation, the sergeant wouldn't tell an officer anything indirectly, choice (B), or imply an order, choice (D). The sergeant *might* delegate orders through another in some situations, choice (C), but the question asks which the sergeant would be *most likely to use*. The answer is (A), direct orders.

30. (B) All of the answers offer errors made in the evaluation process. However, the *most common* rating error is the tendency of evaluators to rate officers higher than they deserve, or (B), leniency.

31. (B) The *type* of police patrol makes little difference in preventing the crimes of murder, choice (C), or sexual assault, choice (D). This leaves a difficult decision between (A), burglary, and (B), auto theft. Since, statistically, most cars are stolen from *on-street* locations, (B) is the best answer. *Directed* or *crime-specific* patrol is the most effective way to prevent the crime of burglary.

32. (A) Deciding who is to do what and when is planning. Answer choices (B), implementing, (C), coordinating, and (D), directing, come *after* the planning process is completed.

33. (C) The higher in the police organization, the lower the span of control. Sergeants (supervisors) have the largest number of people working for them. Choice (D), the only other plausible choice, is incorrect because in most departments detectives are not supervisors.

34. (A) Choices (B), (C), and (D) might well cause situations which are beyond the control of individual officers and are incorrect responses. Answer (A) is correct because, even if excessive, training *would* serve to "guide officers in the performance of their duties" and would be unlikely to result in the situations described.

35. (A) Detectives and personnel assigned to criminal investigations have been chosen either through a testing process, based on exceptional performance, or both. They are performing specialized staff functions and require less *close* supervision.

36. (D) The crimes of burglary, robbery, and prostitution are generally premeditated. Increased police patrol can disrupt, displace, and to a degree prevent these crimes. The crime of murder is often relatively spontaneous and not affected by preventive patrol measures.

37. (B) Choice (A), frequent change of officers in their assignments, would lead to a *less* effective delivery of police services. Since (B), (C), and (D) are *all* effective ways to deliver police services, you must choose the most important statement of the three about effective delivery of police services. Random patrol and overlapping of foot patrols are not as important as assigning the same officers to an area for an extended period of time.

38. (D) The more people a message passes through, the more likely it is to be distorted.

39. (B) Pursuing a minor traffic violator at high speeds creates an unreasonable risk to public safety. The question indicates that the chase is headed into the downtown area at about lunchtime. The danger of a collision almost invariably increases with increased speeds; thus there is more likelihood of serious personal injury or death. The sergeant should radio the officers to stop pursuing the vehicle.

40. (A) Because you're looking for the *least* important trait or skill listed in the answer choices, you must, once again, prioritize. It would be unreasonable for a sergeant to have technical skills in *all* the areas which subordinates will handle: fingerprinting, photography, fatal-accident investigation, and so forth.

41. (D) Because of the way the question and answer choices are worded, you know that false statements must be eliminated. The only false statement is (C) because it uses the word *all.*

42. (C) The sergeant should not have to advise a superior officer in order to take action, as indicated in answer (A), nor is it the sergeant's responsibility to wait for the officer's union steward, as indicated in answer (B). Given the choice between (D), none of the above, and (C), take immediate action, choose (C) because immediate action following an infraction is the most effective.

43. (C) The scene perimeter establishes a secure area in which civilian personnel have been moved to safety and all escape routes for the suspect have been eliminated. The command post should be situated outside this perimeter in a location safe from rifle fire. All police communication, scene direction, planning, negotiations, staging of equipment, and so forth, can then proceed within a secure environment.

44. (A) The terms *policy, procedure,* and *goal are* too broad to be good synonyms for *regulation.* The best synonym is *rule.*

45. (D) Planning is most closely related to organizing.

46. (B) Since *desires* and *wants* mean the same, you can eliminate them. There cannot be more than one right answer unless you are given a choice such as "(A) and (B)." Motivation comes from within. Sergeants can't motivate subordinates to *do* anything. Sergeants can supply only the incentive.

47. (D) Most orders will be willingly obeyed if framed as requests.

48. (B) The objective of the discipline process is *not* to punish, but to correct, teach, train, and coach. The statement is false.

49. (A) The correct answer is *lateral* (horizontal, on the same level) communication.

50. (B) The field sergeant plays the most important part in the training process. After officers graduate from the police academy, it's the sergeant who has the most contact with and influence on probationary officers.

51. (B) The ideal span of control for a line sergeant is five to eight officers.

52. (A) Physiological needs are those which are basic to survival.

53. (B) The traffic division is a specialized unit within a police department. It is created to relieve line units from having to perform traffic-related tasks. Traffic is a *staff* function.

54. (A) Praise in public; criticize in private.

55. (C) Choice (A), fact finding, (B), inspection of the problem, and (D), data analysis, all come after determining that there is a *need*, or a problem, in the first place.

56. (A) True. All items in a police department budget reflect work performed by the department.

57. (A) Even if the consent is in writing, once it is withdrawn, you must advise your subordinates to stop searching. If probable cause exists at that point, the apartment should be secured and a search and seizure warrant obtained.

58. (A) The most important skill of a police supervisor is being able to effectively communicate. Without the ability to communicate, answers (B), (C), and (D) could not take place.

59. (C) The question is *not* asking the basic purpose of the police department, but specifically of patrol services. The purpose of patrol is to eliminate the opportunity for crimes to be committed.

60. (B) False. Police omnipresence means *creating the impression* in the minds of criminals that any criminal activity will result in their immediate arrest.

61. (A) Detectives may be assigned to widely varying roles in a department: youth services, homicide, narcotics, and so forth. Arrest and conviction rates, choices (B) and (C), vary a great deal, depending on assignment. Cases involving stolen property, choice (D), are usually assigned to burglary squad detectives only. The best indicator of performance is the number of assigned cases that are properly cleared. Most departments now use "solvability factors" to indicate types of case clearance. These include such categories as "leads exhausted," "arrest," and "victim cannot identify."

62. (B) The term *modus operandi* refers to the habits and procedures used repeatedly by a criminal to commit crimes.

63. (A) The only opiate among the answer choices is heroin.

64. (C) To suppress in this context means to keep from happening, or prevent. Patrol officers, answer (C), have a more primary duty to suppress crime than do narcotics detectives, tactical units, or SWAT units.

65. (C) It's almost impossible for no physical evidence to be left by a criminal at a crime scene. If none was found, the police probably didn't conduct a thorough enough search.

66. (D) Choices (A), (B), and (C) all provide the basis of police reports.

67. (C) Filtering distorts communication. Answers (A), (B), and (D) all suggest that the sergeant should filter information. The sergeant should, in fact, make sure that information is not filtered, choice (C).

68. (A) Although all three answer choices are hearsay, dying declarations are admissible in court.

69. (C) The key to successful resolution of hostage situations is negotiation. Choices (A), (B), and (D) are too restrictive and leave no room for negotiation.

70. (B) Prior to *Mapp v. Ohio*, which prevents the use, in a criminal trial, of illegally obtained evidence, the exclusionary rule applied only in federal cases.

71. (C) Training is requisite for all officers, regardless of their level.

72. (D) Freedom from unreasonable search and seizure is guaranteed by the Fourth Amendment to the United States Constitution.

73. (C) The term *chain of custody* refers to being able to account for every person who touched, examined, or was in any way involved with the evidence from the moment it was located.

74. (A) Because the question asks what the *first* role of the sergeant is, you must prioritize the answer choices. (A) is the correct answer because coordination must be accomplished before any other choice offered.

75. (A) There is a tendency to answer (B), ensure that the victim is tended to, in this question. *Treat the victim,* or answers similarly worded, is the *correct* answer on many police tests. However, in this particular question, the correct answer is (A), secure the crime scene. The victim can't be treated if he or she is still being assaulted or if the suspect is still on premises and threatening both the victim's and the officer's safety.

76. (B) The only stimulant listed is cocaine.

77. (B) Choices (A) and (D) can be eliminated as being obviously incorrect. Both answers (B) and (C) are plausible, but (B) is the better choice because tool impressions would be more apt to be found on the window sash, not windowsill.

78. (E) The retention of the employee, (A), is outside the scope of the sergeant's responsibilities. The sergeant is, however, guilty of both negligent supervision and negligent training in this situation.

79. (B) False. If *set* up directly at the scene, the command post would be in the line of fire.

80. (C) Either you know this answer through memorization or you don't. The correct answer is Henry's classification plan. Choice (D) is a method of obtaining fingerprints, not a system of classification.

81. (A) True. Discipline is not intended to be a negative process.

82. (C) Alcohol is the drug most commonly abused by members of our profession.

83. (C) Rigor mortis appears three to six hours after death.

84. (A) Inspections have a tendency to raise morale in a police organization.

85. (C) At the sergeant's level, the best estimate of work-force requirements is based on the work that must be done and the people available to do it.

86. (C) The term *postmortem lividity* refers to the fact that after death blood flows to the lowest portion of the body due to gravity. The pooling of blood creates a purplish skin tone.

87. (A) Day-to-day inspection is the best way to find out whether subordinates are performing their jobs properly.

88. (B) *Miranda v Arizona* (1966), concerning suspects' rights during questioning, reaffirmed the decision in *Escobedo v Illinois*.

89. (C) Certainty of punishment is the best deterrent to misconduct.

90. (C) Although choice (A) is true, that doesn't necessarily make it a *dangerous* crime. Choices (B) and (D) are also true but don't explain the dangerous nature of burglary. Choice (C) is the best choice because it directly addresses what the question is asking. Burglars are often armed and use weapons to avoid capture, which creates a potentially very dangerous situation.

91. (C) Notice that the question asks for the *least* important factor. Number of arrests has little to do with quality of performance.

92. (A) A defense attorney's job is to represent their clients to the best of their abilities.

93. (A) The crime scene must be kept, as much as possible, in the condition in which the criminal left it.

94. (C) Because the question asks for the *first* thing the sergeant should do, you must prioritize the answer choices. Sergeants must gather the pertinent facts before they can effectively accomplish (A), (B), or (D).

95. (A) The role of the police is to serve and protect the public. Of the choices given, (A) would best fulfill that role.

96. (A) Without predetermined criteria on which to judge, performance evaluations are subjective.

97. (B) The statement exemplifies organizational integrity.

98. (B) The key to participative management is allowing subordinates to have input into the decision-making process while reserving final decision-making authority for the person *responsible* for accomplishing the work.

99. (A) It's a myth that most alcoholics are skid row bums. Most alcoholics do hold down jobs and work regular hours.

100. (B) Sergeants should delegate only those job tasks that subordinates have the ability to handle. For example, it would be improper for sergeants to delegate internal investigations.

Answer Sheet for Multiple Choice Practice Test 2

Remove this sheet and use it to mark your answers.

Name: _____ Social Security Number: _____/_____/_____

1	(A)	(B)	(C)	(D)		26	(A)	(B)	(C)	(D)
2	(A)	(B)	(C)	(D)		27	(A)	(B)	(C)	(D)
3	(A)	(B)	(C)	(D)		28	(A)	(B)	(C)	(D)
4	(A)	(B)	(C)	(D)		29	(A)	(B)	(C)	(D)
5	(A)	(B)	(C)	(D)		30	(A)	(B)	(C)	(D)
6	(A)	(B)	(C)	(D)		31	(A)	(B)	(C)	(D)
7	(A)	(B)	(C)	(D)		32	(A)	(B)	(C)	(D)
8	(A)	(B)	(C)	(D)		33	(A)	(B)	(C)	(D)
9	(A)	(B)	(C)	(D)		34	(A)	(B)	(C)	(D)
10	(A)	(B)	(C)	(D)		35	(A)	(B)	(C)	(D)
11	(A)	(B)	(C)	(D)		36	(A)	(B)	(C)	(D)
12	(A)	(B)	(C)	(D)		37	(A)	(B)	(C)	(D)
13	(A)	(B)	(C)	(D)		38	(A)	(B)	(C)	(D)
14	(A)	(B)	(C)	(D)		39	(A)	(B)	(C)	(D)
15	(A)	(B)	(C)	(D)		40	(A)	(B)	(C)	(D)
16	(A)	(B)	(C)	(D)		41	(A)	(B)	(C)	(D)
17	(A)	(B)	(C)	(D)		42	(A)	(B)	(C)	(D)
18	(A)	(B)	(C)	(D)		43	(A)	(B)	(C)	(D)
19	(A)	(B)	(C)	(D)		44	(A)	(B)	(C)	(D)
20	(A)	(B)	(C)	(D)		45	(A)	(B)	(C)	(D)
21	(A)	(B)	(C)	(D)		46	(A)	(B)	(C)	(D)
22	(A)	(B)	(C)	(D)		47	(A)	(B)	(C)	(D)
23	(A)	(B)	(C)	(D)		48	(A)	(B)	(C)	(D)
24	(A)	(B)	(C)	(D)		49	(A)	(B)	(C)	(D)
25	(A)	(B)	(C)	(D)		50	(A)	(B)	(C)	(D)

51	(A)	(B)	(C)	(D)		76	(A)	(B)	(C)	(D)
52	(A)	(B)	(C)	(D)		77	(A)	(B)	(C)	(D)
53	(A)	(B)	(C)	(D)		78	(A)	(B)	(C)	(D)
54	(A)	(B)	(C)	(D)		79	(A)	(B)	(C)	(D)
55	(A)	(B)	(C)	(D)		80	(A)	(B)	(C)	(D)
56	(A)	(B)	(C)	(D)		81	(A)	(B)	(C)	(D)
57	(A)	(B)	(C)	(D)		82	(A)	(B)	(C)	(D)
58	(A)	(B)	(C)	(D)		83	(A)	(B)	(C)	(D)
59	(A)	(B)	(C)	(D)		84	(A)	(B)	(C)	(D)
60	(A)	(B)	(C)	(D)		85	(A)	(B)	(C)	(D)
61	(A)	(B)	(C)	(D)		86	(A)	(B)	(C)	(D)
62	(A)	(B)	(C)	(D)		87	(A)	(B)	(C)	(D)
63	(A)	(B)	(C)	(D)		88	(A)	(B)	(C)	(D)
64	(A)	(B)	(C)	(D)		89	(A)	(B)	(C)	(D)
65	(A)	(B)	(C)	(D)		90	(A)	(B)	(C)	(D)
66	(A)	(B)	(C)	(D)		91	(A)	(B)	(C)	(D)
67	(A)	(B)	(C)	(D)		92	(A)	(B)	(C)	(D)
68	(A)	(B)	(C)	(D)		93	(A)	(B)	(C)	(D)
69	(A)	(B)	(C)	(D)		94	(A)	(B)	(C)	(D)
70	(A)	(B)	(C)	(D)		95	(A)	(B)	(C)	(D)
71	(A)	(B)	(C)	(D)		96	(A)	(B)	(C)	(D)
72	(A)	(B)	(C)	(D)		97	(A)	(B)	(C)	(D)
73	(A)	(B)	(C)	(D)		98	(A)	(B)	(C)	(D)
74	(A)	(B)	(C)	(D)		99	(A)	(B)	(C)	(D)
75	(A)	(B)	(C)	(D)		100	(A)	(B)	(C)	(D)

Multiple-Choice Practice Test 2

Directions

This examination consists of 100 multiple-choice and true/false questions. Select the most correct answer. Use the answer sheet provided to record your responses. There is only one correct answer to each question.

Time: 3 hours

1. One advantage of crime-scene sketches over photographs is that crime-scene sketches
    - (A) show the crime scene from all directions at once
    - (B) take longer to create than photographs
    - (C) are more complicated to produce
    - (D) are admissible in court, while photographs are not

2. The *Miranda v. Arizona* decision does not apply in which of the following?
    - (A) field interrogations
    - (B) after custodial arrest
    - (C) after handcuffing a suspect
    - (D) after taking a person into custody

3. Which of the following is an hallucinogenic drug?
    - (A) heroin
    - (B) LSD
    - (C) cocaine
    - (D) alcohol

4. An interrogation is
    - (A) a formal conversation between a police officer and another person to obtain information
    - (B) an interview between a police officer and a suspect
    - (C) the questioning of a person suspected of committing a crime
    - (D) taking a written statement from a witness to a crime

5. Latent prints are
    - (A) visible to the naked eye
    - (B) invisible until enhanced by powders or other chemicals
    - (C) always identifiable
    - (D) inadmissible in court.

6. Which of the following is a correct statement concerning the use of force in effecting an arrest?

   (A) More force can be used in effecting a felony arrest than a misdemeanor arrest

   (B) The size and weight of the suspect is a determining factor in the use of force

   (C) Officers can use pain compliance to arrest a suspect who is peacefully submitting

   (D) Officers should use the minimum force necessary when effecting an arrest

7. Sergeant Ahern develops a budget proposal that outlines a new program to combat open-air drug markets and predicts what results will be achieved. This proposal is an example of

   (A) a line-item budget

   (B) a zero-based budget

   (C) a performance budget

   (D) management by objectives

8. The primary difference between a crime and a tort is that

   (A) a crime does not necessarily result in a tort but a tort necessarily results from a crime

   (B) a crime is civil and a tort is criminal

   (C) a crime is an offense against the state and a tort is a private-injury civil action

   (D) a crime is an offense against a person and a tort is the civil penalty for that crime

9. You are a sergeant assigned to the patrol division. A "robbery in progress" of a package store within your area is communicated via radio. Two units under your supervision are dispatched. One of the units reports he is involved in a minor traffic accident and can't respond. No other units are available. You should

   (A) respond to the scene of the accident

   (B) respond to the scene of the robbery

   (C) order the officer to leave the accident and respond to the robbery

   (D) take up a position between the accident and the robbery

10. Of the following, which would be considered "real evidence"?

    (A) testimony of a witness that a suspect owns a shotgun

    (B) prima facie evidence

    (C) testimony by an expert witness

    (D) a shotgun used in a crime

11. Officer Brown stops a suspect, searches him, and finds cocaine in the suspect's pocket. The suspect is then placed under arrest. The evidence is
    (A) admissible because the search was valid
    (B) inadmissible because the search was made before the arrest
    (C) admissible because the search was incidental to arrest
    (D) inadmissible because there is no proof the substance was cocaine

12. A sergeant reviewing the arrest in question 11 should
    (A) retrain the officer relative to search incidental to arrest
    (B) take no action, since the search was valid
    (C) arrest Officer Brown for violating the suspect's civil rights
    (D) institute disciplinary charges against Officer Brown

13. Which of the following is most unreliable in establishing time of death?
    (A) rigor mortis
    (B) putrefaction
    (C) postmortem lividity
    (D) muscular viscidity

14. Skin popping is injecting a drug directly into a vein.
    (A) true
    (B) false

15. Patrol officers have a responsibility to control drug trafficking within their areas. Patrol officers should target which level of offender?
    (A) organized-crime figures
    (B) mid-level narcotics dealers
    (C) street-level narcotics dealers
    (D) upper-level narcotics dealers

16. The majority of traffic accidents are caused by
    (A) drunk drivers
    (B) speeding
    (C) poor driving habits
    (D) improper traffic enforcement

17. Police officers may use reasonable force to
    (A) effect an arrest
    (B) protect themselves or a third person from injury
    (C) prevent a suicide
    (D) all of the above

18. The exclusionary rule applies to

     (A) police officers

     (B) security guards

     (C) store detectives

     (D) all of the above

19. The sergeant can best measure the productivity of detectives by

     (A) the number of Part 1 crimes investigated

     (B) the number of arrests made

     (C) case clearance

     (D) court convictions

20. The sergeant should deploy officers and equipment

     (A) equally throughout the area to be patrolled

     (B) selectively according to need for police services

     (C) equally according to shift distribution

     (D) none of the above

21. Sergeant Smith is assigning detectives to work during routine operations. They should be assigned to work

     (A) with a partner

     (B) in pairs

     (C) alone

     (D) with a patrol officer

22. Sergeant Johnson is the supervisor of the booking room. Officer Davis brings in a prisoner with a bleeding head wound. The sergeant's first responsibility is to

     (A) ensure that the prisoner receives medical attention

     (B) advise the prisoner of his rights

     (C) advise the prisoner of the citizen-complaint process

     (D) fingerprint and photograph the prisoner

23. Detective Wilson has been assigned to the narcotics squad for three years. Sergeant Morris has noted that she is exhibiting signs of stress and burnout. Sergeant Morris should

     (A) discuss this with Detective Wilson and consider transferring her

     (B) refer the officer to her union representative

     (C) discuss the situation with the officer's peers

     (D) immediately reassign the officer

24. Sergeant Johnson has given Officer Mendez a job assignment and later found that he is not performing it properly. Sergeant Johnson should first determine whether Officer Mendez

    (A) has a behavioral problem that is interfering with his work

    (B) has performed this task before

    (C) is motivated to perform the job

    (D) understands Sergeant Johnson's instructions

25. Proper distribution of personnel ensures that the right number of people is working in the right place at the right time.

    (A) true

    (B) false

26. The Fifth Amendment to the Constitution deals with

    (A) search and seizure

    (B) right to counsel

    (C) self-incrimination

    (D) freedom of the press

27. A "frisk" is defined as the

    (A) search of a person for evidence of a crime

    (B) search of a person for narcotics

    (C) search of a person for incriminating evidence

    (D) pat down of a person's outer garments for the officer's safety

28. The first organized metropolitan police force was established in 1829 by

    (A) O. W. Wilson

    (B) Sir John Peavail

    (C) Sir Robert Peel

    (D) Richard B. Chamberlain

29. Which Supreme Court decision deals with stop and frisk?

    (A) *Powers v. Idaho*

    (B) *Terry v. Ohio*

    (C) *Miranda v. Arizona*

    (D) *Chimed v. Illinois*

30. Our physiological system's response to stress is

    (A) highly evolved, resulting in our present-day adaptive stage

    (B) still based on a fight/flight response

    (C) poorly organized but highly evolved

    (D) based on our pituitary complex

31. The sergeant's primary duty at the scene of a labor/management strike at a hospital is to

    (A) maintain law and order

    (B) allow for the entrance and exit of emergency room staff

    (C) limit picketing to areas designated by court injunction

    (D) confer with both labor and management relative to noncriminal disputes

32. Sergeant Donovan is appointed the supervisor of a newly formed traffic enforcement unit. He is directed by Captain Johnson to develop a policy, procedure, and goal statement for the unit. Which of the following would be the best goal statement?

    (A) to take enforcement action against traffic violators

    (B) to deter traffic violations from occurring

    (C) to increase voluntary compliance with traffic regulations

    (D) to prevent traffic accidents

33. Which of the following is not a privileged communication?

    (A) attorney/client

    (B) husband/wife

    (C) clergyman/penitent

    (D) physician/patient

34. In a criminal prosecution, it is necessary to prove there was a "criminal cause." This criminal cause is also known as

    (A) modus operandi

    (B) corpus delicti

    (C) prima facie evidence

    (D) res gestae

35. To be admissible in court, evidence must be

    (A) relevant

    (B) material

    (C) competent

    (D) all of the above

36. In illegal sports betting, past posting is

    (A) placing a bet on a race that has already been run and won

    (B) a sports line obtained on the day of the contest

    (C) placing a bet on a race that is being run

    (D) a bookkeeping practice in which payouts are deducted only after the following day's wagers are made

37. When giving instruction to this subordinates, Sergeant Killen always frames his words in terms of orders. This is an example of

    (A) autocratic supervision
    (B) democratic supervision
    (C) participatory supervision
    (D) free-rein supervision

38. Sergeant Lewis believes that her subordinates will do a good job if the work is explained to them and they are told what is expected of them. This is an example of

    (A) free-rein supervision
    (B) a Theory X management style
    (C) a Theory Y management style
    (D) participative leadership

39. Sergeant Jennings has given Officer Donovan a verbal warning for reporting to work late. The next day, Officer Donovan reports for duty late again and is given documented counseling. This is an example of

    (A) positive discipline
    (B) negative discipline
    (C) progressive discipline
    (D) training

40. Sergeant Howard learns that a rumor is spreading throughout the department that an officer has been arrested. Sergeant Howard should

    (A) take no action, since he does not have all of the facts
    (B) refer personnel to the department advocate
    (C) refer personnel to their union representative
    (D) determine the pertinent facts of the incident and advise his subordinates

41. One of the primary advantages of a formal evaluation process is that it

    (A) serves to give the sergeant supervisory control over subordinates
    (B) motivates officers by providing feedback on their performance
    (C) serves as a rank-ordering tool for promotional examinations
    (D) identifies areas in which the sergeant needs to concentrate for subordinate direction

42. While working the front desk, Sergeant Kowalski receives a call from the media asking the name of a person killed in a traffic accident. Sergeant Kowalski has the information but isn't certain a next of kin has been notified. She should

  (A) release the name of the person to the media
  (B) advise the caller that she doesn't have the report
  (C) advise the media to call the commanding officer
  (D) tell the caller that she can't release the name until she's certain a next of kin has been notified

43. Of the following, which is the most important factor in deciding the type of patrol for a specific area?

  (A) number of citizen complaints against police officers
  (B) calls for police services within the area
  (C) number of residents in the area
  (D) number of foot beats and cruisers in adjoining areas

44. Sergeant Downing is assigned to monitor a picket line consisting of off-duty police officers contesting stalled union contract negotiations. His personal opinion is that the officers are right. Which of the following actions should he take?

  (A) Advise the officers of his feelings but enforce the law
  (B) Monitor the picket line but refrain from direct action
  (C) Ensure that the law is enforced impartially
  (D) Ensure that the picket line is photographed for department review

45. A new policy on writing arrest reports has been instituted, and training has been given to all personnel. The sergeant determines if the new policy is being followed by

  (A) controlling subordinates within his or her span of control
  (B) giving further training on the new procedure
  (C) directing that all arrest reports be completed properly
  (D) inspecting arrest reports to see if the new policy is being followed

46. Police supervisors should train their personnel

  (A) periodically
  (B) on all new material
  (C) at every opportunity
  (D) whenever necessary

47. Sergeant Horowitz responds to the scene of a fire in an apartment building. Officer Carlson reports that an elderly woman on the first floor is refusing to vacate her apartment. The fire is rapidly spreading, and the elderly woman is in immediate danger. Sergeant Horowitz should

    (A) notify communications and request assistance

    (B) remove the elderly woman to a position of safety

    (C) instruct the officer to notify the fire department as soon as they arrive

    (D) request assistance from other tenants in taking the woman out of her apartment

48. An officer has stopped a vehicle for a routine traffic violation. The driver has the windows of the car rolled up and the doors locked and is refusing to speak with the officer. There is a young child in the vehicle. The officer has called a sergeant to the scene and explained the situation. The sergeant should

    (A) instruct the officer to gain forcible entry into the vehicle

    (B) instruct the officer to issue a ticket to the driver

    (C) attempt to communicate with the operator of the vehicle

    (D) assist the officer in gaining access to the vehicle

49. Allowing officers to bid their shifts by seniority is considered to be

    (A) desirable; people work better on a permanent as opposed to a rotating schedule

    (B) undesirable; people work better on a rotating schedule

    (C) desirable; human resources can be deployed more efficiently if they are not on a rotating schedule

    (D) undesirable; statistics indicate that a permanent schedule results in increased employee lost time

50. Which of the following is a Part 1 crime?

    (A) auto theft

    (B) pick-pocketing

    (C) possession of marijuana

    (D) prostitution

51. The best method of judging a police department's performance is by

    (A) crime statistics

    (B) arrest rates

    (C) citizen satisfaction

    (D) conviction rates

52. Sergeant Jackson has responded to an "officer in trouble" call within his area. His first duty upon arriving at the scene is to

    (A) render necessary assistance to the officer in trouble
    (B) determine if units assigned have responded
    (C) make an assessment of the need for additional personnel
    (D) authorize a cancellation if no additional help is required

53. A sergeant should order the termination of a police vehicle pursuit in which of the following circumstances?

    (A) for minor misdemeanor and traffic offenses
    (B) during inclement weather
    (C) when the pursuit poses a threat of imminent injury to another person
    (D) when the pursuing officer has reason to believe the driver of the vehicle is impaired

54. The first responsibility of a sergeant arriving at the scene of a hostage situation is to

    (A) prevent the escape of the perpetrator
    (B) take command and assess the situation
    (C) secure the premises
    (D) establish an interim command post

55. Sergeant Chin is working the front desk. He receives a phone call from a person who gives detailed information that Officer Peterson is selling drugs from his police vehicle. The caller refuses to give his name. Sergeant Chin should

    (A) take no action, since the complaint was anonymous
    (B) inform the caller that anonymous complaints cannot be investigated
    (C) advise Officer Peterson of the complaint and instruct him to submit a report
    (D) document the contents of the phone call and forward the report to the officer's commanding officer

56. The sergeant should ensure that subordinates conduct a thorough inspection of their vehicles' equipment

    (A) daily, prior to leaving the station
    (B) once each week
    (C) periodically, when time permits
    (D) a maximum of three times per week

57. In which of the following cases would it be appropriate to refer an officer to the department's stress unit?

    (A) an officer who has been suspended for drinking on duty

    (B) an officer who has shot and killed a suspect

    (C) an officer who lives out of town and has been arrested during a domestic dispute

    (D) all of the above

58. An officer under your direct supervision is assigned to routine traffic duty in a busy city intersection. An "officer in trouble" call is transmitted via radio at a location directly across the street. The officer responds, assists, and is injured. His response is

    (A) inappropriate; he should have remained at his post

    (B) appropriate; an officer who was nearby was calling for assistance

    (C) inappropriate; he was not dispatched to the scene

    (D) inappropriate; he did not receive permission from a supervisor

59. In preparing a police budget, which step would come first?

    (A) determining the dollar amount of the budget

    (B) planning what needs to be done

    (C) determining objectives

    (D) assigning dollar costs to organizational plans

60. Most communication in a police organization moves

    (A) from the top, downward

    (B) laterally

    (C) from the bottom, upward

    (D) horizontally

61. The police union contract is binding on

    (A) labor only

    (B) management and labor

    (C) management only

    (D) the police union only

62. Contingency plans are developed to deal with

    (A) day-to-day operations

    (B) budget implementation

    (C) inspectional objectives

    (D) emergency situations

63. Officer Hernandez approaches Sergeant Gallagher with a grievance relative to being denied a day off. The sergeant has had occasion recently to discipline the officer for being late for work and for failure to respond to radio calls. He advises the officer that if he paid more attention to his work, his request for a day off would probably be approved. The sergeant's action is

   (A) improper; the sergeant should act on the grievance

   (B) proper; the sergeant is using the situation to motivate the officer

   (C) improper; the sergeant should refer the officer to his union steward

   (D) proper; the sergeant has wide latitude in accepting or rejecting employee grievances

64. Sergeant Jennings is conducting a firearm inspection at roll call and finds that Officer Donnely, vice president of the police union, is carrying unauthorized ammunition. Sergeant Jennings should

   (A) take appropriate disciplinary action and ensure that Officer Donnely has the proper ammunition prior to going on patrol

   (B) issue the officer the proper ammunition, advising him of the consequences of a repeat offense

   (C) advise the officer to obtain the proper ammunition prior to going on patrol

   (D) advise the lieutenant of the situation and obtain direction prior to proceeding with any action

65. Sergeant Carlson follows all the rules and regulations of the department to the letter and demands the same from those under his supervision. He is inflexible and disciplines subordinates for even minor mistakes. His supervisory style is most closely related to which of the following?

   (A) autocratic

   (B) democratic

   (C) free-rein

   (D) Theory Y

66. Detective Novak arrests a high school student, Paula Erickson, for possession of a marijuana cigarette. Detective Novak then supplies the student with five bags of marijuana to sell to other students as part of a sting operation. She refuses, but then is convinced by the detective that it would be in her own best interest. She is arrested by other officers on the way to the sting operation. Do the above facts tend to show entrapment?

   (A) Yes; the student was influenced to commit the crime by the detective

   (B) No; the student took an affirmative step in committing a crime

67. Officer Scott responds to the scene of a robbery in progress at a package store. Upon arrival she finds the victim unconscious and bleeding profusely from a stab wound to his side. At the same time the officer sees a suspect running out the back door. The officer should first

    (A) notify headquarters and pursue the suspect

    (B) ask a witness to render first aid to the victim and pursue the suspect

    (C) render first aid to the victim and notify headquarters

    (D) telephone headquarters, request an ambulance, and then pursue the suspect

68. Which amendment to the United States Constitution deals with self-incrimination?

    (A) the Second Amendment

    (B) the Fourth Amendment

    (C) the Fifth Amendment

    (D) the Sixth Amendment

69. Which of the following is an exception to the hearsay rule?

    (A) indirect evidence

    (B) physical evidence

    (C) best evidence

    (D) res gestae

70. The exclusionary rule originally resulted from which of the following court decisions?

    (A) *Weeks v. United States*

    (B) *Terry v. Ohio*

    (C) *Chimel v. California*

    (D) *Miranda v. Arizona*

71. Sergeant Downing is called to the apartment of an elderly man who officers believe has a mental disorder. The man has not committed a crime. The sergeant determines that the man is a danger to himself and others. The sergeant should

    (A) have the man arrested and brought to the station

    (B) have the man taken into custody and released to his family

    (C) have the man taken into custody and brought to a treatment facility

    (D) take no police action, as the man has not committed a crime

72. Crime-scene fingerprints are most likely to be found

    (A) inside the building in which a crime was committed

    (B) at the point of entry by the criminal

    (C) at the point of exit by the criminal

    (D) at the primary location of the offense

73. Sergeant Moriarty is assigned the task of designing a plan to increase the effectiveness of patrol resources within his area. The sergeant should first
    (A) collect and analyze crime data in the area
    (B) evaluate the courses of action available to him
    (C) define the problem as an objective
    (D) prepare a plan for review and approval

74. Sergeant Franklin has been advised by Lieutenant Edwards of a high incidence rate of muggings in a city park between the hours of 1800 and 2100. The best type of patrol for Sergeant Franklin to institute in the park area is
    (A) directed patrol
    (B) preventive patrol
    (C) foot patrol
    (D) team patrol

75. An inspection process designed to measure compliance with the department's goals, policies, and procedures is known as
    (A) coordinating
    (B) planning
    (C) controlling
    (D) directing

76. Sociologists contend that crime can never be totally eliminated. Of the following, which criminal act is most likely to be eliminated by the police?
    (A) prostitution
    (B) murder
    (C) robbery
    (D) none of the above

77. The primary cause of supervisory failure in interpersonal communication is
    (A) failure to listen
    (B) not obtaining feedback
    (C) filtering
    (D) physical barriers

78. Which of the following is a line function within a police organization?
    (A) records division
    (B) police academy
    (C) patrol division
    (D) internal affairs division

79. Which of the following investigations would it be proper for a sergeant to delegate to a subordinate?

    (A) the investigation of a minor complaint against a police officer

    (B) a sensitive investigation relative to a civilian police employee

    (C) a traffic accident between two off-duty police officers

    (D) none of the above

80. Sergeant Heald has noted a widespread increase in street robbery throughout his district. Which of the following tactics is most likely to reduce this type of crime?

    (A) random patrol

    (B) decoy operations

    (C) proactive patrol

    (D) passive patrol

81. Sergeant Connors is frequently heard to tell his subordinates, "If you have a problem, don't tell me. I have enough of my own." This type of supervision is most closely related to

    (A) autocratic

    (B) democratic

    (C) laissez-faire

    (D) participative

82. Of the following officers, with whom should sergeants be spending the most time?

    (A) a probationary police officer

    (B) a veteran officer newly assigned to the unit

    (C) an officer recently promoted to detective

    (D) an officer returning from extended sick leave

83. A veteran officer, who previously has been an exceptional employee, begins exhibiting signs of stress. He is argumentative and short-tempered with the public, and his appearance is less than adequate. Such symptoms most often point to

    (A) a problem off the job

    (B) a substance abuse problem

    (C) a problem with the officer's peers

    (D) the need for a transfer

84. Sergeant Schwartz has conducted an investigation in which there is a preponderance of evidence to believe that Officer Stringer has violated the department's firearms guidelines. Sergeant Schwartz should

    (A) counsel the officer

    (B) recommend that the officer be retrained

    (C) submit appropriate disciplinary charges

    (D) continue the investigation, as preponderance of evidence is too limiting to draw a conclusion

85. Just prior to roll call, Officer Parish advises Sergeant Small that she is taking a prescribed medication that has side effects which include double vision. The appropriate action for the sergeant to take is to

    (A) place the officer in an inside job for the shift

    (B) take appropriate disciplinary action against the officer

    (C) put the officer on sick leave

    (D) put the officer with a partner for the shift

86. Sergeant Peterson learns that a local merchant is offering free food and coffee to officers frequenting his establishment. This practice is

    (A) acceptable, as long as the merchant is not seeking anything in return

    (B) unacceptable, but so minor as not to be a form of police corruption

    (C) acceptable, as long as the officers first offer payment and the merchant refuses to accept it

    (D) unacceptable; gratuities are a form of police corruption

87. Sergeant Morrison has reviewed Officer Donovan's incident reports and found that he is not following the correct departmental procedures. Sergeant Morrison advises Officer Donovan of his mistakes and the correct procedure. Officer Donovan is still not completing the reports properly; however, he is an excellent officer and normally follows instructions well. Sergeant Morrison should

    (A) counsel Officer Donovan and advise him that further errors would call for disciplinary action

    (B) retrain the officer again prior to disciplining him

    (C) ensure that proper communication is taking place

    (D) give the officer a stern warning and inspect all future reports

88. The statement "Leaders are born, not made" is

    (A) true; some people are born with inherent qualities that make them future leaders

    (B) false; people become leaders through making the most of their skills and abilities

    (C) true; higher intelligence and increased life chances produce leaders

    (D) false; leadership is an extrinsic quality possessed by all people

89. Which of the following statements about motivation is false?

    (A) Officers can't be motivated to do anything; it must come from within

    (B) Money is the prime motivator in the workplace

    (C) Motivation is an intrinsic quality; different people are motivated by different things

    (D) Sergeants can influence officers and provide the stimulus for motivation to take place

90. Before sergeants can communicate a message to officers they must

    (A) ensure that the message is clear and concise

    (B) ensure that proper feedback mechanisms are in place

    (C) clearly understand what is to be communicated

    (D) remove all physical barriers to effective communication

91. Officer Reynolds asks Sergeant Nielson to explain a criminal statute which Sergeant Nielson is not familiar with. It would be most proper for the sergeant to

    (A) instruct the officer to look up the statute and get back to him on it

    (B) advise the officer to see the desk sergeant about the statute

    (C) advise the officer that he is not familiar with the statute and look it up with him

    (D) advise the officer that he is not familiar with the statute and tell him to look it up

92. Many police departments use line-item budgeting in their fiscal management. The primary advantage of this form of budget preparation is that it

    (A) provides for integrating planning, budgeting, and control into one process

    (B) specifically relates budget items to objectives

    (C) provides flexibility in making changes in the budget

    (D) simplifies year-to-year comparison

93. In which of the following cases would it be proper for Sergeant Pawlina to instruct an officer to search a suspect and the area under the suspect's control?

    (A) in a high-crime area in which they are alone and where there is suspected criminal behavior on the part of a person

    (B) after briefly detaining the suspect of muggings within their district

    (C) after making an arrest for a motor vehicle violation in which incarceration is required

    (D) after having a high degree of suspicion that a suspect has committed a narcotics offense

94. Sergeant Kubiak has given a group of police officers at a special event traffic duty assignments. Upon inspecting, she finds that an officer is absent from his post. She should first

    (A) direct traffic until the officer returns

    (B) find out where the officer is

    (C) have another officer do the traffic duty

    (D) draft appropriate disciplinary charges

95. Sergeant D' Arnica is the booking room supervisor. One of his duties is the setting of bond for persons arrested. The purpose of bond is to

    (A) ensure a person access to legal counsel

    (B) ensure that a person appears in court

    (C) ensure timely adjudication of the judicial process

    (D) prevent unnecessary detainment of a person

96. Of the following, in which area is it most important for a sergeant to be highly skilled?

    (A) motivation of employees

    (B) highly technical job knowledge

    (C) human relations

    (D) forensics

97. Sergeant Gutska responds to the scene of a sexual assault and is informed by a detective that the suspect has made an "exculpatory" statement. Sergeant Gutska can infer that the suspect

    (A) lied to the detective relative to his alibi

    (B) denied any guilt in the case

    (C) admitted that he committed the crime

    (D) implicated another suspect in the commission of the crime

98. An officer working alone in a high-crime area, who approaches a person acting suspiciously, has a right to pat down the suspect's outer garments for his own protection.

    (A) true

    (B) false

99. Upon arriving at the scene of a homicide, Sergeant Newton observes the victim lying on his back, with postmortem lividity clearly present on his stomach. This indicates that the victim

    (A) suffered a fatal wound to the back

    (B) was lying on his stomach at the time of his death

    (C) was turned over from his stomach onto his back

    (D) was transported to where he was found

100. Crack cocaine is normally
      (A) smoked
      (B) skin popped
      (C) snorted
      (D) mainlined

Scoring Multiple-Choice Practice Test 2—Answer Key

As you did with Multiple-Choice Practice Test 1, use the following Answer Key to determine areas in which you're still having difficulty and concentrate on these areas in your studying. The code which immediately follows the correct answer to each question will assist you in filling out the Self-Evaluation Topic Chart that follows.

Code			
Administration	A	Patrol Techniques	P
Communication	C	Supervision	S
Investigation	I		

1. A (I)	26. C (I)	51. C (A)	76. D (A)
2. A (I)	27. D (P)	52. A (S)	77. A (C)
3. B (I)	28. C (A)	53. C (S)	78. C (A)
4. C (I)	29. B (P)	54. B (S)	79. D (S)
5. B (I)	30. B (A)	55. D (S)	80. C (P)
6. D (P)	31. A (A)	56. A (S)	81. C (S)
7. C (A)	32. C (A)	57. D (S)	82. A (S)
8. C (A)	33. D (I)	58. B (S)	83. A (S)
9. B (S)	34. B (I)	59. C (A)	84. C (S)
10. D (I)	35. D (I)	60. A (C)	85. C (S)
11. B (P)	36. A (I)	61. B (A)	86. D (A)
12. A (S)	37. A (S)	62. D (A)	87. C (C)
13. D (I)	38. C (S)	63. A(S)	88. B (A)
14. B (I)	39. C (S)	64. A (S)	89. B (A)
15. C (P)	40. D (S)	65. A (S)	90. C (C)
16. C (P)	41. B (S)	66. A (P)	91. C (S)
17. D (P)	42. D (S)	67. C (P)	92. D (A)
18. A (A)	43. B (P)	68. C (I)	93. C (I)
19. C (S)	44. C (S)	69. D (I)	94. B (S)
20. B (S)	45. D (S)	70. A (A)	95. B (A)
21. C (S)	46. C (S)	71. C (S)	96. C (S)
22. A (S)	47. B (S)	72. B (I)	97. C (I)
23. A (S)	48. C (P)	73. C (A)	98. A (P)
24. D (C)	49. A (A)	74. A (S)	99. C (I)
25. A (A)	50. A (A)	75. C (A)	100. A(I)

Self-Evaluation Topic Chart

To assess your progress in each area, check the space marked "right" or "wrong" for each question, mark the total of the right answers in the space below, and compare your result with the evaluation given. Then fill out the Overall Score chart that follows to compute your final score. As you study, concentrate your efforts in those areas in which you are still having difficulty.

ADMINISTRATION			COMMUNICATION			INVESTIGATION		
Question Number	Right	Wrong	Question Number	Right	Wrong	Question Number	Right	Wrong
7			24			22		
8			60			41		
18			77			57		
25			87			61		
28			90			62		
30						63		
31						65		
32						68		
49						70		
50						72		
51						73		
59						76		
61						77		
62						80		
70						83		
73						86		
75						88		
76						90		
78						92		
86						93		
88						97		
89						99		
92						100		
95								

Number Right:
10-11 Excellent
9 Fair
8 Fair
Under 8 Poor

Number Right:
8-9 Excellent
7 Fair
6 Fair
Under 6 Poor

Number Right:
19-20 Excellent
17-18 Good
14-16 Fair
Under 14 Poor

PATROL TECHNIQUES			SUPERVISION					
Question Number	Right	Wrong	Question Number	Right	Wrong	Question Number	Right	Wrong
6			9			54		
11			12			55		
15			19			56		
16			20			57		
17			21			58		
27			22			63		
29			23			64		
43			37			65		
48			38			71		
66			39			74		
67			40			79		
80			41			81		
98			42			82		
			44			83		
			45			84		
			46			85		
			47			91		
			52			94		
			53			96		

Number Right	Number Right	Overall Score	Number Right
11-12 Excellent	45-48 Excellent	Administration	_____
10 Good	41-44 Good	Communication	_____
9 Fair	37-40 Fair	Investigation	_____
Under 9 Poor	Under 37 Poor	Patrol Techniques	_____
		Supervision	
		Final Score _____	

Answers and Analysis for Multiple-Choice Practice Test 2

1. (A) Circle the word *advantage*. Choices (B) and (C) are *disadvantages* in using crime-scene sketches, and (D) is an incorrect statement. Crime-scene photographs show the scene only from the simple perspective of the camera.

2. (A) *Miranda v. Arizona* deals with self-incrimination. The Miranda warnings must be given when a person has been deprived of his or her freedom of movement in a significant way. Choices (B), (C), and (D) all indicate physical detainment, while choice (A), field interrogations, does not.

3. (B) Heroin, cocaine, and alcohol are not hallucinogenic drugs. LSD is.

4. (C) A police interrogation is more than is offered in choice (A), a *conversation*. Interrogation is questioning a specific person relative to his or her involvement in a crime. (B) and (D) are incorrect choices.

5. (B) The word *latent* is derived from the Latin word *latens*, meaning *to lie hidden*. Latent fingerprints are invisible until enhanced by powders or chemicals.

6. (D) A basic premise of law enforcement is that only the minimum amount of force necessary to effect an arrest is permissible.

7. (C) Whenever a test question involving police budgets gives a prediction or estimates an outcome based on pursuing a specific policy, it's a *performance budget*. Sergeant Ahern is stating that he has a certain amount of human and physical resources and can accomplish a specific goal relative to open-air drug markets. He is predicting that, if given a certain amount of resources, he can accomplish a specific objective or performance level.

8. (C) A *tort is a* civil action that may or may not result from criminal conduct, which makes (A) and (B) incorrect choices. A tort *may involve a* civil penalty resulting from criminal behavior, as mentioned in (D), but it is not itself the penalty.

9. (B) You know from the question that, of the two patrol units dispatched to the robbery, one is still responding and the other is involved in a traffic accident. Choice (D) has you, the sergeant, doing nothing. Ordering an officer to leave the scene of a traffic accident, as offered in choice (C), would require exigent circumstances (which the question does not mention) after you assessed the situation. There is no reason for you to respond to the accident, (A), instead of the robbery. The correct answer is (B), respond to the scene of the robbery.

10. (D) *Real evidence* is tangible. While prima facie evidence, choice (B), *might* be tangible, it is not necessarily so. The only tangible evidence offered in the answer choices is (D), a shotgun used in a crime.

11. (B) Don't confuse this with *Terry v. Ohio* (pat down of the outer garments for the officer's protection). A *pat down is a limited* search. Officer Brown searched, *then* arrested. Had

he probable cause to arrest and found the cocaine in a search subsequent to arrest, the evidence would have been admissible. But in this case, the evidence is inadmissible because the search was made before the arrest.

12. (A) Choice (B) is incorrect, since the search was not valid. Officer Brown may have used incorrect procedure, but that doesn't call for his arrest, as is offered in (C), or negative discipline, as cited in (D). A sergeant should retrain the officer relative to proper search and arrest procedures.

13. (D) This is a question designed to confuse. Choices (A), (B), and (C) are fairly reliable in establishing the time of death under certain circumstances. Choice (D), muscular viscidity, has nothing to do with establishing time of death. Thus, it is the most *unreliable* and is the correct answer.

14. (B) Injecting a drug directly into a vein is *mainlining*. Injecting a drug into a muscle or just under the skin is *skin popping*.

15. (C) Choices (A), (B), and (D) are generally the responsibility of a specialized unit. But street-level dealers fall within the scope of the patrol officer.

16. (C) The majority of traffic accidents are caused by poor driving habits.

17. (D) The key word in the question is *reasonable*. Choices (A), (B), and (C) are all appropriate reasons to use reasonable force.

18. (A) The exclusionary rule applies only to federal, state, or local *government* agents. Security guards, (B), and store detectives, (C), are not government agents.

19. (C) Numbers of arrests, court convictions, and Part 1 crimes investigated have little to do with productivity, but cases cleared do.

20. (B) Deploying officers *equally*, (A) and (B), shows a lack of planning and crime analysis. Officers should be deployed according to the need for police services.

21. (C) There are few situations requiring officers or detectives to be assigned with a partner (A). Answer (B), in pairs, and (D), with a patrol officer, are the same as (A), only stated differently.

22. (A) Giving aid to the injured prior to any other action *is usually* the correct answer on police promotional examinations.

23. (A) It is not the sergeant's role to refer officers to their union steward as stated in (B). There may be cases when the sergeant would seek information from an officer's peers, as offered in (C), but this is generally not a good practice. Reassigning the officer *immediately*, (D), is too arbitrary. Of the answers offered, (A) is the most correct.

24. (D) Prioritize your answers. In the absence of information other than that given in the question, Sergeant Johnson must ensure that Officer Mendez understands his instructions.

25. (A) True. This function is closely related to planning—deciding who is to do what and when.

26. (C) Memorize the amendments to the Constitution having the greatest impact on our profession. The correct answer is self-incrimination.

27. (D) Although a *frisk is* technically a limited search, the intent of the *Terry v. Ohio* decision is to balance the rights of citizens with a legitimate concern for the safety of police officers. *A frisk is not* a search for criminal cause as offered in choices (A), (B), and (C).

28. (C) Sir Robert Peel organized the first metropolitan police force, in England, in 1829.

29. (B) *Terry v. Ohio,* deals with stop and frisk. Memorize the basics of Supreme Court decisions of importance in policing.

30. (B) Our physiological system has not changed and is still based on a fight/flight response system.

31. (A) Although choices (B) and (C) and, to a more limited extent, (D) may be duties of a sergeant in this case, the word *primary in* the question should alert you to look for the *most* important duty of the sergeant, which is (A), maintain law and order.

32. (C) The question is asking for the best *goal* statement. The voluntary compliance of citizens with statutes, ordinances, and regulations is a fundamental goal of law enforcement. Choice (A) is a method of achieving (C), and choices (B) and (D) are by-products of (C), but the goal is voluntary compliance.

33. (D) Don't be confused by the fact that many physician/patient records require a search warrant with the principle behind privileged communication. Choices (A), (B), and (C) have enjoyed privileged communication status going back to common law.

34. (B) *Criminal cause* is the same as *corpus delicti,* body of the crime or the totality of circumstances surrounding a crime.

35. (D) In order to be admissible in court, evidence must pass the three-part test of being relevant, material, and competent.

36. (A) Past posting is placing a bet on a race that has already been run and won. In other words, a person is placing a bet on a race, which he or she already knows the results of.

37. (A) Democratic supervision, (B), and participatory supervision, (C), are basically the same, allowing subordinates to give their input while retaining final decision-making authority. Thus, both choices can be eliminated. Free-rein supervision, (A), is turning over decision-making authority to subordinates and is also incorrect. Autocratic supervision involves giving instruction as orders.

38. (C) There is a suggestion here that Sergeant Lewis is turning over decision-making authority, so choice (A), free-rein supervision, can be eliminated, leaving only two possible choices. Participative leadership, (D), involves gathering input from subordinates prior to making a decision that will affect them. The information given in the question does not in-

dicate that subordinates necessarily will have *input*. It merely states that the sergeant will explain the work and the criteria under which it is to be performed. The correct answer is (C), Theory Y management style.

39. (C) This is a case of progressive discipline.

40. (D) Taking no action, (A), is almost always incorrect in a promotional examination. A *department advocate*, (B), is a position in a large police organization filled by a high-ranking officer serving as a trier of fact in a disciplinary hearing. The sergeant should not refer anyone to the union representative, as offered in (C). The sergeant should find out the facts and advise all personnel.

41. (B) The question asks for the *primary* advantage of the formal evaluation process. The main reason performance evaluations are completed is to advise officers of whether or not they are performing their jobs in a proper manner. For most officers, the answer will be "yes" they are doing the job properly. For others, it will serve to advise them on how to improve. In most cases, this does motivate people because it gives them feedback from their supervisor. The purpose of employee evaluations is not to provide control, as offered in (A), or to direct officers, (D). Nor is it to rank-order personnel for promotion, (C). Studies indicate that people perform better when they receive feedback on how they are doing.

42. (D) Many officers think that, due to the freedom-of-information laws, all information in the hands of the police must be released to the media. As is the case in most aspects of law enforcement, reasonableness and common sense are your guidelines. Until the sergeant is certain a next of kin has been notified, the name should not be released.

43. (B) Circle the words *most important* and *type of patrol*. The number of citizen complaints against police officers, (A), has little relationship to the question and can be eliminated. The number of residents in an area, (C), would increase the number of calls for service but wouldn't dictate the *type* of patrol. The number of foot beats and cruisers in adjoining areas would be taken into consideration but isn't the *most important* factor in deciding the type of patrol. The correct answer is (B), the number of calls for police services within the area.

44. (C) In advising the officers of his personal feelings, (A), Sergeant Downing would be doing a disservice to his department even if he does then, in fact, enforce the law. Doing nothing, (B), is not what is expected from a supervisor. Picket lines are often photographed and videotaped, (D), but the answer choice that is most correct is (C), to impartially enforce the law.

45. (D) How do supervisors determine whether their subordinates are performing their jobs properly? This question appears here in another form. On police exams, basic principles and concepts are often repeated but phrased differently. More often than not, the correct answer to the above question is by *conducting inspections*. The correct answer is (D), inspecting reports to see if the new policy is being followed.

46. (C) Training is one of the primary duties of the police sergeant. All four answer choices are correct statements, but the best answer is (C), train at every opportunity.

47. (B) The key words in this question are *immediate danger*. Recognizing the key words makes the answer rather obvious—(B), remove the elderly woman to a position of safety.

48. (C) The driver of the vehicle is exhibiting abnormal behavior. There is a young child in the vehicle. The tendency of many officers is to select (A), instruct the officer to gain forcible entry into the vehicle, as the answer. They choose (A) because it's action-oriented. However, by prioritizing the answer choices and re-creating the scenario, answer (C), attempt to communicate with the operator of the vehicle, becomes the better choice.

49. (A) Rotating schedules contribute to lost efficiency, increase time lost to illness and injury, and produce employee stress. People work better on a permanent, as opposed to a rotating, schedule.

50. (A) The only Part 1 crime among the choices listed is (A), auto theft.

51. (C) Crime statistics, arrest rates, and conviction rates are not good indicators of a police department's performance. Citizen satisfaction is.

52. (A) Once again, the question is asking what the sergeant should do *first* upon arriving at a situation. Avoid reading information into the question that isn't there or making it more complicated than it is. All of the choices mention actions that the sergeant might take, but only one should be taken first. Many officers incorrectly answer (C), make an assessment of the need for additional personnel. The *most* correct answer is to render necessary assistance to the officer in trouble.

53. (C) The question doesn't explain why the vehicle is being pursued. In the absence of further information, the correct answer is (C), when the pursuit poses a threat of imminent injury to another person.

54. (B) The first responsibility of a Sergeant responding to a hostage situation is to take command and assess the situation.

55. (D) Document the contents of the phone calls and forward the report to the officer's commanding officer.

56. (A) Police vehicles should be inspected daily prior to leaving the station.

57. (D) All of the above. All of these situations A, B C require a referral to the departments stress unit.

58. (B) Consider which of the answer choices makes the most common sense given the situation presented. An officer is calling for assistance. The question states that another officer is on *routine* traffic duty directly across the street. It's true that he didn't remain at his post, (A), he was not dispatched to the scene, (C), and he did not receive permission from his supervisor, (D). These are all rules in many police departments that deal with day-to-day operations. However, there are exigent circumstances here, and in this case, it was appropriate to respond to an officer who was nearby calling for assistance.

59. (C) Before a determination can be made of how much money it will cost, (A), or what needs to be done, (B), or what the dollar figure is, (D), a decision must be made on what the overall objectives are.

60. (A) Communication in pyramid-type organizations, such as police departments, moves most often from the top downward.

61. (B) Once a labor/management contract agreement is signed, its contents are binding on both management and labor.

62. (D) Contingency plans always deal with emergency situations.

63. (A) The fact that the sergeant has had recent occasion to discipline the officer should not enter into the decision-making process as to his grievance relative to his being denied a day off. Most union contracts contain specific language concerning the process used to grant days off to employees, and the sergeant should investigate the complaint to determine whether it is valid or invalid.

64. (A) Having unauthorized ammunition is both a serious departmental offense and a vicarious-liability issue once the supervisor has knowledge of it. The fact that the officer is vice president of the police union must have no bearing on the sergeant's actions. A warning, as offered in choice (B), is generally appropriate for minor infractions, which is not the case here. Choice (C) is not appropriate for an offense of this seriousness, and choice (D) passes a decision upward that should be made at the sergeant's level.

65. (A) The key words in the question are *demands, inflexible,* and *disciplines,* all indicative of an autocratic supervisory style.

66. (A) A high school student is involved here—someone from 15 to 18 years old. Note that she *refuses, is convinced* to attempt to sell the substance, and is *supplied* with the marijuana by a police detective. All of these facts indicate entrapment.

67. (C) A police officer's duty is to give aid to the victim, even at the expense of letting the suspect go. Notifying headquarters and pursuing the suspect, (A), leaves the victim unconscious and bleeding without any help. Asking a witness to render aid to an unconscious and bleeding person, (B), a witness who may or may not be trained in medical emergencies, may lead to civil action against the officer and the department. Choice (13) is the same as choice (A) except that the officer is requesting an ambulance. The officer should render first aid to the victim and notify headquarters.

68. (C) The Fifth Amendment to the United States Constitution deals with self-incrimination.

69. (D) Res gestae is a spontaneous utterance made by a suspect prior to an officer having an opportunity to advise the suspect of his or her constitutional rights under *Miranda v. Arizona.* It is an exception to the hearsay rule.

70. (A) Notice that choices (A), (B), and (C) all specify states. Answer (A), *Weeks v. United States,* means that the decision was on the federal level. The exclusionary rule was originally

a decision at the federal level and was later applied to the individual states by other court decisions.

71. (C) The key words are *mental disorder* and a *danger to himself* Choice (A) would be appropriate only if the person had committed a crime. Releasing the person to his family, (B), doesn't ensure that the man will receive medical attention. Taking no police action is contrary to the purpose on which our profession is founded: serve and protect. The sergeant should have the man taken into custody and brought to a treatment facility.

72. (B) Fingerprints are most likely to be found at the point of entry.

73. (C) The question is asking you what the *first* step in the planning process is. Defining the problem as a clear objective must come first in order for (A), (B), or (D) to be useful.

74. (A) Whether the area is patrolled in vehicles or on foot, the best type of patrol for crime-specific activity within a small geographical area is a directed patrol.

75. (C) Controlling is an ongoing inspection process, in many departments assigned to a separate unit that reports directly to the chief of police. However, controlling is also a function of each supervisor, manager, and administrator within an organization.

76. (D) The question gives its own answer. If crime can never be totally eliminated, then (A), (B), and (C) are not viable choices. Neither crime in general nor any one specific type of crime ever has or ever will be eliminated as long as human beings are human beings. The only way we can ever eliminate crime is to make it legal.

77. (A) Communication can't take place unless both the sender and the receiver are listening to one another. Communication is an *exchange* of information. Failure to listen is the most common reason interpersonal communication breaks down. Proper listening techniques must be developed if superior communication is to take place.

78. (C) The patrol division, the backbone of a police department, is a line function within a police organization.

79. (D) To delegate means to turn one's work over to another. While it's true that the sergeant should seek to delegate tasks downward, there are some that can't be delegated. All three situations mentioned are either sensitive or those in which a sergeant may have to take disciplinary action.

80. (C) The use of undercover officers to flash rolls of money or use other such techniques to pose as potential targets for street robbery (decoy operations, B) not only is dangerous, but also limits the scope of the operation to a small area, requiring the use of large numbers of officers to ensure officer safety. The question asks for the best tactic to reduce *widespread* robberies *throughout* the district. Random patrol is not a tactic but the theory that officers shouldn't establish a specific pattern as to time or place, which a criminal can watch and then plan for. Passive patrol, (D), occurs when officers rove their districts waiting for the dispatcher to direct them to a call. The correct answer is (C), proactive patrol. This tactic maximizes patrol time by having officers actively stop suspicious persons for field checks

throughout the district and make a large number of motor vehicle and pedestrian checks. Research indicates that this tactic has the most effect in decreasing the level of street robberies.

81. (C) Laissez-faire supervision most often means *anything goes.* The question indicates that the sergeant doesn't want to be advised of any problems or concerns.

82. (A) Sergeants should be spending the most time with probationary police officers. Since such officers are still being trained in the basics of the profession, sergeants should spend more time with them than with veteran officers, as offered in choices (B) and (C), or with an officer returning from leave, as given in choice (D).

83. (A) The type of behavior described in the question is most indicative that the officer is having a problem off the job.

84. (C) *Preponderance of evidence* means that the facts tend to sway more one way than another. If the facts indicate that there is more evidence than not that an officer violated the department's firearms guidelines, the sergeant should submit appropriate disciplinary charges.

85. (C) If the officer is taking medication that produces double vision then she shouldn't be working in any capacity. Of the answer choices listed, the most viable is (C), to put the officer on the sick list. This is a vicarious-liability situation for the sergeant, the officer, and the department.

86. (D) The acceptance of gifts, favors, or other gratuities, however small, is a form of police corruption and is unacceptable.

87. (C) Circle *excellent officer* and *normally follows instructions well.* If this is not a concern relative to behavior and if past evaluation of the officer isn't indicative of a performance problem, Sergeant Morrison would be correct to first look to himself and ensure that proper communication is taking place. Sergeant Morrison should obtain feedback from the officer when giving direction to ensure that the officer understands what he is explaining to him.

88. (B) The statement made in the question is a myth and is false. People are not born with inherent leadership skills and abilities. Some people have more opportunity than others to develop the attributes of leadership; however, most become leaders by making the most of their skills and abilities.

89. (B) The question is asking for a false statement. Choice (A) is true. You can't motivate another to do anything; you can only supply the incentive. (C) is true. Different people are influenced to act by different stimuli. (D) is true. Sergeants can provide the influence to motivate people. The only false statement is (B). Money is *not* the prime motivator in the workplace because once it is received (pay raise, bonus, etc.), it fails to remain a motivator.

90. (C) Because all of the answer choices are important in effective communication, you must be very careful to understand what it is that the question is asking. Note the word *Before.* Choices (A) and (B) should be taken care of either during or after communication, not before. This leaves (C) and (D) to choose between. Removing all physical barriers to communication, (D), is important, but it will do little good if the sender doesn't have a clear understanding of what is being communicated to the receiver.

91. (C) You can't bluff your way through with subordinates, as in choices (A) and (B), and expect them to look to you for guidance and direction in the future. Choice (D) is all right, but the sergeant is losing a valuable opportunity to coach and train the subordinate. The best answer option is to advise the officer that he is not familiar with the statute and look it up with him.

92. (D) Choices (A), (B), and (C) are advantages that line-item budgeting does not produce. Line-item budgets merely list human and physical resources and allocate a dollar amount to each. There is no relationship to planning and control, explanation of objectives, or flexibility in making changes. But a line-item budget *does* provide a clear comparison of expenditures from year to year.

93. (C) Police officers cannot search persons and the area under their control for *suspected criminal behavior,* (A), or for *suspicion of an offense,* (D), or after a legal detainment, (B). The key to this question is in the use of the words *arrest* and *incarceration* in choice (C). A police officer can search the person and the area under his or her immediate control at the time of a custodial arrest.

94. (B) The sergeant should first find out where the officer is because the officer may be injured or involved in some type of altercation and unable to get to his radio. Choices (C) and (D) are viable alternatives under certain circumstances, but only after (B) has been accomplished.

95. (B) The purpose of bond is to ensure that a person appears in court. The prediction is that if a person provides money for release from incarceration, he or she will appear in court at a future date rather than forfeit the money.

96. (C) You're looking for the *most important* skill of those listed. People are our most important asset.

97. (C) *Exculpatory* is a common legal term meaning culpable. The suspect here admitted his guilt in the crime.

98. (A) *Terry v. Ohio.* Given the scenario as outlined in this question, the officer would have the right to pat down a suspect's outer garments for his own safety.

99. (C) Lividity stains flow to the lowest portion of the body due to gravity. If the victim was found lying on his back, but the lividity stains were on his stomach, we know that the body was rolled over after death. The correct answer is (C), the victim was turned over from his stomach onto his back.

100. (A) Crack got its name because it makes a crackling sound when it's smoked.

7

Oral Practice Test

◆ ◆ ◆

This section contains a battery of questions, covering a wide range of supervisory topics, designed to sharpen your skill level and improve your verbal communication ability.

The more realistic you make your practice exams, the better you'll do at the real thing, so simulate an actual oral board in your own home. Set up the table with three chairs behind it for the panelists and a chair in front of the table where you'll sit—don't forget the stuffed animals, and don't worry about feeling silly; you'll feel a lot sillier if you come out of the oral knowing you didn't do as well as you could have. Have a friend or a family member record a series of questions for you (eight or nine is plenty) or actually sit where one of the panelists will be and ask you the questions. Use a video camera with sound capability to record your practice sessions and evaluate your progress. Repeat the process with a new set of questions or the same questions phrased differently. Review the video recordings of your practice sessions. Try writing out your responses to the questions prior to taping. Most important, practice, practice, practice.

Most orals for the rank of police sergeant last from 30–40 minutes—two to three questions per panelist, with follow-up questions from each, plus short opening and closing remarks gives you three or four minutes to respond to each question. Time your answers accordingly. Talking about a specific topic for four minutes is longer than it seems when you see it in writing. Try it. It's not as easy as it sounds.

Unless you'll be taking a "technical oral", only a limited number of concepts can be covered in this type of testing process. The same questions are often used, but they may be phrased differently. The following questions are in sequences of three, asking the same thing in three different ways. Although there often isn't a definitive right or wrong answer to oral questions, each sequence is followed by a discussion of the supervisory concepts that should be covered in your answer. You may wish to adapt them to your own department's standards.

Oral Board Questions and Analysis

1. As a sergeant, how will you determine whether your officers are properly performing their jobs?

1. As a sergeant, what mechanisms will you use to evaluate your subordinates' job performances?

1. What criteria will you use to determine whether your officers are appropriately performing their job assignments?

ANALYSIS How can you tell that people are performing their jobs properly? In policing, we accomplish this by *inspecting* human and physical resources and monitoring job performance (people and things—police officers, systems, and procedures). The rules and regulations, procedural manuals, department orders, the sergeant's experience level and training, etc., establish standard criteria on which to judge officer performance. Your answer should include an inspection of people by observing them perform their job tasks. Such inspection is accomplished by accompanying them on calls for service, by listening to radio transmissions and responses, and by *monitoring* and observing their actual work performance. Inspection of systems and procedures involves reviewing officers' reports, monthly calls for service records (time off on calls, number of calls responded to, time spent while en route to calls, etc.), and the officers' training records, internal affairs profiles, and personnel files. Your answer should also include what you will do if the performance is not satisfactory. Coaching, teaching, training, modeling techniques, progressive discipline, and documentation should all be covered in your answer.

2. You are a patrol sergeant working the midnight shift. An officer under your supervision does not respond to a radio call or repeated attempts to contact him. You find him behind a gas station sleeping in the front seat of his cruiser. How would you handle this situation?

2. While on routine patrol you decide to inspect the two beat officers assigned to a city housing project. They have an office in the project in which to write their reports and take walk-in complaints from citizens. Upon entering, you find both officers sleeping. What action would you take?

2. You are advised by the patrol lieutenant that there has been a fire at a jewelry store on a previous shift. The owner has requested that an officer be stationed at the location to prevent looting. Upon inspecting, you find the officer in a back room sleeping in a chair. The officer states that she "didn't feel well." Please tell the board what steps you would take.

ANALYSIS No matter how the question is asked, we still have an officer sleeping on duty. This is a violation of the rules and regulations (code of conduct, manual, etc.) in every police department. The officer is placing himself and others in danger, not properly performing his job assignment, placing himself and the department in a vicarious liability situation, and disparaging the reputation of the department. The officer must be referred for disciplinary action. Your answer should also include an evaluation of whether the officer is mentally and physically able to continue working, a counseling session to determine the cause for sleeping (physical, mental, shift work, poor health habits, etc.), and a plan to closely inspect the officer in the future to ensure that it doesn't happen again.

3. You are a sergeant inspecting officers at roll call. You find an officer in the back row unstable on his feel and smell a strong odor of alcohol in his breath. What action would you take?

3. You are a sergeant assigned to the detective division and upon entering the locker room see a detective, who is on duty, take several sips from a pint bottle of vodka and then put the bottle back in his locker. How would you handle this situation?

3. You are a sergeant assigned to the narcotics squad. A search warrant is planned where armed resistance is expected. After the briefing and while the detectives are putting on their vests, you go into the men's room and see a detective at the washstand vomiting. On the shelf next to him is a bottle containing alcohol. He admits to having "one shot" to calm his nerves. He doesn't appear to be intoxicated. What will you do?

ANALYSIS It doesn't matter whether the subordinate is actually intoxicated or is just observed drinking alcohol. In either case, the sergeant's duty is clear; the subordinate must be relieved of duty, his service revolver confiscate, and appropriate disciplinary action taken or recommended. The subordinate should be referred to the department's stress or EAP unit, counseled, and closely monitored upon return to duty. In cases of an officer assigned to an especially sensitive assignment, such as the narcotics division or squad, the officer should be transferred.

4. What leadership style will you feel most comfortable with as a police supervisor?

4. There are many management and supervisory styles. Which do you feel is best for a police sergeant in your department?

4. Sergeants are the most important supervisors in a police department. Please tell this board what supervisory techniques you will use to maximize the potential of your subordinates.

ANALYSIS You want the board to recognize that you know the various management theories. Give a brief description of these theories: participative (democratic), autocratic, free-rein, laissez-faire, Theory X, and Theory Y. Since no one management or supervisory style is best for policing, you may want to expound on situational leadership for motivation of subordinates, participative management for day-to-day operations, and autocratic supervision in emergency situations.

5. You are a patrol sergeant and respond to a hostage situation. Several officers are at the scene. Almost immediately upon your arrival, a suspect wielding a gun exits the building with a hostage and begins walking up the street. What action would you take?

5. You respond to a call of an active robbery of a package store. Upon arriving you find that two armed men are inside and holding several customers at gunpoint. How would you handle this situation?

5. You respond to the scene of a domestic dispute and are advised by your officers that a husband is inside who has a knife to his wife's throat and who is refusing to release her or come out. What steps would you take in this situation?

ANALYSIS The first role of a sergeant in a situation as depicted in these questions is to assess the incident and then advise headquarters of the situation (through use of the radio or, if this is a tactical problem, by land line), prevent the escape of the suspects, establish an inner and outer perimeter, evacuate the area, establish a command post, request tactical and hostage negotiating teams, begin negotiating if necessary, and use appropriate force if the situation deteriorates. Note: The board is almost certain to ask follow-up questions that will put you in a position where you have to make a decision to act. For example, the suspect kills a hostage and is about to kill another. What will you do now? If you respond that you would continue to negotiate, a panelist may then say, "Okay, the suspect just killed a second hostage and is threatening to kill a third." At some point you're going to have to implement offensive action. At an oral board, it's better to do it sooner than later, but only after all of the sequential steps have been taken.

6. You are asked by the patrol captain to give all officers roll call training on the department's firearms guidelines. How would you accomplish this task?

6. You are advised by your lieutenant that you are to give a two-hour block of training to police academy recruits relative to search and seizure. What steps would you take?

6. Over a period of time, you note an increase in cruiser traffic accidents involving vehicular pursuits. What supervisory actions would you take?

ANALYSIS Any oral board question relative to the training of subordinates requires a sequential approach. Your answer should include research of the subject, preparation of a lesson plan, type of teaching method (lecture, video, flip chart, blackboard, etc.), use of handouts, evaluation instrument to obtain feedback on whether the training was successful, and recording the training for vicarious liability and documentation purposes.

7. A vehicle is being pursued by an officer for a minor traffic violation. You monitor the pursuit via the police radio and instruct the officer to terminate the chase of the vehicle. He ignores your instructions, continues the chase, and pulls the vehicle over. What supervisory action would you take?

7. At roll call you advise all walking patrols that they are not to ride with the area car at any time during their shifts, with the exception of going to their posts and back to headquarters at the end of their tours. While on patrol, you observe an officer assigned to a beat off his post and riding in a cruiser. What action would you take?

7. You respond to a call of an active fight in a bar. Upon arrival, you find that the situation is under control and instruct several officers who are not needed to return to their assigned areas. You leave but, upon driving through the area 15 minutes later, find one officer who has not followed your instructions and is still at the scene. What would you do?

ANALYSIS Use care in answering this type of question. Many candidates tend to automatically recommend negative discipline when an order is not obeyed or instructions given by a supervisor are not followed. However, two other steps must be taken first. Did the subordinate understand what was being communicated? Why didn't the officer follow the instructions? Was there a reason that would be acceptable if the officer explained his actions? If the subordinate did understand or should have understood the communication and there is no extenuating circumstance, then disciplinary action should be invoked. Your answer should also include remarks concerning future monitoring of the officer and documentation of the incident.

8. You are a patrol sergeant dispatched to the scene of a domestic dispute involving an off-duty police officer. Upon arrival, you learn that the officer has assaulted his wife and that she has been taken to a hospital. What supervisory action would you take?

8. You are dispatched to the scene where a search warrant for narcotics has been executed. The detective in charge advises you that an off-duty officer was found at the location and to be in possession of two vials of crack cocaine. What steps would you take?

8. You respond to the scene of the burglary of a package store. Upon arrival at the back of the store, you look through the window and see an officer take some money out of the register and put it into her front pocket. When you confront the officer, she admits to stealing the money. How would you handle this situation?

ANALYSIS If an officer, on or off duty, commits a crime in the sergeant's presence or the sergeant has probable cause to believe the officer has committed a crime, an arrest must be made. Depending on your department, either the arrest is immediate or an arrest warrant must be applied for. Your answer should include a logical progression of steps. Assess the situation, gather the facts through the investigative process, determine if a crime was committed, if so, arrest, make the proper notifications, relieve from duty, advise EAP or the stress unit, take appropriate disciplinary action, and monitor the officer closely if she is allowed back to work.

9. How do you, as a sergeant, decide the type of patrol that is most advantageous for a particular situation or area?

9. Please tell this board what you feel are the advantages and disadvantages of motorized patrol versus foot patrol.

9. In what circumstances would you recommend to your patrol commander the use of foot patrol for a specific area?

ANALYSIS These questions give you an opportunity to highlight your technical job knowledge. Your answer should include a brief overview of the types of patrol and the purposes of each, the reason walking beats are more appropriate in certain areas than in others, the factors that enter into a decision to recommend various patrols (foot patrol, directed patrol, park and ride, etc.), the advantages of motorized patrol over foot patrol and the disadvantages of having officers on foot as opposed to riding in a cruiser, and the advantages and disadvantages of having two officers in a single cruiser.

10. Crime analysis is an important tool for the police supervisor. Please explain to this board the purpose of crime analysis and how you would use this information as a police sergeant?

10. What crime analysis information do you feel is important for a police supervisor?

10. It is important for police sergeants to keep their subordinates informed. What types of information would you want to pass along to officers under your supervision?

ANALYSIS Crime analysis is also called "operations analysis" in many police departments. It is a description of crime trends and patterns after review of investigative reports and statistical information. Your answer should cover what crime analysis is and how it's used to concentrate patrol efforts at specific locations and times, its relationship to modus operandi patterns, the type of crime analysis done by your department, how this information is communicated throughout the department, how you as a supervisor will communicate this information to your subordinates, and what method you will use to ensure that subordinates are acting on the information which you provide them.

11. Please explain to this board what you know about the types of discipline and the disciplinary process.

11. You are a sergeant assigned to the patrol division. You inspect an officer's arrest report and find that he has left out several pieces of key information. How would you handle this situation?

11. An officer under your direct supervision has reported for duty out of uniform. You counsel the officer and ensure that he is properly uniformed prior to leaving the station. The next day, the officer reports for duty without his badge or field jacket. What steps would you take?

ANALYSIS Your answer should include a statement of the purpose of the disciplinary process; the types of discipline (positive, negative, and progressive); the fact that you intend to coach, teach, and train, but that you will use negative discipline for repeat offenses; how discipline is documented and why; and what you will do to inspect and monitor the officer in the future. Don't forget the "hot-stove rule," to criticize in private and praise in public, to gather all the facts, and to be fair and consistent.

12. You become aware that a subordinate under your direction has improperly destroyed a small amount of marijuana and let a suspect go. How would you handle this?

12. You are a patrol sergeant and accompany several narcotics detectives on a search warrant. The detectives seize a large amount of cocaine in the apartment, some heroin, and a small amount of LSD. Upon reviewing the arrest report, you note that the LSD has been left off the evidence part of the report. You are advised by the arresting officer that he "flushed it down the toilet because the court won't prosecute such a small amount." How do you feel about this?

12. Upon returning from a search warrant you observe a detective separate the evidence and place a marijuana pipe and a small bong on his desk as a decoration. Both were taken from the apartment of a drug dealer. What supervisory action would you take?

ANALYSIS Destroying evidence or converting it to one's own use is a violation of the rules of all police departments. The initial steps to be included in your answer are fairly simple: Communicate to the subordinate that the behavior or action is improper and why, take appropriate disciplinary action, and document. However, in some parts of the country, the conduct described in the questions may be considered criminal. In that case, all of the above steps must be taken and, additionally, the case must be reviewed for criminal prosecution. You may also want to add that you would follow up with inspections to ensure that other officers are not performing similar acts.

13. The lack of upward mobility in a police department is often a concern to employees. As a newly appointed sergeant, what methods will you use to motivate your officers?

13. Burnout is a persistent problem in law enforcement. Could you tell this board how you would recognize employees who are exhibiting signs of stress overload and what you would do about it?

13. As a newly appointed sergeant, how will you go about supervising officers with whom you have worked side by side for many years?

ANALYSIS This question gives you an opportunity to showcase your knowledge about motivation (Maslow, Herzberg, etc.) and leadership. Included in your answer should be an overview of what motivation is, what you will do to motivate your subordinates, the importance of interpersonal communication, your knowledge of the symptoms of stress, referral to the stress unit or EAP program, and leadership styles, including the one you will use and why.

14. You respond to the scene of a street fight. Two officers have arrested a suspect and placed him in the cruiser prior to your arrival. You note that he is bleeding slightly from a head wound. As you're walking back to your cruiser, you're approached by a citizen who tells you he saw one of the officers get into the back-seat of the cruiser with the prisoner and beat him about the head with a blackjack. The citizen states that the prisoner was in handcuffs and offering no resistance. What supervisory action would you take?

14. You are walking by an interrogation room and hear someone screaming. Upon opening the door, you observe a suspect handcuffed to a chair, bleeding from the mouth, and two detectives hovering over him. The suspect states, "They beat me up." What would you do?

14. You are dispatched to the scene of an officer-involved shooting. Upon investigating, you learn that a juvenile suspect has been shot in the back by an officer upon fleeing the scene of a theft of newspapers from a paper box. How would you handle this situation?

ANALYSIS Candidates have a tendency to begin answering this question with severe punitive action prior to gathering all of the facts. Your answer should indicate that you would take immediate steps to curtail any abuse of a prisoner, conduct a complete, thorough investigation, and arrest if a crime had been committed in your presence. But if you lacked probable cause for immediate arrest, you would recommend appropriate criminal charges through the affidavit process, and departmental charges would be forthcoming. Obviously, you would also ensure that the proper notifications take place.

15. An officer, who has been under your supervision for several years, advises you that he is having severe financial problems. He states that he is divorced and is having trouble making his child support payments. He fears that his wages will be attached. How would you handle this?

15. A newly appointed officer approaches you and asks if she can speak with you in private. She tells you that she loves the job, but her husband is urging her to quit because of the shift work involved. What would you advise the officer to do?

15. A veteran officer, who always keeps to himself and seldom speaks with supervisors, approaches you and states, "I think I have a problem. I can't seem to stop drinking and I'm afraid I'm going to lose my wife and kids." What action would you take?

ANALYSIS The sergeant is often seen as a parent figure by subordinates. In each of these cases, an officer is seeking out the sergeant for advice on a problem occurring off the job.

Your answer should show the panel that you recognize this as an opportunity to be of assistance to the officer and thus your organization. A discussion of communications techniques and listening skills should be included in your response, along with a referral to the EAP, stress unit, or outside agency if more appropriate. Some sort of follow-up or monitoring of the subordinate must be addressed, along with motivational theory and human relations.

8 Assessment Center Practice Test

How to Take the In-Basket Practice Test

The assessment center is a flexible testing method that can be readily adapted in order to evaluate candidates individually or in groups. Because the test exercises are designed around specific organizational problems under a variety of situations and circumstances, your test may be structured differently from the one offered here. However, the testing concept follows an established pattern, and the principle on which this method of testing is based remains the same: to predict the supervisory potential of candidates for promotion. If your department is going to use an assessment center to test you for promotion, then learn all you can about this method of testing by going to the library and bookstores and doing additional research on assessment center testing. Knowing what to expect will add points to your score.

You should not see the text of the following informational and in-basket items or the text of the phone calls before you begin the practice exam.

The sample assessment center test designed for this guide will give you an overview of how this type of testing works and practical experience in actually taking an assessment center in-basket examination. Because there are many ways to handle the problems presented in this exercise and still be correct, the answers provided should not be treated as the only correct answers.

The material offered in this guide and the sample test will give you the information you need to plan an intensive study program aimed at achieving a high score. However, no book can re-create the pressure-packed atmosphere generated by assessment center testing. Most of the exercises require you to directly interact with other candidates and role players, creating enormous pressure on candidates to perform. Don't be surprised if you're mentally and physically drained after going through the assessment center testing process. But early preparation will give you an *edge* on your competitors.

The practice exercise you are about to take consists of three components:

1. the in-basket exercise
2. an index of in-basket items
3. an analysis and discussion of the in-basket exercise

Follow the directions carefully. They outline the materials needed and the time in which the test must be completed. Contained in the in-basket exercise are five incoming phone calls. To make the test more realistic, have a friend or family member record the phone calls. While you're taking the in-basket examination and writing your responses, have them play one phone call from the recording every 12 minutes. For example, activate the first call 12 minutes into the exam, the second at 24 minutes, and so forth.

I repeat . . . **you should not see the text of the following informational and in-basket items or the text of the phone calls before you begin the practice exam. Before you do anything else,** give this book to the person who will record your phone calls and have him or her follow these instructions:

ATTENTION SUPPORT PERSON

1. Cut out all informational and in-basket items on pages 201–249 on the lines indicated.

2. Put all of this material in a large manila envelope to be given to the candidate at the beginning of the practice exam.

3. Cut out page 251, the text of the five telephone calls, and use it to record them. If you will be present while the candidate takes the practice exam, record the telephone calls one after the other, with only a little space between them. You will play one phone call approximately every 12 minutes during the exam. If you will not be present while the candidate takes the practice exam, record the phone calls with approximately 12 minutes of blank space between them so that the candidate can allow the recording to run throughout the exam.

In-Basket Exercise

Materials required: pen, paper, highlighter
Time: 1 hour and 15 minutes

Directions

You are a police sergeant working the 1500–2300 shift in the patrol division (squad B) of the Centerville police department on Saturday, February 21. Your name is Sergeant Michael Flynn.

Handle the in-basket exercise in accordance with the established procedure of your police department. Think of yourself as a sergeant and act accordingly. You are required to respond to the in-basket problems *in the manner in which you would handle them as a sergeant in real life. Each response must be in writing and reflect actual behavior.* For example, your response to an incoming telephone call must be written and should reflect how you would have handled the caller or situation.

Each of your responses should be written directly on the piece of correspondence that you're addressing or, if you require more space, on a separate piece of paper, clearly identifying the material or correspondence you're responding to (for example, "Memo from Captain Walker Regarding Smith Complaint"). The action you take on all incoming phone calls must be written on a separate sheet of paper. Write the number of the phone call you're dealing with (if one is given) or clearly identify the subject of the phone call (for example, "Call from Sergeant Bell Regarding Property Room Theft") before each written response.

The following information is provided as part of the testing process:

1. Detective division resources consist of a normal complement for a Saturday evening shift in your department.
2. There is a seven-officer special detail operating in the Hill area of the city to combat street-level narcotics activity.
3. There is a motorcycle detail consisting of four officers working within the downtown area.
4. There is a traffic-enforcement unit consisting of three officers working throughout the city.
5. Patrol division staffing levels are normal.
6. The union contract is the same as is used in your department.

INFORMATIONAL ITEMS

CENTERVILLE, USA

Centerville was formed in the early 1800s, growing out of the fur-trading activity along a large Midwest river. The city has a population of over 400,000 and is culturally and ethnically diverse, with approximately 53% white residents, 37% black, and 9.5% Hispanic and Oriental. Centerville, once heavily dependent on the railroad and meatpacking industries, has seen considerable growth in agricultural products, telecommunications, light industry, and insurance, all of which are large employers. A major employer, AI Firearms, Incorporated, is located in a poverty-stricken downtown area of the city and recently laid off 450 workers, who are now leading a labor strike against the plant.

Centerville has a mayor/city manager/city council form of government. The city manager is appointed by the city council, which consists of nine elected officials including the mayor. The mayor has no real power other than being one of the nine council members. An election was recently held in the city, and four of the nine city council members are new. The mayor has served for two years and is in disfavor with the present city council.

Centerville has one daily newspaper, which recently reported widespread corruption in the city's public-works department and called for a grand jury investigation. The newspaper article also hinted at problems in the police department's traffic division relative to the proceeds from city parking meters.

There is a major east/west highway through the city, and on weekends, as many as 300,000 vehicles pass through Centerville. There are several state and private colleges in the city, with a total enrollment of over 20,000 students. The Centerville police department has 832 sworn officers and 93 civilian employees. The chief of police, Frank Simpson, has been with the department for the past thirty-four years. He was promoted to chief five years ago. The department has two assistant and three deputy chiefs of police. The department operates under a pyramid organizational structure, and Chief Simpson believes in managing by objectives. The department was reorganized by Chief Simpson several months ago, and new personnel were placed in key positions throughout the department. The morale of the department is low due to the reorganization. The police union is very powerful.

The average salary for police officers is $24,900 yearly, with supervisory personnel making approximately six percent more than patrol officers. Chief Simpson reports directly to the city manager and enjoys a good relationship with her. In general, the department has a well-educated force, with the average officer having fourteen years of formal education. Many of the lower-ranking officers have college degrees and resent superior officers who do not. The union president is up for reelection and has a strong fight on his hands due to a bid-shift section in the union contract, which the younger officers on the force want to repeal and the veteran members want to keep. The average length of service for a police officer is currently 6.7 years.

CENTERVILLE POLITICAL STRUCTURE

Mayor

The mayor serves along with the city council as the legislative and policy-making body of the municipal government—receiving community and citizen comment, having responsibility for enacting city ordinances, appropriating funds to conduct city business, and providing policy direction to the administration.

City Council

The city council consists of nine members elected by district for two-year terms in the odd years. By charter, the council has the power to provide for the organization of the various city departments, agencies, and offices and to conduct and operate them; to create, alter, abolish, assign, and reassign divisions, bureaus, offices, and agencies; to transfer functions and activities; to consolidate and reorganize departments; and to determine the number, titles, qualifications, powers, duties, and compensation of all officers and employees of the city.

City Manager

The city manager manages administrative affairs of the city and carries out the policies enacted by the city council. The city manager is the chief executive officer of the city and is responsible to the city council for the effective and efficient management of all departments and agencies of city government.

Personnel

The personnel department provides city departments with an efficient personnel management system by planning and controlling divisional programs and monitoring all personnel transactions to assure conformance to federal and state statutes, city charter, ordinances, personnel rules and regulations, and collective-bargaining agreements.

Fire

The fire department protects, by means of prevention or suppression, life and property against the dangers of fire and other natural or man-made disasters and responds to those events in order to minimize the losses of life and property.

Police

The police department, through the effective utilization of its resources, provides for the preservation of the public peace, the apprehension of criminals, the protection of the rights of persons and property, and the enforcement of the laws of the state and the ordinances of the city.

Public Works

The public works department provides those essential services to the community that will assure safe, clean, and well-maintained streets; a safe and reliable city fleet; well-maintained city buildings and facilities; sanitary and cost-effective waste collection; and the efficient flow of traffic and transportation throughout the city.

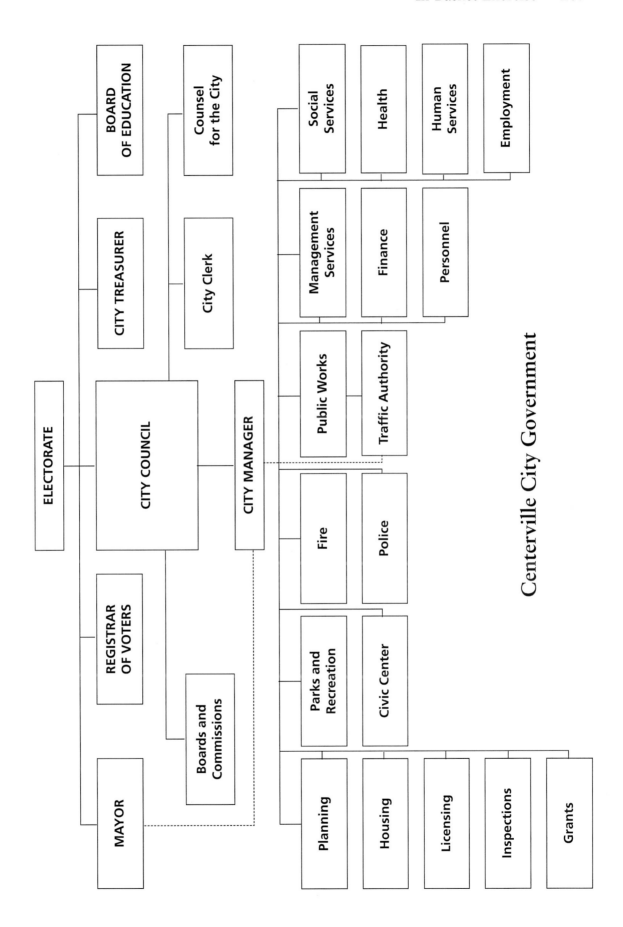

Centerville City Government

Centerville Police Organizational Chart

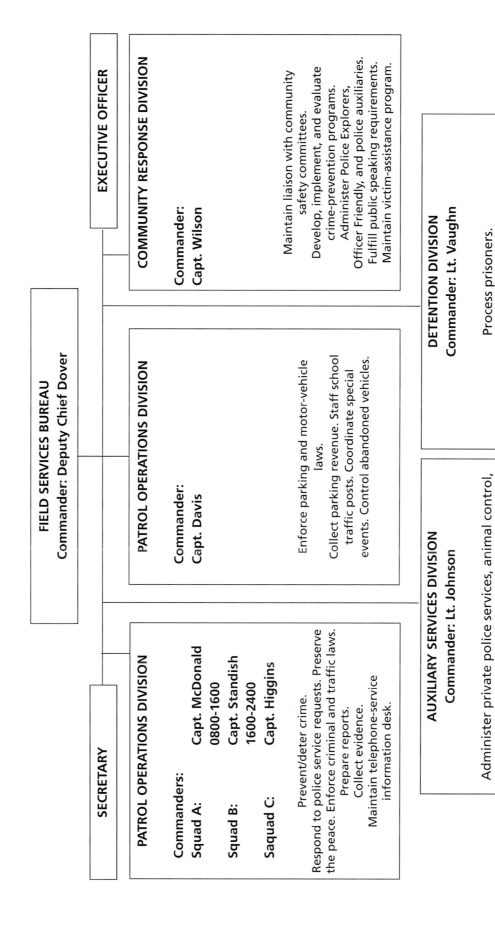

SECRETARY

EXECUTIVE OFFICER

FIELD SERVICES BUREAU
Commander: Deputy Chief Dover

COMMUNITY RESPONSE DIVISION

Commander:
Capt. Wilson

Maintain liaison with community safety committees. Develop, implement, and evaluate crime-prevention programs. Administer Police Explorers, Officer Friendly, and police auxiliaries. Fulfill public speaking requirements. Maintain victim-assistance program.

PATROL OPERATIONS DIVISION

Commander:
Capt. Davis

Enforce parking and motor-vehicle laws.
Collect parking revenue. Staff school traffic posts. Coordinate special events. Control abandoned vehicles.

PATROL OPERATIONS DIVISION

Commanders:
Squad A: Capt. McDonald
            0800-1600
Squad B: Capt. Standish
            1600-2400
Saquad C: Capt. Higgins

Prevent/deter crime.
Respond to police service requests. Preserve the peace. Enforce criminal and traffic laws.
Prepare reports.
Collect evidence.
Maintain telephone-service information desk.

DETENTION DIVISION
Commander: Lt. Vaughn

Process prisoners.
Hold prisoners for arraignment. Process prisoners for bail.

AUXILIARY SERVICES DIVISION
Commander: Lt. Johnson

Administer private police services, animal control, and police overtime.

POLITICAL ACTIVITIES OF
CENTERVILLE CLASSIFIED CITY EMPLOYEES

State Law 76-424 concerns political activities of municipal and state employees in the classified service. This interpretation of the law is intended as a guide and not as a formal legal opinion.

The law permits employees in the classified service to

1. Vote as they choose and to express opinions on political candidates and subjects.

2. Participate actively in political management and campaigns. Such activity may include but is not limited to

   (a) Membership and holding office in a political party, organization, or club.

   (b) Campaigning for a candidate in a partisan election by making speeches, writing on behalf of a candidate, or soliciting votes in support of or in opposition to a candidate.

   (c) Making contributions of time and money to political parties.

The law prohibits municipal employees in the classified service from

1. The use of official authority or influence to affect or interfere with an election or nomination for office.

2. Actual candidacy for elective office in a political partisan election.

3. The solicitation of funds or anything of value directly or indirectly from a party, committee, organization, agency, or person for political purposes.

4. The utilization of municipal funds, supplies, vehicles, or facilities to secure support for or oppose any candidate, party, or issue in a political partisan election.

5. Engaging in political activities permitted by law while on duty or within any period of time during which an employee is expected to perform services for which he or she receives compensation from the municipality.

This law supersedes the city charter, the personnel rules and regulations, and present labor agreements on the issue of political activity.

In-Basket Items

CITY OF CENTERVILLE
INTERDEPARTMENT ROUTING SLIP

	Name		Check and Forward
1.	_____		_____
2.	_____		_____
3.	_____		_____

_____ YOUR INFORMATION

_____ REPLY DIRECTLY TO CORRESPONDENT

_____ PREPARE REPLY WITH MY SIGNATURE

__X___ INVESTIGATE AND REPORT

_____ SUBMIT RECOMMENDATIONS AND COMMENTS

_____ DISCUSS WITH ME

_____ NECESSARY ACTION

__X___ IMMEDIATE ACTION

__X___ RETURN *Investigative plan by 2/23*

_____YOUR FILE

REMARKS *Please investigate this complaint.*

I need your investigative plan by 2/23 _____

_____

Thanks

_____

__2/20__	__E. Standish__
Date	**Signature**

CENTERVILLE POLICE DEPARTMENT
INTERNAL AFFAIRS DIVISION

Citizen Complaint

Complainant's
Name: _____ Charles Poteat _____ D.O.B. _____ 12/18/1962 _____

Address _____ 61 Anawan Street, Centerville _____

Home Phone: _____ 246-4832 _____ Business Phone: _____ 278-3129 _____

Location of Incident: _____ Park and Main Streets _____

Complaint
Against:
Name: _____ M. Bailey _____ Rank: _____ Patrol Officer _____
Badge Number: _____ 76 _____

Name: _____ J. Mackey _____ Rank: _____ Patrol Officer _____
Badge Number: _____ 176 _____

Complaint: I was walking in the area of Main and Park Streets when I was stopped by two officers. The officers held me down and searched me. One of the officers also punched me in the stomach. The officers then arrested me. When I got to the police station, I found that my $200 was missing.

Witnesses:
Name: _____ Mr. Stubby Sears _____ Phone _____ 278-0130 _____

Address _____ 21 Broad Street, Centerville _____

Complaint received by:
Name: _____ John Riggins _____ Rank: _____ Sergeant _____ Date _____ 02/20/-- _____

CPD Form 72 (revised)

2 copies to IAD
1 copy to complainant

CENTERVILLE POLICE DEPARTMENT
Unusual Occurrence Report

Date of incident: __02/21/--__   Case Number: ___23326___

Time occurred: ___1325 hours___

Location: ___821 Holyoke Avenue, Centerville___

1. This report prepared by __Sergeant T. Butler__

   Under the supervision of ___Captain Joseph McDonald___

2. **Synopsis of the incident:** On the above date and time, Juno's Jewelry store was entered by two masked men with shotguns. The store owner was beaten by one man while the other filled a sack with jewelry. Upon their exit, shots were fired into the ceiling.

3. **Persons injured/property damage:** Angelo Juno, D.O.B. 4/8/45, the store owner, received cuts and bruises about the head. Treated and released at Seabrook Hospital.

4. **Police action taken/persons arrested:** Units responded. A broadcast was put out for the suspects.

5. **Citizen Complaints:** Yes _____ No ___X___ If yes, explain:

6. **Summary of findings/recommendations:** None

7. **Notifications made/time:** Deputy Chief Dover 1340 hours
                      8D 1340 hours
                      Detective division 1340 hours

CPD Form 63

CITY OF CENTERVILLE
INTERDEPARTMENT MEMORANDUM

Name: ___Sergeant Flynn_____   Date _____2/21/--_____

From: ___Captain Standish_____

Subject: Officer Rhodes

Officer Rhodes approached me on 2/20 and requested three hours
unofficial comp time, which he says you granted him last week. I denied
the request. Please look into this matter and advise me by 2/24.

February 18, 20—

Sergeant Michael Flynn
Centerville Police Department
80 Jennings Road
Centerville, USA 06925

Dear Sergeant Flynn:

My daughter, Paula Dickson, age 17, of 123 Andover St., Centerville, received a motor vehicle summons on February 17 on Andover St. She was cited for "speeding" going 48 miles per hour in a 28 zone. Her court date is February 27.

Mike, we have known each other for a long time, and I was wondering if there is anything you can do for Paula to resolve this matter. I would really appreciate it if you could take care of this for me. Please write or call to let me know.

Thanks in advance,

Andy

Andrew P. Dickson
Centerville City Councilman
800 Main Street
Centerville

CENTERVILLE POLICE DEPARTMENT

Report of Disciplinary Infraction

Complete in duplicate when report required by CPD Order 4-2 "Disciplinary Procedure," Par. IV A.1 and 2.

SECTION I

Name of employee: _Paul Churchill_   Rank: _officer_

Division: _patrol_   Date of infraction: _02/20/--_

SECTION II

Infraction charged: _Violation of CPD Code of Conduct_

	Article	Section	Title of Offense
1.	V	5.04	Inattentive to duty
2.			
3.			

Explain infraction(s) in detail (list witness if any):

On this date, the undersigned observed the above officer standing outside his cruiser talking to a female just after he and another unit had been dispatched to an active burglary. He made no attempt to immediately answer the call.

To the best of our knowledge, is this a second or subsequent offense to any of the code sections cited? If so, specify:

Unknown

Immediate corrective action taken, if any (if any of the infractions call for an oral reprimand and the reprimand has been issued, so state and attach to a copy):

None

Date: _02/20/--_   Submitted by: _Sergeant Trautman_

CPD Form 80
Revised

CITY OF CENTERVILLE
Application for Attendance at
Training/Education Activity

1. Name: __Simoni, John P.__ 2. Rank: __Officer__

3. Assignment: __Simoni, John P.__ _____ __Officer__
            Unit   **Division**   **Bureau**

4. Training/education activity requested: __Arson Investigation Seminar__

5. Date(s) of attendance: __February 28, 20--__

   Total Days: __1__

6. **Reason for request:** I would like to learn about the crime of arson. I am very interested in this field and believe it would benefit the department.

7. Location of activity: __Hilton Hotel, Centerville__

8. Sponsor/conducted by: __Municipal Police Training Academy__

9. Cost (include registration, tuition, travel, etc.): __$100__

10. Applicant's Signature: __John P. Simoni__

   Date: __02/21__

11. **Commanding officer:** App. _____ Disapp. _____ Date _____

12. **Bureau chief:** App. _____ Disapp. _____ Date _____

13. **Police academy:** App. _____ Disapp. _____ Date _____

14. **Chief of police:** App. _____ Disapp. _____ Date _____

15. **Reason for disapproval:** _____

16. **Personnel unit:** _____ Order issue date: _____

CPD Form 41 (1-85) Revised

CITY OF CENTERVILLE
INTERDEPARTMENT MEMORANDUM

To: Sergeant Flynn   Date: 2/21

From: Deputy Chief Dover

Subject: Officer Casco

Please review the attached Probationary Police Officer Report (CPD forms 26) and CPD Form 190. This officer was appointed to the department on August 15, 20—, and completed the Police Academy on February 22, 20—. As you can see, he will be off probation of February 23. Prepare a recommendation to me immediately.

For this problem, the following CPD Form 26 represents 12 completed forms over this evaluation period.

CENTERVILLE POLICE DEPARTMENT
Probationary Police Officer
Performance Evaluation Report

Employee's name: _Paul Casco_

Date of employment: _08/15/--_

Evaluation for period   BEGINNING: _02/24/--_

                                  ENDING: _02/22/--_

Method of assigning overall evaluations:

Thoroughly competent: Thorough competent evaluations are earned on all critical factors.

Acceptable: Acceptable evaluations are earned on one or more critical factors, and no below standard evaluations are earned on any critical factors.

Below standard: Below standard evaluations are earned on one or more critical factors.

CRITICAL PERFORMANCE FACTOR EVALUATION

CRITICAL FACTOR

1. **Communication Skills:** _Acceptable_
2. **Interpersonal skills:** _Thoroughly competent_
3. **Ability to apply laws, rules, and procedures:** _Thoroughly competent_
4. **Ability to take initiative and successfully complete all job assignments:** _Thoroughly competent_
5. **Ability to exercise command and make decisions:** _Thoroughly competent_
6. **Skill in the use and care of police equipment:** _Below standard_
7. **Skill in the legal and effective use of police force:** _Thoroughly competent_
8. **Ability to conduct effective patrol operations:** _Thoroughly competent_

Performance Evaluation Documentation Sheets must be completed for each critical factor which is given an evaluation of below standard.

Evaluator's name: _____

Title: _____

Signature: _____

Date: _____

CPD Form 26

CENTERVILLE POLICE DEPARTMENT
Probationary Police Officer
Performance Evaluation Documental Sheet

Employee's name: Paul Casco

Date of employment: 08/15/--

Critical factor: Vehicle operation

Evaluator's name: Michael Stevens

Evaluator's signature: *Michael Stevens*

Title: Field Training Officer

Documentation of performance: Officer has not been able to operate a police cruiser, as he has not passed his proficiency driving test at the skid pan school. I've tried to work with the officer alone, but he seems to freeze up

CPD Form 190

CENTERVILLE POLICE DEPARTMENT
Expenditure Request

Bureau: Field Services Bureau   **Division:** Patrol

Person requesting item: Officer Paul Johnson

Item requested: narcotics identification kit

Suggested vendor:

     Name: Newton Labs

     Address: 123 Vescott St, Lamont, WY

     Phone: (310) 338-1996

Estimated cost per unit: _____

     Number: _____

     Total: _____

Justification for request: The chemicals in the present kit are several years old and need to be replaced.

_____

Reviewed by division commander

_____

Authorized by bureau commander

CPD Form 98

CENTERVILLE POLICE DEPARTMENT
COMMUNITY-RESPONSE DIVISION
Block Watch/Community Leaders Meeting Report

Meeting/visit date: 2/19/--

Location: 113 Ansonia Street, Centerville

Meeting held with: Teresa Jennings/approximately 20 block watch members

Time Started: 1815   Time Ended: 1940

Concerns presented to police officer during meeting/visit:

Undersigned met with entire block watch group during their monthly meeting. Member stated that their area is infested with drug dealers, who sell openly on the street corners, and they want increased patrols.

Action taken by police officer:

Recommend notifying vice and narcotics division of groups concerns.

Report prepared by: Officer Lemner   Date: 02/19/--

Reviewed by: _____

Remarks:

CPD Form 12

CENTERVILLE POLICE DEPARTMENT

Field Sergeant Actvity Report

Date: _____

Squad: _____

I. **Supervisory activity:**

II. **Assigned inspections:**

III. **Self-generated inspections:**

IV. **Other assigned duties:**

V. **Comments and recommendations:**

_____

Sergeant's signature

CPD Form 346

CENTERVILLE POLICE DEPARTMENT
Unusual Occurrence Report

Date of incident: 2/21/--   Case Number: 23332

Time occurred: 1415 hours

Location: 1325 Main Street, Centerville

1. **This report prepared by:** Sergeant Rowlands

   Under the supervision of: Captain McDonald

2. **Synopsis of the incident:** Units 192/193, Officers Weston and Ramos, operating vehicle 227, were transporting prisoner to detention, and upon stopping for a traffic signal, they were struck in the rear by another vehicle.

3. **Persons injured/property damage:** Cruiser 227 sustained minor damage to the rear end. There were no injuries to the officers or prisoner.

4. **Police action taken/persons arrested:** Mr. John Rollins, D.O.B. 5/8/1953, or 129 Seymour Drive, Centerville, was issued a summons for 14-240, failure to drive a reasonable distance apart.

5. **Citizen complaints:** Yes_____   No _____ If yes, explain:

6. **Summary of findings/recommendations:** The driver of the police vehicle was not at fault in this traffic accident.

7. **Notifications made/time:** Patrol commander 1420 hours
   Evidentiary services 1430 hours

CPD Form 63

CITY OF CENTERVILLE
INTERDEPARTMENT MEMORANDUM

To: Sergeant MIchael Flynn, Squad B   **Date:** 2/21/--

From: Lieutenant Andrew Paulson, Inspection Division

Subject: Officer Anthony Sweeney

On February 20, I personally observed Officer Sweeney sleeping in a room adjacent to the executive officer's desk. The executive officer, Sergeant Wooding, was out of the building on an assignment at the time. I have requested a written report from Officer Sweeney on two occasions and have not received same. Please look into this and take appropriate action.

CITY OF CENTERVILLE
INTERDEPARTMENT ROUTING SLIP

Check and Forward

1. <u>Sergeant Flynn</u>   ☐

2. _____   ☐

3. _____   ☐

__X__ YOUR INFORMATION

_____ REPLY DIRECTLY TO CORRESPONDENT

_____ PREPARE REPLY WITH MY SIGNATURE

_____ INVESTIGATE AND REPORT

_____ SUBMIT RECOMMENDATIONS AND COMMENTS

_____ DISCUSS WITH ME

__X__ NECESSARY ACTION

_____ IMMEDIATE ACTION

_____ RETURN

_____ YOUR FILE

REMARKS: <u>Prepare a written report to me detailing the action taken relative to these</u>
<u>robberies. Reply by 2/21</u>

_____

_____

_____

_____2/21_____   _____ Deputy Chief Dover
                                                Signature

CRIME-ANALYSIS UNIT
CONFIDENTIAL—POLICE USE ONLY
Crime Pattern Bulletin

To: Deputy Chief, ISB

Deputy Chief, FSB

Date: 2/20/--

The Crime-Analysis Unit has observed the following crime pattern: Street robberies in the lower Blue Hills Avenue area.

General Time Pattern:

Sun:	3
Mon:	1
Tues:	0
Wed:	1
Thurs:	5
Fri:	2
Sat:	1

Hours: 1800-2300

Modus: Normally two or more BM's will attack a single victim. Five incidents involved weapons (three guns, two knives.)

Suspect Descriptions:

Sex	Race	Age	Height	Weight	Comments
M	B	16-20	5'8"	150	
M	B	23			Light skinned
M	B	13		125	
M	B	17-19		160-170	Dark skinned
M	B	20	6'	180	Short hair
M	B	20	5'6"	150	Brown Hair

Remarks:

Distribution:

X	Chief of Police	X	CSU-CPU	X	Intel.
X	Patrol Cmdrs.	X	Cmdr. ISB	X	Cmdr. FSB
	C.A. Property	X	C.A. Persons	X	Y.S.D.
X	E.S.D.				

Patrol Units: 19, 20, 27, 124, 110

CITY OF CENTERVILLE
INTERDEPARTMENT ROUTING SLIP

Check and Forward

1. *Sergeant Flynn* ☐

2. _____ ☐

3. _____ ☐

_____ YOUR INFORMATION

_____ REPLY DIRECTLY TO CORRESPONDENT

_____ PREPARE REPLY WITH MY SIGNATURE

_____ INVESTIGATE AND REPORT

_____ SUBMIT RECOMMENDATIONS AND COMMENTS

_____ DISCUSS WITH ME

__X__ NECESSARY ACTION

_____ IMMEDIATE ACTION

__X__ RETURN by 2/24

_____ YOUR FILE

REMARKS: *Please respond to each complain of The Citizen Advisory Committee dealing with Patrol Squad B*

_____

_____

_____

2/20	*E. Standish*
	Signature

CITY OF CENTERVILLE
INTERDEPARTMENT MEMORANDUM

To: __Deputy Chief Dover__   Date: __2/20/--__

From: __Frank Simpson, Chief of Police__

Subject: __Complaints made by Police/Citizen Advisory Committee – February meeting.__

On February 19, I met with the Police/Citizen Advisory Committee. The following locations were identified by committee members as areas of criminal or disorderly conduct. Please have the appropriate personnel from your bureau look into these problems and respond with action taken by February 24.

1. (Patrol A and B) Complaint of loiterers trespassing in the rear of the drugstore on the corner of Blue Hills and Burnham Streets.

2. (Traffic) Complaint of speeders – Chandler and Dart Streets.

3. (Traffic) Complaint of speeders on Brookfield Street near Flatbush Avenue between 1430 and 1630 hours.

4. (Patrol A) Complaint of vandalism, thefts from vehicles, and general harassment of personnel in the area of the board of education building on Atlantic Street.

5. (Patrol A and B) Request for extra attention for trespassers in the rear of the bank at park and Broad Streets.

6. (Patrol A and B) Complaint that alternate side parking is not being enforced on Monroe Street.

7. (Patrol A and B) Request from southwest representative, Ann DeVeau, to communicate with officers in her area. Chief Simpson indicated that the area sergeant should see her.

8. (Patrol A and B) Written complaint from Parkville representatives that the parking situation in the Parkville area has gotten much worse on Saturdays during the last month. Requests strict enforcement in this area.

Phone Calls

Call 1

Sergeant Flynn, this is Officer Riggins down at A1 Firearms. As you know, A1 is on strike and the situation here has been getting progressively more difficult to control. We just had an incident that's causing big problems. One of the recently hired strike breakers just drove his car through the picket line and hit a striking worker. The injured worker is a 30 year old woman, and she has a serious head injury. We arrested the driver of the car, but now several fights have broken out. I didn't want to go over the radio with this because then the media will be all over us. What do you want me to do?

   Exam proctor's voice: In making your response to this phone call, you should be aware that both your lieutenant and your captain are unavailable.

Call 2

Sergeant Flynn, this is Officer Sloan at the front desk. There are two state police officers out here with an arrest warrant for Officer John Peters. The warrant charges Officer Peters with sexual assault in the first degree. Officer Peters is working a downtown beat right now. What do you want me to do?

Call 3

Sergeant Flynn, this is Lou Blance of Channel 17 action news. I heard they shot the clerk at Juno's Jewelry Store today. How about a few quotes? We're rolling the recording right now.

Call 4

Sergeant Flynn, this is Officer Reynolds in records. City councilman Casey is on the telephone and is asking for an arrest records check on one of his opponent's major campaign workers. We're not supposed to do this, but he says it's OK. What should we do? How do you want me to handle this?

Call 5

Sergeant Flynn, this is Officer Caron. I'm down here at the Golden Oak Café with my girlfriend, and there's something going on here you should know. Officer Jensen's down here, and he's had way too much to drink. Right now, he's at the bar waving his badge and gun around pretending he's on a raid. He's already gotten into a beef with one guy, and I'm scared he's going to do something stupid. I feel like a turncoat calling you, but, Like I said, I'm scared there's going to be an accident. What do you want me to do?

Index of In-Basket Exercise Items

Inter-department Routing Slip from Deputy Chief Dover concerning robbery Crime pattern Bulletin

Crime Pattern Bulletin concerning robberies in the Blue Hills Avenue area

Inter-department Routing Slip from Captain Standish with request to respond to Citizen Advisory Committee complaints

Inter-department Memorandum from Chief Simpson to Deputy Chief Dover concerning Police/Citizen Advisory Committee complaints

Text of Phone Calls 1 through 5

Analysis and Discussion of In-Basket Exercise

Informational Item

Informational items are included with the test material for several reasons. The test creates a single framework in which all of the candidates receive exactly the same information. Some of the material in the informational items may be important and relevant to the effective completion of the in-basket examination. However, much of it is added only to determine whether you can prioritize information and to add pressure to the test-taking process.

When you take an assessment center in-basket exam, first quickly scan the informational items you're given. Use your highlighter to pick out key points. Do not over mark. For example, you might highlight the "Centerville, USA" material as follows (areas underlined show areas you might highlight):

CENTERVILLE, USA

Centerville was formed in the early 1800s growing out of the fur-trading activity along a large Midwest river. The city has a population of over 400,000 and is culturally and ethnically diverse, with approximately 53% white residents, 37% black, and 9.5% Hispanic and Oriental. Centerville, once heavily dependent on the railroad and meat packing industries, has seen considerable growth in agricultural products, telecommunications, light industry, and insurance, all of which are large employers. A major employer, A1 Firearms, Incorporated, is located in a poverty-stricken downtown area of the city and recently laid off 450 workers, who are now leading a labor strike against the plant.

Centerville has a mayor/city manager/city council form of government. The city manager is appointed by the city council, which consists of nine elected officials including the mayor. The mayor has no real power other than being one of the nice council members. An election was recently held in the city, and four of the nine city council members are new. The mayor has served for two years and is in disfavor with the present city council.

Centerville has one daily newspaper, which recently reported widespread corruption in the city's public-works department and called for a grand jury investigation. The newspaper article also hinted at problems in the police department's traffic division relative to the proceeds from city parking meters.

There is a major east/west highway through the city, and on weekends, as many as 300,000 vehicles pass through Centerville There are several state and private colleges in the city, with a total enrollment of over 20,000 students. The Centerville police department has 832 sworn officers and 93 civilian employees. The chief of police, Frank Simpson, has been with the department for the past thirty-four years. He was promoted to chief five years ago. The department has two assistant and three deputy chiefs of police. The department operates under a pyramid organizational structure, and Chief Simpson believes in managing by objectives. The department was reorganized by Chief Simpson several months ago, and new personnel were placed in key positions throughout the department. The morale of the department is low due to the reorganization. The police union is very powerful.

The average salary for police officers is $24,900 yearly, with supervisory personnel making approximately six percent more than patrol officers. Chief Simpson reports directly to the city manager and enjoys a good relationship with her. In general, the department has a well educated force, with the average officer having fourteen years of formal education. Many of the lower-ranking officers have college degrees and resent superior officers who do not. The union president is up for reelection and has a strong fight on his hand due to a bid-shift section in the union contract, which the younger officers ion the force want to repeal and the veteran members want to keep. The average length of service for a police officer is currently 6-7 years.

In-Basket Items

After scanning the informational items and highlighting important information, scan all the remaining in-basket items. Now you must prioritize the in-basket items from most important to least, placing the most important on the top of your stack of papers, as they would be the ones you would work on first.

Phone Calls

You will have written your responses to the phone calls on a separate piece of paper. Although you have no way of knowing exactly when the phone will ring and how far you will have progressed through your in-basket items when it does, the following analysis includes model responses to those calls at likely intervals.

Prioritized Items, Phone Calls, and Model Responses

1. Unusual Occurrence Report – Juno's Jewelry Store

Remember that the directions indicate that you are working the 1500-2300 shift. In most police departments, there is a roll call or briefing held at a central location for officers working from 1600-2400 hours. Items for this briefing would claim top priority for a sergeant completing an actual in-basket in real life. The robbery at Juno's Jewelry Store occurred less than two hours ago. One appropriate response to this item is as follows:

> Write this directly on the form

> Place your initials here to show it's your writing and that you've reviewed this item

Call detective division to get an update on information in UOR relative to robbery and suspects. Read at roll call 1600 hours, 2/21/ MF

CENTERVILLE POLICE DEPARTMENT
Unusual Occurrence Report

> Note date of incident. Today

Date of incident: 02/21/--   Case Number: 23326

Time occurred: 1325 hours

Location: 821 Holyoke Avenue, Centerville

> Note time of incident. Less than two hours ago

1. This report prepared by Sergeant T. Butler

   Under the supervision of Captain Joseph McDonald

2. **Synopsis of the incident:** On the above date and time, Juno's Jewelry store was entered by two masked men with shotguns. The store owner was beaten by one man while the other filled a sack with jewelry. Upon their exit, shots were fired into the ceiling.

3. **Persons injured/property damage:** Angelo Juno, D.O.B. 4/8/45, the store owner, received cuts and bruises about the head. Treated and released at Seabrook Hospital.

4. **Police action taken/persons arrested:** Units responded. A broadcast was put out for the suspects.

5. **Citizen Complaints:** Yes _____ No __X__ If yes, explain:

6. **Summary of findings/recommendations:** None

7. **Notifications made/time:** Deputy Chief Dover 1340 hours
   8D 1340 hours
   Detective division 1340 hours

CPD Form 63

2. Routing Slip and Note from Deputy Chief Dover – Crime Pattern Bulletin

This is another roll-call informational item, and as such, it should be attended to immediately. The Crime Pattern Bulletin must be read at roll call so that all officers (especially those working in the lower Blue Hills Avenue area) will be informed of specific patterns of criminal activity. Since the information is crime and location specific, a good tactic is to put out a special detail in the area to work specifically on the problem. Depending on the procedures of your department, you would either implement a special detail or recommend it to your lieutenant or patrol commander. Following is one way to handle these two pieces of correspondence:

CITY OF CENTERVILLE
INTERDEPARTMENT ROUTING SLIP

Name   Check and
                                                              Forward

1. *Sergeant Flynn* _____   _____

2. _____   _____

3. _____   _____

*X*____ YOUR INFORMATION

_____ REPLY DIRECTLY TO CORRESPONDENT

_____ PREPARE REPLY WITH MY SIGNATURE

_____ INVESTIGATE AND REPORT

_____ SUBMIT RECOMMENDATIONS AND COMMENTS

_____ DISCUSS WITH ME

*X*____ NECESSARY ACTION

_____ IMMEDIATE ACTION

_____ RETURN *Investigative plan by 2/23*

_____ YOUR FILE

REMARKS *Prepare a written report to me detailing the action taken*
relative to these robberies. Reply by 2/21 _____

_____

2/21 _____   _____ *Deputy Chief Dover* _____
                                            Signature

Margin note (left, pointing to REMARKS): Note that a report is due and that it must be written

Margin note (lower left, pointing to signature): Note the sender of this information

Margin note (bottom, pointing to date): Note the due date. Today.

Write your response directly on this form or, if you require more space, write it on a separate piece of paper.

CRIME-ANALYSIS UNIT
Crime Pattern Bulletin

To: Deputy Chief, ISB

Deputy Chief, FSB

Date: 2/20/--

The Crime-Analysis Unit has observed the following crime pattern: Street robberies in the lower Blue Hills Avenue area.

Note—crime and location specific

General Time Pattern:

Sun: 3

Mon: 1

Tues: 0

Wed: 1

Thurs: 5

Fri: 2

Sat: 1

Hours: 1800-2300

Modus: Normally two or more BM's will attack a single victim. Five incidents involved weapons (three guns, two knives.)

Suspect Descriptions:

Sex	Race	Age	Height	Weight	Comments
M	B	16-20	5'8"	150	
M	B	23			Light skinned
M	B	13		125	
M	B	17-19		160-170	Dark skinned
M	B	20	6'	180	Short hair
M	B	20	5'6"	150	Brown Hair

Remarks:

Distribution:

X	Chief of Police	X	CSU-CPU	X	Intel.
X	Patrol Cmdrs.	X	Cmdr. ISB	X	Cmdr. FSB
	C.A. Property	X	C.A. Persons	X	Y.S.D.
X	E.S.D.				

Patrol Units: 19, 20, 27, 124, 110

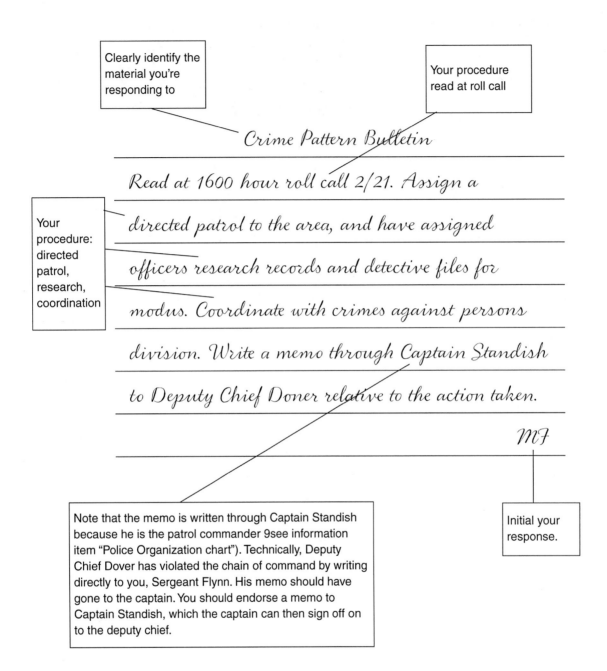

Clearly identify the material you're responding to

Your procedure read at roll call

Your procedure: directed patrol, research, coordination

Crime Pattern Bulletin

Read at 1600 hour roll call 2/21. Assign a directed patrol to the area, and have assigned officers research records and detective files for modus. Coordinate with crimes against persons division. Write a memo through Captain Standish to Deputy Chief Doner relative to the action taken.

MF

Note that the memo is written through Captain Standish because he is the patrol commander 9see information item "Police Organization chart"). Technically, Deputy Chief Dover has violated the chain of command by writing directly to you, Sergeant Flynn. His memo should have gone to the captain. You should endorse a memo to Captain Standish, which the captain can then sign off on to the deputy chief.

Initial your response.

3. Expenditure Request for Narcotics Identification Kit

Handle as follows:

Write your response directly on the form

Your initials

Note that needed information is left out. You would not sign a request where the price is not specified.

Return to officer to complete form. Price, etc., left out. MF

CENTERVILLE POLICE DEPARTMENT
Expenditure Request

Bureau: Field Services Bureau   **Division:** Patrol

Person requesting item: Officer Paul Johnson

Item requested: narcotics identification kit

Suggested vendor:

Name: Newton Labs

Address: 123 Vescott St, Lamont, WY

Phone: (310) 338-1996

Estimated cost per unit: _____

Number: _____

Total: _____

Justification for request: The chemicals in the present kit are several years old and need to be replaced.

_____
Reviewed by division commander

_____
Authorized by bureau commander

CPD Form 98

4. Routing Slip with Note from Captain Standish. Citizen Complaint against officers Bailey and Mackey

One correct response might be as follows:

> Note the due date and that it is the *investigative plan*, not the *investigation*, that must be completed by this date.

CITY OF CENTERVILLE
INTERDEPARTMENT ROUTING SLIP

Check and Forward

1. _Sergeant Flynn_ ☐

2. _____ ☐

3. _____ ☑

_____	YOUR INFORMATION
_____	REPLY DIRECTLY TO CORRESPONDENT
_____	PREPARE REPLY WITH MY SIGNATURE
_X_	INVESTIGATE AND REPORT
_____	SUBMIT RECOMMENDATIONS AND COMMENTS
_____	DISCUSS WITH ME
_____	NECESSARY ACTION
_X_	IMMEDIATE ACTION
_X_	RETURN *Investigative plan by 2/23*
_____	YOUR FILE

REMARKS: _Please investigate this complaint. I need your investigative plan_

_by 2/23_ _____

_____

_____

2/20   E. Standish

Write your response directly on this form, or if you require more space, write it on a separate piece of paper.

CENTERVILLE POLICE DEPARTMENT
INTERNAL AFFAIRS DIVISION

Citizen Complaint

Note name of complainant

Complainant's
Name: __Charles Poteat__   D.O.B. __12/18/1962__

Address __61 Anawan Street, Centerville__

Home Phone: __246-4832__   Business Phone: __278-3129__

Location of Incident: __Park and Main Streets__

Complaint
Against:

Name: __M. Bailey__   Rank: __Patrol Officer__

Badge Number: __76__

Note name of officers

Name: __J. Mackey__   Rank: __Patrol Officer__

Badge Number: __176__

Complaint: I was walking in the area of Main and Park Streets when I was stopped by two officers. The officers held me down and searched me. One of the officers also punched me in the stomach. The officers then arrested me. When I got to the police station, I found that my $200 was missing.

Note allegations

Witnesses:
Name: __Mr. Stubby Sears__   Phone __278-0130__

Address __21 Broad Street, Centerville__

Complaint received by:

Name: __John Riggins__   Rank: __Sergeant__   Date __02/20/--__

CPD Form 72 (revised)

2 copies to IAD

1 copy to complainant

Indicating that you're making a note to file to work on this at a later date.

Clearly identify the material you're responding to.

Citizen Complaint against Bailey and

Mackey Tickler file for 2/23

Call Mr. Poteat to set up an appointment

for an interview. Determine when officers

Bailey and Mackey are working to

interview them. Review their internal

affairs and personnel files.

MF

Initial your response.

Your procedure: Call Poteat, locate Bailey and Mackey for interview, review their files.

5. Telephone Call – A1 Firearms

At approximately this point in the examination, you may hear your first telephone call. The exam proctor has required you to make a decision by advising you that your lieutenant and your captain are unavailable. You might respond as follows:

> Clearly identify the call you're responding to with an appropriate name or with a number, if one is given for the call (for example, telephone call number 1).

> Recall the information item "Centerville, USA" concerning the magnitude of the strike and the location of A1 Firearms.

> Recall the informational item concerning the four officer unit in the downtown area.

> Recall the informational item concerning the four officer unit in the downtown area.

> Recall the informational item concerning the four officer unit in the downtown area.

Telephone Call – A1 Firearms

I would advise officer Riggins that I would immediately respond to the scene. I would contact the supervisor of the Communications division and determine what area units were available in the area and have them dispatched to A1 Firearms. If no units were available I would have the four motorcycle officers in the downtown area dispatched to the scene. Upon arrival, I would assess the situation and determine if additional officers were needed. I would advise the patrol lieutenant or captain of my actions as quickly as possible. Once the situation had stabilized, I would direct personnel back to their regular assignments.

MF

> Your initials

6. Letter from City Councilman Dickson

It would be appropriate to handle this item in the following way:

> Recall the information item concerning the suggestion of problems in the traffic division. Realize that this could be a delicate area.

> Note that the letter is personal; it has not come through a superior.

February 18, 20—

Sergeant Michael Flynn
Centerville Police Department
80 Jennings Road
Centerville, USA 06925

Dear Sergeant Flynn:

My daughter, Paula Dickson, age 17, of 123 Andover St., Centerville, received a motor vehicle summons on February 17 on Andover St. She was cited for "speeding" going 48 miles per hour in a 28 zone. Her court date is February 27.

> Note that you've known each other a long time.

Mike, we have known each other for a long time, and I was wondering if there is anything you can do for Paula to resolve this matter. I would really appreciate it if you could take care of this for me. Please write or call to let me know.

Thanks in advance,

Andy

Andrew P. Dickson
Centerville City Councilman
800 Main Street
Centerville

> Your procedure: respond promptly, be tactful, and advise your immediate supervisor.

I would call Councilman Dickson and advise him of the departments policy relative to a motor vehicle summons and, as tactfully as possible, suggest he hire an attorney to represent his daughter in court. I would then write a memo to my immediate supervisor detailing the action taken and attach the letter from Councilman Dickson to it.

> Write your response directly on the letter.

> Initial your response.

MF

7. Memo from Captain Standish Relative to Officer Rhodes
Following is one correct response to this memo:

CITY OF CENTERVILLE
INTERDEPARTMENT MEMORANDUM

Name: Sergeant Flynn   Date 2/21/--

From: Captain Standish

Subject: Officer Rhodes

Officer Rhodes approached me on 2/20 and requested three hours unofficial comp time, which he says you granted him last week. I denied the request. Please look into this matter and advise me by 2/24.

Ticker for 2/24. If time permits, contact Officer Rhodes and advise him that under the present union contract "unofficial compensatory time" is not permitted. Write a memo to Captain Standish explain the action taken.

MF

Note due date. Three days from now.

Your procedure; file for future action, advise Officer Rhodes, reply to captain.

Write your response directly on the memo.

Your initials

This response assumes your familiarity with your *own* union contract. If the unofficial comp time regulation is *not* a part of your contract, you would, of course, have to answer this differently. Also, informational items might include a union contract for the fictional town. If this were the case, you would refer to that contract for guidelines here.

8. Telephone Call from officer Sloan at Front Desk – Arrest Warrant for Officer on Duty

Following is one appropriate response:

> Clearly identify the call you're responding to.

> Write your response on a separate piece of paper.

Telephone Call - Warrant for Officer Peters

I would handle this matter personally by meeting with the state police officers and reviewing the arrest warrant to ensure its validity. If the warrant was valid, I would notify the patrol commander and arrange a private location within police headquarters for officer peters to respond and assist the state police in serving their arrest warrant. I would notify the Employee Assistance Unit. The offense is a felony, and the union contract calls for a supervision from duty. By notifying the patrol commander who is outside the bargaining union, it would then be his decision on the administrative steps to take relative to the officers' future duty status and the retention of his service revolver. Sergeants cannot suspend officers under the current contract but can relieve offices from duty. If the patrol commander wasn't available, I would relieve Officer Peters from duty.

MF

> Your procedure: handle personally, review and establish validity of warrant, ensure privacy, contact EAU, consider union contract terms.

> Recall informational item concerning union power.

> Response to this call again assumes your knowledge of your own contract or is based on information supplied to you concerning a fictional city's contract.

> Your initials

9. Application for Attendance at Training/Education Activity – Officer Simoni

> Write your response directly on this form or, if you require more space, write it on a separate piece of paper.

CITY OF CENTERVILLE
Application for Attendance at
Training/Education Activity

1. Name: __Simoni, John P.__   2. Rank: __Officer__

3. Assignment: __Simoni, John P.__   __Patrol__   __Officer__
                Unit   **Division**

Bureau

> Note training requested

4. Training/education activity requested: __Arson Investigation Seminar__

> Note date of training

5. Date(s) of attendance: __February 28, 20--__

    Total Days: __1__

6. **Reason for request:** I would like to learn about the crime of arson. I am very interested in this field and believe it would benefit the department.

7. Location of activity: __Hilton Hotel, Centerville__

> Note training agency

8. Sponsor/conducted by: __Municipal Police Training Academy__

9. Cost (include registration, tuition, travel, etc.): __$100__

10. Applicant's Signature: _John P. Simoni_

    Date: __02/21__

11. **Commanding officer:**   App. _____   Disapp. _____   Date _____

12. **Bureau chief:**   App. _____   Disapp. _____   Date _____

> Note that sergeant not listed

13. **Police academy:**   App. _____   Disapp. _____   Date _____

14. **Chief of police:**   App. _____   Disapp. _____   Date _____

15. **Reason for disapproval:** _____

16. **Personnel unit:** _____   **Order issue date:** _____

Clearly identify the material you're responding to.

Name found on form

Application for Training - Officer Simoni I

would telephone the Municipal Police

Training Academy to determine if this

particular course is designed for patrol officers

or if it's designed for personnel assigned to

specialized division. If it's designed for patrol

officers, I would attach a memo to Captain

Standish recommending approval or

disapproval. Once a decision was reached by the

Captain, I would inform Officer Simoni.

If the application was disapproved, I would

advise the officer of the reason for the decision.

MF

Your procedure: Call to investigate course, send memo to captain, inform officer.

Because there is no place on the form for a sergeant to sign off on.

Your initials

10. Memo from Deputy Chief Dover
    Probationary Police Officer Performance Evaluation Report
    Documentation Sheet

CITY OF CENTERVILLE
INTERDEPARTMENT MEMORANDUM

To: Sergeant Flynn   Date: 2/21

From: Deputy Chief Dover

Subject: Officer Casco

Please review the attached Probationary Police
Officer Report (CPD forms 26) and CPD Form
190. This officer was appointed to the
department on August 15, 20—, and completed
the Police Academy on February 22, 20—. As
you can see, he will be off probation of February
23. Prepare a recommendation to me
immediately.

Note
action
required

Note
immediate
action

Write your response directly on the form or if you need more
space, on a separate piece of paper.

This form represents
12 CPD Forms 26

CENTERVILLE POLICE DEPARTMENT
Probationary Police Officer
Performance Evaluation Report

Employee's name: Paul Casco

Date of employment: 08/15/--

Evaluation for period   BEGINNING: 02/24/--

   ENDING: 02/22/--

Method of assigning overall evaluations:

Thoroughly competent: Thorough competent evaluations are earned on all critical factors.

Acceptable: Acceptable evaluations are earned on one or more critical factors, and no below standard evaluations are earned on any critical factors.

Below standard: Below standard evaluations are earned on one or more critical factors.

CRITICAL PERFORMANCE FACTOR EVALUATION

CRITICAL FACTOR

1. **Communication Skills:** Acceptable

2. **Interpersonal skills:** Thoroughly competent

3. **Ability to apply laws, rules, and procedures:** Thoroughly competent

4. **Ability to take initiative and successfully complete all job assignments:** Thoroughly competent

Note rating. Requires your decision on retention.

5. **Ability to exercise command and make decisions:** Thoroughly competent

6. **Skill in the use and care of police equipment:** Below standard

7. **Skill in the legal and effective use of police force:** Thoroughly competent

8. **Ability to conduct effective patrol operations:** Thoroughly competent

Performance Evaluation Documentation Sheets must be completed for each critical factor which is given an evaluation of below standard.

Evaluator's name: Michael Flynn

Title: Sergeant

Signature: Michael Flynn

Date: 2/21

CPD Form 26

Fill in this.

Sign "Michael Flynn" since that is your name for the test.

CENTERVILLE POLICE DEPARTMENT
Probationary Police Officer
Performance Evaluation Documental Sheet

Employee's name: Paul Casco

Date of employment: 08/15/--

Critical factor: Vehicle operation

Evaluator's name: Michael Stevens

Evaluator's signature: *Michael Stevens*

Title: Field Training Officer

No need to sign this form. Already signed by Stevens.

Documentation of performance: Officer has not been able to operate a police cruiser, as he has not passed his proficiency driving test at the skid pan school. I've tried to work with the officer alone, but he seems to freeze up

Note reason for "below standard" rating.

CPD Form 190

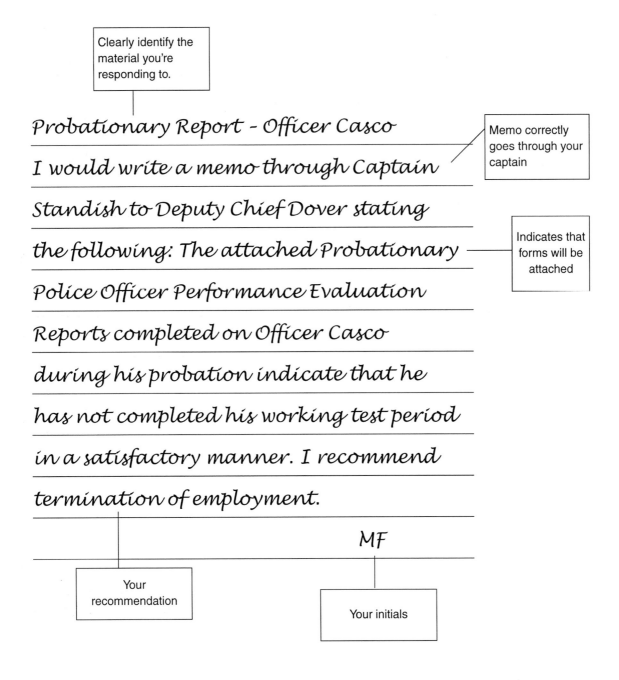

Clearly identify the material you're responding to.

Probationary Report - Officer Casco

Memo correctly goes through your captain

I would write a memo through Captain

Standish to Deputy Chief Dover stating

Indicates that forms will be attached

the following: The attached Probationary

Police Officer Performance Evaluation

Reports completed on Officer Casco

during his probation indicate that he

has not completed his working test period

in a satisfactory manner. I recommend

termination of employment.

MF

Your recommendation

Your initials

11. Unusual Occurrence Report

This is a routine piece of correspondence. Handle as follows:

> Initial the report to indicate that you've reviewed it. No other action is required.

CENTERVILLE POLICE DEPARTMENT
Unusual Occurrence Report   MF

Date of incident: 2/21/--   Case Number: 23332

Time occurred: 1415 hours

Location: 1325 Main Street, Centerville

1. **This report prepared by:** Sergeant Rowlands

   Under the supervision of: Captain McDonald

2. **Synopsis of the incident:** Units 192/193, Officers Weston and Ramos, operating vehicle 227, were transporting prisoner to detention, and upon stopping for a traffic signal, they were struck in the rear by another vehicle.

3. **Persons injured/property damage:** Cruiser 227 sustained minor damage to the rear end. There were no injuries to the officers or prisoner.

4. **Police action taken/persons arrested:** Mr. John Rollins, D.O.B. 5/8/1953, or 129 Seymour Drive, Centerville, was issued a summons for 14-240, failure to drive a reasonable distance apart.

5. **Citizen complaints:** Yes_____ No _____ If yes, explain:

6. **Summary of findings/recommendations:** The driver of the police vehicle was not at fault in this traffic accident.

7. **Notifications made/time:** Patrol commander 1420 hours
   Evidentiary services 1430 hours

CPD Form 63

12. Telephone Call from Lou Blance of Channel 17

One correct response is the following:

> Clearly identify the call you're responding to.

Telephone Call - Lou Blance, Channel 17

I would advise Mr. Blance that I was still in the process of reviewing the previous shifts paperwork and would be happy to call him to give a synopsis later in the evening.

MF

> Note that the fact that the recording is playing does not necessarily mean that you must directly, or at that moment, respond to a request. There are appropriate occasions for delaying response.

> Your initials

13. Memo from Lieutenant Paulson Relative to Officer Sweeney Sleeping on Duty

---

CITY OF CENTERVILLE
INTERDEPARTMENT MEMORANDUM

To: Sergeant Michael Flynn, Squad B   **Date:** 2/21/--

From: Lieutenant Andrew Paulson, Inspection Division

Subject: Officer Anthony Sweeney

On February 20, I personally observed Officer Sweeney sleeping in a room adjacent to the executive officer's desk. The executive officer, Sergeant Wooding, was out of the building on an assignment at the time. I have requested a written report from Officer Sweeney on two occasions and have not received same. Please look into this and take appropriate action.

Tickler file for 2/24. Interview and obtain a report from Officer Sweeney. Forward completed report and memo to Lieutenant Paulson.

MF

Note that there is no due date, so you're making a note to remind yourself to complete this work at a later date.

Write your response directly on memo

Since Lieutenant Paulson indicates that he's been trying to get written report from officer Sweeney, follow up with report and memo to him.

Your initials

14. Routing slip with Note from Captain Standish; Police/Citizen Advisory Committee Complaints

Write this response directly on this form or, if you require more space, write it on a separate piece of paper

---

CITY OF CENTERVILLE
INTERDEPARTMENT ROUTING SLIP

Check and
Forward

1. *Sergeant Flynn* ☐

2. _____ ☐

3. _____ ☐

_____	YOUR INFORMATION
_____	REPLY DIRECTLY TO CORRESPONDENT
_____	PREPARE REPLY WITH MY SIGNATURE
_____	INVESTIGATE AND REPORT
_____	SUBMIT RECOMMENDATIONS AND COMMENTS
_____	DISCUSS WITH ME
__X__	NECESSARY ACTION
_____	IMMEDIATE ACTION
__X__	RETURN *by 2/24*
_____	YOUR FILE

Note due date: 2/24

REMARKS: *Please respond to each complaint of The Citizen Advisory Committee dealing with Patrol Squad B.*

Note that a response is required

Note that you are to respond only to complaints involving squad B.

2/21   *E. Standish*

Signature

CITY OF CENTERVILLE
INTERDEPARTMENT MEMORANDUM

To: __Deputy Chief Dover__   Date: __2/20/--__

From: __Frank Simpson, Chief of Police__

Subject: __Complaints made by Police/Citizen Advisory Committee –__
__February meeting.__

On February 19, I met with the Police/Citizen Advisory Committee. The following locations were identified by committee members as areas of criminal or disorderly conduct. Please have the appropriate personnel from your bureau look into these problems and respond with action taken by February 24.

1. (Patrol A and B) Complaint of loiterers trespassing in the rear of the drugstore on the corner of Blue Hills and Burnham Streets.

2. (Traffic) Complaint of speeders – Chandler and Dart Streets.

3. (Traffic) Complaint of speeders on Brookfield Street near Flatbush Avenue between 1430 and 1630 hours.

4. (Patrol A) Complaint of vandalism, thefts from vehicles, and general harassment of personnel in the area of the board of education building on Atlantic Street.

5. (Patrol A and B) Request for extra attention for trespassers in the rear of the bank at park and Broad Streets.

6. (Patrol A and B) Complaint that alternate side parking is not being enforced on Monroe Street.

7. (Patrol A and B) Request from southwest representative, Ann DeVeau, to communicate with officers in her area. Chief Simpson indicated that the area sergeant should see her.

8. (Patrol A and B) Written complaint from Parkville representatives that the parking situation in the Parkville area has gotten much worse on Saturdays during the last month. Requests strict enforcement in this area.

Items 1 and 5 through 8 involve Squad B

Note specific request by Ann DeVeau

Since the due date is 2/24, work must be assigned and responses gathered as soon as possible to allow captain time to advise deputy chief.

Clearly identify the material you're responding to.

Response to items 1, 5, 6, and 8

Response to item 7

Memo should be in your captain's name

Your initials

Police/Citizen Advisory Committee

Complaints

I would advise the area units and

beat officers relative to the

complaints in numbers 1, 5, 6 and

8 and require a written response by

the end of their shift. I would

telephone Ms. DeVeau and arrange

to meet with her personally. After

receiving the responses from the

various officers, I would write a

memo in Captain Stand'sh's name

to Depute Chief Dover detailing the

results of the action taken.

MF

15. Telephone Call from Officer Reynolds Regarding Councilman Casey

One correct response is as follows:

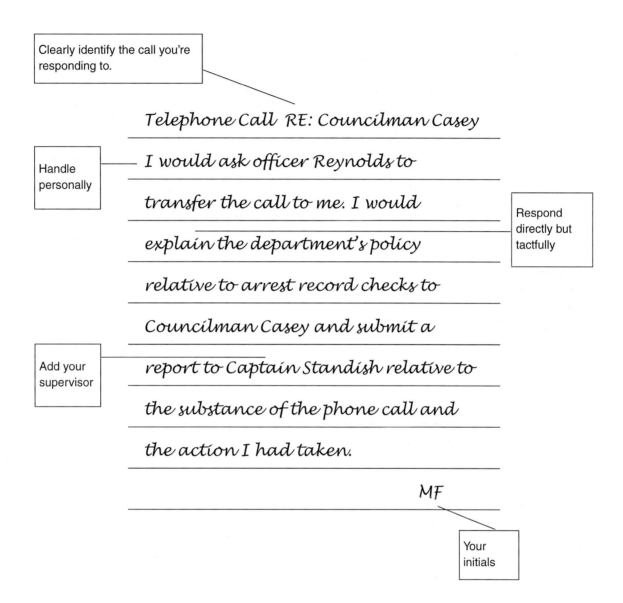

Clearly identify the call you're responding to.

Telephone Call RE: Councilman Casey

Handle personally

I would ask officer Reynolds to

transfer the call to me. I would

Respond directly but tactfully

explain the department's policy

relative to arrest record checks to

Councilman Casey and submit a

Add your supervisor

report to Captain Standish relative to

the substance of the phone call and

the action I had taken.

MF

Your initials

16. Block Watch/Community leaders Meeting Report
You might respond as follows:

> Write your response directly on the form or, if you require more space, write it on a separate piece of paper

> Your initials

> Your procedure: read at roll call, coordinate with vice and narcotics, require report from officers, supply due date

> As per recommendation below

> Note problem reported

> Note recommended action

Reviewed. Advise area units and beat officers at role call. Ensure a copy of UDR is sent to vice and narcotics division. Require activity report from area officers with due date of 2/28 as to action take.   MF

CENTERVILLE POLICE DEPARTMENT
COMMUNITY-RESPONSE DIVISION
Block Watch/Community Leaders Meeting Report

Meeting/visit date: ___2/19/--___

Location: ___113 Ansonia Street, Centerville___

Meeting held with: ___Teresa Jennings/approximately 20 block watch members___

Time Started: ___1815___   Time Ended: ___1940___

Concerns presented to police officer during meeting/visit:

Undersigned met with entire block watch group during their monthly meeting. Member stated that their area is infested with drug dealers, who sell openly on the street corners, and they want increased patrols.

Action taken by police officer:

Recommend notifying vice and narcotics division of groups concerns.

Report prepared by: ___Officer Lemner___   Date: ___02/19/--___

Reviewed by: _____

Remarks:

CPD Form 12

17. Report of Disciplinary Infraction – Officer Churchill
This one is quickly disposed of:

> Your initials, to show that you've reviewed

MF

CENTERVILLE POLICE DEPARTMENT
Report of Disciplinary Infraction

Complete in duplicate when report required by CPD Order 4-2 "Disciplinary Procedure," Par. IV A.1 and 2.

SECTION I

Name of employee: _Paul Churchill_   Rank: _officer_

Division: _patrol_   Date of infraction: _02/20/--_

SECTION II

Infraction charged: _Violation of CPD Code of Conduct_

	Article	Section	Title of Offense
1.	V	5.04	Inattentive to duty
2.			
3.			

Explain infraction(s) in detail (list witness if any):

On this date, the undersigned observed the above officer standing outside his cruiser talking to a female just after he and another unit had been dispatched to an active burglary. He made no attempt to immediately answer the call.

To the best of our knowledge, is this a second or subsequent offense to any of the code sections cited? If so, specify:

Unknown

Immediate corrective action taken, if any (if any of the infractions call for an oral reprimand and the reprimand has been issued, so state and attach to a copy):

None

Date: _02/20/--_   Submitted by: _Sergeant Trautman_

CPD Form 80
Revised 12-90

> Sergeant Trautman has already taken action – no other action required.

18. **Telephone Call from officer Caron Regarding Officer Intoxicated at the Golden Oak Café**

This call demands an immediate response to the scene. A correct answer is as follows:

> Clearly identify the call you're responding to.

Respond personally to scene

Telephone Call - RE: Officer Intoxicated

I would instruct Officer Caron to remain at the café and advise him that I was responding. I would request an additional unit to respond with me to the location. Upon arrival, I would

Your procedure: assess the situation, determine if crime has been committed

assess the situation, and if Officer Jensen was committing a crime in my presence, I would place him under arrest. If he was not committing a crime in my presence, I would determine if there was a complaint being lodged against him by the proprietor. If not, I would require a report from Officer Caron, assess Officer Jensen's condition, and based on the facts, make a determination if the department's code of conduct had been violated. If so, I would take appropriate disciplinary action. I would prepare a report relative to the incident and forward same to Captain Standish.

MF

Your procedure: require report from Officer Caron.

Your procedure: assess officer's condition, determine if code of conduct violated.

Your procedure: take disciplinary action if appropriate

Your Procedure: advise captain.

> Your initials

19. Field Sergeant Activity Report

The correct response is to fill out the report:

CENTERVILLE POLICE DEPARTMENT

Field Sergeant Actvity Report

Date: _____2/21_____

Squad: _____B_____

I. **Supervisory activity:** *Attended 1440 and 1540 roll calls. Deployed special detail relative to crime pattern bulletin and robbery in Blue Hill Ave area. Responded to strike at A1 Firearms and off duty officer incident at the Golden Oak Café. Coordinated service of arrest warrant on CPD officer. See attached reports for details.*

II. **Assigned inspections:** *RE: Citizen Advisory Board - Assigned complaints to area officers. Inspected Blue Hill and Burnham, no activity. Personal contact made with Ms DeVeau and meeting scheduled, full report to follow. Assigned Block Watch information relative to narcotics trafficking to area officers and coordinated with vice and narcotics.*

III. **Self-generated inspections:**

IV. **Other assigned duties:** *IAD complaint against Officers Bailey and Mackey. Completion of Probationary Officer Reports. Review of squad A prosecutor and investigative reports.*

V. **Comments and recommendations:** *Recommend increasing personnel at strike detail, A1 Firearms, by four officers due to increased tensions and use of strike breakers.*

_____

Michael Flynn

Sergeant's signature

CPD Form 346

9 Glossary of Key Terms

Glossary

Ability – An intrinsic trait further developed through training, education, or experience.

Apprehension of Authority – The result of task-oriented, autocratic supervision. Under such authority, subordinates become reluctant to make decisions on routine matters, having received the impression from their supervisor that they will be criticized for even minor mistakes. This behavior results in lost efficiency, effectiveness, and productivity. Often, in an effort to solve the problem, closer supervision is applied, which serves only to heighten employee anxiety even further.

Assessment Center – A testing process in which candidates participate in a series of systematic, job-related, true-to-life, mock situations while being observed and graded by experts in policing.

Budget – A police budget details the amount of money needed to deliver police services in a community. It is an estimate of the need for human resources (people – their salaries, benefits, and training) and physical resources (such as cruisers, desks, computers and forms). In larger police department, division commanders (patrol, traffic, investigations, and so forth) prepare a projected estimate of the personnel and equipment needed to perform job tasks leading toward organizational objectives. This identification of personnel and equipment is then translated into a monetary figure, accompanied by a report justifying the predicted expenditure. The report is then submitted through the chain of command and revised at each level through which it passes prior to being forwarded to the chief of police.

Each level reviewing the proposed budget may revise and return it to the division commander for further documentation of the need for a particular expenditure. The chief of police and his or her staff (which often includes a civilian budge analyst) then reviews the requests from the various components of the department and prioritizes them based on their impact on the overall ability of the department to fulfill the objectives as perceived by the chief of police. The chief of police may revise the budget upward or downward in a specific area or eliminate personnel positions and/or equipment packages. Then, depending on the cities form of government, the budget is submitted to the city manager or mayor.

A **performance budget** details the cost of specific programs and activities within police departments, such as traffic or detective divisions. Objectives are outlined and tied directly to a monetary figure depicting levels of service that can be provided, depending on the amount of money allocated.

In a **zero-based budget,** the total amount of money authorized for the entire city budget for a fiscal year is predetermined by the city manager, mayor, council, etc. Department heads (police chief, fire chief, parks and recreation manager, and so forth) are then advised of the amount of money allocated for their individual departments. The police chief submits a budget based on the projection and estimates what level of police service can be provided with the amount of money allocated.

Certified List for Promotion – A rank-ordered list of candidates who have passed all testing and other requirements and are eligible for promotion.

Command – Command provides organizational structure, direction, and goals through which people work in order to accomplish the department's objectives.

Command Post – A command post is established under emergency conditions. It consists of a base of operations, or staging area, for personnel and equipment. It may be located in such areas as an office building, apartment, patrol vehicle, or SWAT truck and is used for planning, organizing, directing and communicating. It should be close to, but not directly exposed to, the emergency situation. Conditions which may require setting up a command post include, among others, hostage situations, barricaded persons, public demonstrations, and civil disorders.

Command Presence – The intrinsic qualities of a leader. Factors contributing to command presence include military bearing, self-discipline, appearance, integrity, honesty, poise, the ability to instill in officers a willingness to follow, creating a vision which others adopt, pulling people upwards, granting first-class citizenship to officers in the organization, and influencing people through presence.

Command Staff – Command staff is made up of officers who have, in their own right, no formal authority due to rank but do have the approval of and speak for a supervisor or ranking officer. Example: Officer Jennings (the captain's executive officer) informs Sergeant Wilson what the captain would like Wilson to attend a community meeting.

Communication – Whenever two or more people come together, some form of communication takes place. The ability to communicate clearly and effectively is an important trait of a good supervisor. Poor communication results in misdirection, confusion, lost efficiency and productivity, and duplication of effort.

> The purpose of **downward communication** is to provide officers with the information they need to perform their jobs. Most information in a police organization moves from the top downward through written or face-to-face communication channels.
>
> **Formal communication** provides organizational structure and consists of SOP's, orders, correspondence, and other written messages that communicate the "official policy" of a police department.
>
> **Informal communication** develops when formal channels of communication don't exist or fail to meet the needs of officers. Informal communication consists of "it grapevines" or "rumor mills" that distort and filter messages.
>
> **Lateral (horizontal) communication** – In routine matters, officers in one unit or division would not have to confer with officers of another unit or division in order to perform everyday job assignments. Such communication would be unnecessarily restrictive and is a frequent cause of lack of productivity. But decisions involving matters which a subordinate doesn't have the authority to act on should be reviewed by a supervisor. And supervisors of separate units or divisions should at times confer (laterally) to decide the best course of action to achieve the organizational goals.

In **upward communication,** the flow of information is from the lower levels of the organization upward to the top. Without upward communication, police administrators would not have the information needed to plan or make decisions.

Communication Net – Due to the complexity of police organizations, there is often filtering and lack of communication. The term communication net refers to the various channels (upward, lateral, downward) that communication must pass through from sender to receiver. The degree of accuracy of the communication and the time consumed as the communication moves through the channels have a direct effect on the clarity of the message.

Community Relations – Good community relations promote feelings of trust, pride, and rapport between a police department and community it serves.

Conference – A conference involves an exchange of ideas, opinions, and communication between officers in order to solve or prevent a problem. It is often used as a forum for planning, organizing, and coordinating.

At the sergeant's level, a **staff conference** is called in order to give direction on the implementation of procedure and to gather feedback on improving work performance.

A **vertical staff conference** is used primarily by the chief of police or other high-ranking members of the department to quickly communicate with all levels and ranks. Representatives from different ranks attend the meeting so that direct, face-to-face communication takes place and information can be brought back to various levels of the organization.

Controlling – Controlling is the influencing and guiding of officers toward organizational objectives through observation, inspection, communication, modeling, and reviewing reports and records. The sergeant is responsible for ensuring that officers perform their jobs properly, follow orders and procedures, and behave within the guidelines established by the organization.

Coordination – The sergeant's responsibility is to ensure that the goals of the police department are accomplished by coordinating personnel under his or her control. Such coordination is accomplished by developing plans detailing what will be done, who will do it, when it will be done, and how job tasks are to be implemented. The coordination of diverse individual and group tasks to accomplish organizational goals is facilitated by the proper use of personnel and equipment, improving the capability of the department to deliver police services effectively and efficiently.

Crime – A crime is anything that society says is a crime and has the authority to punish.

Crime Repression/Suppression – Crime repression (suppression) involves creating an atmosphere in which criminal offenders believe that the opportunity to commit a crime doesn't exist or that the crime will result in immediate arrest.

Crime-Scene Preservation – In proper crime-scene preservation, the location at which a crime occurred is kept in exactly the same condition as it was left in by the criminal.

Decision-Making – Making decisions is one of the primary roles of the supervisor. Failure to decide what to do, how it's to be done, and who is to do it is detrimental to morale and the organization's efficiency. The axiom "Even a bad decision is better than no decision at all" can often be applied to "doing" professions like policing.

Delegation of Work – Delegation of work is the turning over or entrusting of one's work to another while remaining accountable for its completion. When supervisors assign tasks to subordinates, they must also give them the authority needed to complete the assignment. Subordinates can't be held responsible for job tasks for which they lack the power or resources needed to accomplish those tasks. Proper delegation requires the assignment of work to the lowest level capable of getting it done, which allows supervisors to use their time more efficiently and effectively.

Direction – Through direction, subordinates are guided toward job-task accomplishment.

Discipline – A supervisor uses the disciplinary process to accomplish organizational objectives through people. Discipline is the coaching, training, and instructing of subordinates in behavior, skill proficiency, and ways to improve their job performance. Because sergeants are closes to and have the most contact with subordinates, they are the key to an effective disciplinary process in a police department. In cases calling for disciplinary action, the sergeant should evaluate all of the factors involved, document, and initiate disciplinary action.

Discipline should be **administered** in private. The sergeant should inform subordinates exactly what is lacking in their job performance or behavior, what needs to be done to bring their performance or behavior up to an acceptable level, and what consequence will occur if they don't do as required. The sergeant should be fair, consistent, and impartial, conducting frequent inspections so that systematic failures can be promptly corrected.

Positive discipline is not punishment. It is teaching, counseling, and instructing of subordinates in order to encourage them to improve their work performance. As it is the case in all disciplinary actions, documentation is required.

Negative discipline is used when positive discipline has not worked or in the case of repeated or serious violations of department regulations, rules, procedures, or policies. It is punishment designed to enforce standards, deter others, and control behavior. Documentation of the disciplinary action is required. Negative discipline should always be done in private except in emergency situations.

Progressive discipline – The disciplinary process should always be progressively stronger for each offense, depending on its seriousness. A logical progression consists of counseling, verbal reprimand, written reprimand, suspension, and termination. Such a progression should be used except in cases of sever misconduct requiring acceleration of the process.

Division of Work – Division of work involves the grouping of job tasks and functions in order to improve efficiency and effectiveness.

Eligible List For Promotion – A list of applicants who have successfully completed the testing process for promotion.

Emergency Situation – The sergeant's role in an emergency situation is to immediately evaluate and advise headquarters of the situation and to deploy personnel and equipment to prevent it from escalating.

Esprit de Corps – The concept of esprit de corps is closely related to that of morale and consists of organizational pride and a sense of ownership of an responsibility to and for the department. It is the intangible elements that cause people to take pride in being part of an organization and which fulfill their value systems, needs, beliefs and wants.

Exception Principle – The exception principle relates to the term *completed staff work*. Work should be performed at the lowest level possible in the police department. Sergeants should not have to act on routine matters that could be handled at a lower level. Their time and expertise should be reserved for matters that can be handled only at their level.

Feedback – Feedback is part of the verbal communication process and is a combination of facial expressions, gestures, and body language that indicate whether understanding has or has not taken place.

Field Inquiry – Field inquiry is based on the principle that the opportunity to apprehend a criminal and prevent crime increases with the number of people interviewed and the frequency with which they are interviewed in the field.

Filtering – When communication takes place and is later repeated to someone else, the facts tend to be changes, blurred, or distorted. The change in the meaning of communication as it is passed from one person to another is known as *filtering*.

Grievance – A grievance is based on an employee's perception that a job-related factor is unfair, improper, or inequitable.

> It is the **sergeant's responsibility** to identify employee concerns before they affect the efficiency of the police department. Because sergeants are the closes level of supervision to the majority of the work force and have the most direct contact with subordinates, they have the best opportunity to handle officer concerns.

Information Dissemination – The sergeant has a responsibility to ensure that all officers receive current information and are informed of all criminal activity prior to leaving roll call for their job assignments.

Inspection – Inspection is a systematic review of department procedures, systems, methods of operation, equipment, and human resources in order to improve efficiency, effectiveness, and productivity.

Interrogation – Interrogation is communication consisting of questioning a person in order to obtain information.

Interview – In an interview, communication takes place between two or more persons for the purpose of exchanging ideas or sharing information.

Job Dimensions – Job dimensions are the duties and responsibilities of an individual, broken down into specific job tasks necessary for proper performance.

Labor Disputes – The sergeant's role in a labor dispute is to ensure that both labor and management are treated equally and fairly and that the law is enforced without favoritism for either side.

Leadership Styles –

> **Autocratic leaders** are task-oriented. They tend to stress rules and regulations and don't use participative management techniques. This style of leadership motivates b y fear rather than by inspiration and doesn't work well for extended periods of time. However, this style does work in emergency situations where a more focused direction and control of officers is important.

> **Democratic (participative) leaders** seek input from subordinates and allow them to e part o the decision making process while reserving final decision making authority for themselves.

> **Free-rein (laissez-faire) leaders** take little part in the decision making process and consistently forward, up the chain of command, matters that should be decided at their level. Free-rein leaders give no assistance to their subordinates and allow them to make their own decisions.

Line Function – The term *line function* describes those officers in a police department engaged in activities directly related to immediate response to citizens' calls for police service. For example, officers assigned to the patrol division arc line officers, while those assigned to the training or records division, which support the work of the patrol division, are staff officers.

Lines of Authority – The term *lines of authority* is closely related to the term chain of command. All officers must know where they fit within the organization in terms of rank, assignment, and job responsibility. In a semi military profession, lines of authority establish who the officers' first-line supervisor is and the scope of that supervisor's authority. Lines of authority clearly delineate the responsibility for completion of job tasks throughout the department and describe those individuals who have the authority to delegate work to lower levels.

Management Information System – In order to properly plan, members of a police department must have a wide range of information, including crime patterns, modus operandi, reports on calls for police service, budgetary items, utilization of equipment records, and so forth. The system of coordination and distribution of information through the various communication channels in a police department is known as the *management information system*.

Management Styles – Management is the process of directing human and equipment resources in an efficient and effective manner so that the goals of the organization can be reached.

Management by objectives is a management style that puts emphasis on getting the job done by determining goals which will fulfill organizational responsibilities. These objectives are communicated to subordinates, usually in writing, and times are established by which specific parts of the objectives must be met. For example, the objective might be to increase the number of block-watch meetings attended by personnel by ten percent. In order to accomplish this goal, 25 block-watch meetings must be attended each quarter of the fiscal year.

Theory X management assumes that people dislike work and that autocratic behavior is necessary to control subordinates. A Theory X manager does not believe in participative management and informs subordinates of their roles without their input.

Theory Y management assumes that people will achieve goals through self direction. A Theory Y manager often uses participative management techniques to motivate subordinates toward organizational goals.

Modeling Techniques - In using modeling techniques, job coaches, supervisors, or trainers *show* the trainee how to perform the job task by performing it themselves from simple to complex states and then having the trainee repeat the task in the same way under direct supervision. The sergeant models behavior over a period of time to set an example for a subordinate to follow.

Modus Operandi – *Modus operandi* is a Latin term meaning *method of operation* – the method in which a criminal operates, the habits and procedures used repeatedly by a criminal to commit crime.

Monitoring – In monitoring, the sergeant determines whether subordinates are properly carrying out their assignments by reviewing data-analysis reports concerning officer productivity, conducting frequent field inspections of officers handling calls for service, observing officer response to calls for service, checking the condition of officers' beats and areas, reviewing reports, and conducting training sessions.

Morale – The term morale is closely related to the term *esprit de corps*. Good morale exists when a person wants to reach organizational objectives and sees them as personally valuable. Good morale embodies a spirit of enthusiasm and a sense of pulling toward a common goal, making the organization function more efficiently and effectively.

Motivation – Motivation is the influencing of one person by another to encourage positive behavior.

Operations Analysis (Crime Analysis) – In operations analysis, information is compiled and analyzed in order to plan, organize, direct, and coordinate police services. Examples of operations analysis are the compiling of crime statistics, crime patterns, and calls for service.

Orders – If subordinates understand why an order is necessary, they will be more likely to carry it out effectively. The sergeant should not place responsibility for giving or enforcing orders on a higher authority, but should act as if the orders are coming from him or her. After issuing an order, the sergeant should follow up to ensure compliance.

Operational orders describe the procedures to be followed during special events such as VIP visits, funerals, and public demonstrations.

Organizational Integrity – One who possesses organizational integrity puts the police organization ahead of personal interests, seeing that the interests of the organization prevail in each situation.

Organizational Pyramid – An organizational pyramid is a chart or diagram showing the command structure and reporting responsibilities from the top of an organization to the bottom.

Its purpose is to functionally group job tasks and associate them with the department's goals. Such a chart shows the chain of command of the department in an organizational format.

Patrol –

> **Establishing the location of foot patrols –** A combination of factors contribute to whether a specific area can be served more effectively through the use of foot patrol or through the use of vehicular patrol. Factors indicating the use of foot patrol include (1) high density population within small geographic areas, such as housing projects or shopping malls, (2) locations having high volumes of pedestrian and/or vehicular traffic, such as downtown or business areas, and (3) condensed areas experiencing high levels of crime and repeated calls for police service.

> **Determining the size and boundaries of foot patrols –** Foot patrols should conform to the natural boundaries that area adjacent to the area, which include (1) main streets and traffic arteries, (2) rivers, bridges, and parks, and (3) highways and highway connectors. Other factors to be considered include the number and types of calls for service within walking distance in a specific area, the type of area (housing projects, downtown, residential, etc.), and the safety of assigned officers.

> **Advantages of foot patrol versus vehicular patrol –** Officers on foot patrol can make more personal contacts with citizens and have more of an opportunity to perform community relations services than do officers in patrol cars. They can handle calls within their areas, relieving line cars from having to respond to minor calls for service. They can devote more of their time to special concerns, such as traffic congestion, bars, illegal parking, and so forth.

> **Disadvantages of foot patrol versus vehicular patrol –** Cruisers can cover larger areas in less time than can officers on foot. Foot patrol officers are limited to the equipment they can carry with them, while patrol cars can be equipped with emergency equipment, such as first-aid supplies, flares, oxygen, and special weapons. Vehicles can respond to emergency situations faster than can officers on foot. Supervision of foot patrols is more time consuming and costly than is supervision of officers in vehicles.

> **Importance of random patrol –** patrol, whether in a vehicle or on foot, should not establish a particular pattern which a criminal can observe and use to aid in the planning and commission of a crime.

> **Vehicular patrol –** To determine the effectiveness of vehicular patrol, consider factors similar to those used in making decisions about foot patrols: (1) calls for police service, (2) size of the area to be patrolled, (3) topography of the area and type of buildings, (4) density of population in the area, (5) amount of vehicular and pedestrian traffic, and (6) officer safety.

> With **one-person vehicular patrol,** the coverage of an area can be twice what it would be with two-person patrol (by using two patrol vehicles and putting a single officer in each).

> A **two-person vehicular patrol** is implemented in areas in which there is a high frequency of arrests and/or finding of weapons on persons. This type of patrol is costly to implement but is a valid alternative when the safety of police officers is involved.

Patrol Division – The patrol division is the backbone of a police department, directly responsible for the delivery of police service to the community.

Performance Evaluation – One of the primary duties of the police sergeant is to inform subordinates of how they can improve their job performances. In order to accomplish this task, the sergeant must make an evaluation of the subordinate against specific criteria. The evaluation can consist of a formal, written document or may take the form of immediate, on-the-spot correction. In either case, communicating with emp0olyees is required to ensure that subordinates understand what is expected of them. Another purpose of performance evaluations is to motivate officers to higher achievements or to bring marginal employees up to an acceptable level of work performance. The following errors are common in performance evaluations.

> The **error of central tendency** is the inclination of supervisors to rate subordinates neither high nor low, but rather consistently in the middle, to avoid having to document either superior or inadequate performance.

> The **halo effect** is an error in the rating of subordinate's performance based on an overall impression rather than against specific identifiable criteria.

> **Leniency** is the most common error in evaluating officer performance, involving the supervisor's tendency to rate officers higher than they deserve in order to avoid an unpleasant confrontation, because of a lack of proper training, or based on the belief that the evaluation is without merit.

Personnel Distribution – Appropriate distribution of personnel means using the right number of people, at the right time, to accomplish organizational goals.

Planning – Planning is deciding in advance what must be done, who will do it, when they will do it, and what equipment is necessary to accomplish it.

> **Long-range plans** outline methods of obtaining long-term goals.

> **Procedural plans** are the guidelines and standard operating procedures outlining who is responsible to do what, when, and under what circumstances. They establish day-to-day operation tasks for personnel, units, squads, divisions and bureaus in a police department.

> **Short-range plans** outline procedures for completion of tasks immediately or over a short period of time in order to accomplish organizational goals.

> **Tactical plans** are those for handling emergency situations, such as civil disorders, bomb threats, and crime scenes.

Police Omnipresence – The term police *omnipresence* refers to the perception on the part of the criminals that the police are everywhere and that if they commit a criminal act, they will be apprehended immediately.

Police Role – The role of police is the protection of life and property and the prevention of crime – to preserve and protect the people.

Policies – Policies are formalized plans designed to guide and direct personnel in the performance of their duties.

POSDCORB – The acronym stands for planning, organizing, staffing ,directing, coordinating, reporting, and budgeting as they relate to supervision and management.

Praise – Praise in public; criticize in private.

Report Checking – The sergeant should routinely check a subordinate's reports to ensure that they are being properly written.

Reporting – Reporting involves an exchange of information between supervisor and subordinates.

Rules and Regulations – Rules and regulations are plans containing specific guidelines for behavior and job performance.

Seniority – The amount of time that an officer has been working for a police department, usually calculated from the date he or she was sworn in, is labeled *seniority*.

Span of Control – The term span of control refers to the number of officers a sergeant can effectively supervise and control. Factors which influence a sergeant's span of control include (1) the sergeant's experience and ability, (2) the types of tasks that subordinates are performing, (3) the experience and morale of subordinates, and (4) the conditions under which job tasks are to be performed and the physical resources available to assist in performing them.

Staff Function – The term staff function describes all work in a police department that doesn't deal directly with the public in the field, such as the records division, training, fiscal management, and so form.

Staffing – Staffing is the personnel function of selection, training, testing, etc.

Supervision – Supervision involves the leading, coordinating, controlling, and directing of subordinates toward accomplishment of organizational job tasks.

> **Close supervision** uses specific instructions to subordinates and allows them only minimum discretion.

> **Over Supervision** is usually a result of a lack of supervisory experience, characterized by poor delegation skills, It is task-oriented behavior and give subordinates the perception that they will be corrected for even minor mistakes, a perception that is also known as *apprehension of authority*.

> **Supervision of officers outside a sergeant's unit** is generally not appropriate. Such behavior violates the principle of unity of command. Circumstances in which a sergeant *should* take control of officers outside his or her unit include emergency situations and employee misconduct.

Tests – Promotional tests involve a systematic procedure in which the individual being tested is presented with a set of constructed questions that will allow the tester to make a prediction of whether the person being tested has what the test is designed to measure.

Generic test questions – Generic test questions are those that do not reflect a specific police department's method of operations but instead deal with universally accepted principles of policing.

Job surveys – Job surveys are used in test analysis to ensure validity. In performing a job survey, the test analyst meets with a sampling of people in the job classification for which the test is being created and asks questions designed to determine what steps are required to perform the job in question successfully.

Nontraditional oral tests – This testing process evaluates a candidate on abilities that have been determined to be necessary for successful job performance. The tests involve an interview before three or more panel members who evaluate a candidate's intrinsic and behavioral qualities, communication skills, appearance, and organizational integrity.

Traditional oral tests – This testing process evaluates a candidate on abilities that have been determined to be necessary for successful job performance. The tests involve an interview before three or more panel members who evaluate a candidate's intrinsic and behavioral qualities, communication skills, appearance, and organizational integrity.

Test reliability – For a promotional test to be reliable, it must consistently and dependably measure those characteristics needed to perform a job properly over a period of time.

Test validity – For a promotional test to be valid, the questions must specifically relate to performing the job for which the test is being given.

Unity of Command – The term unity of command refers to the fact that each person in a police organization should be under the direct supervision of one person and report to only one supervisor – that is, one person should be in charge of each situation. This procedure improves the efficiency and effectiveness of the organization. When unity of command is absent, the result is duplication of effort, over supervision, lost productivity, and confusion on the part of subordinates.

Notes

Notes

Notes

Notes

Notes

Notes